D0518965

ON HISTORIANS

ON HISTORIANS

J. H. Hexter

Reappraisals of some of the makers of modern history

COLLINS
St James's Place, London
1979

William Collins Sons & Co Ltd
London · Glasgow · Sydney · Auckland
Toronto · Johannesburg

First published 1979
© J. H. Hexter 1979
ISBN 0 00 216623 2

Set in Baskerville

Made and Printed in Great Britain by
William Collins Sons & Co Ltd Glasgow

To my colleagues of
the Department of History, Yale University 1964-1978,
living and dead, gentlemen and scholars

Acknowledgments

I am grateful for permission to reprint my previously published essays. Chapter 2 originally appeared in the *Journal of Modern History* 22 (1951) :257-261 (copyright 1951 by the University of Chicago) ; Chapter 3, in the *Journal of Modern History* 44 (1972) :480-539; Chapter 4, in the *Journal of British Studies* 8 (1968) :22-78; Chapter 5, in the *TLS*, Oct. 24, 1975; Chapter 6, in *History and Theory* 16 (1977) :306-337. I wrote Chapter 6 at the Institute for Advanced Study with the support of the National Endowment for the Humanities, grant number FC10503.

For the essay on Braudel and the Mediterranean, I needed and received special help. I owe to Professor Robert Harding of Yale University the acquisition and tabulation of the data from the *Annuaires* of the VIe section, 1965–1971. I am also obligated to him for rapidly dispatching to me many of the works of scholars associated with the so-called *Annales* school. I am further indebted to him for illuminating conversations about the operation of the *Annales*-VIe section enterprise. In this matter I am also indebted to my former colleagues at Yale University, Raymond Kierstead, Robert Lopez, and Harry Miskimin. Professor Miskimin also gave me useful advice on weighing some of the statistics in *La Méditerranée*. My wife, Ruth Hexter, compiled the statistics on the size and growth of several historical journals from 1929 to the present, identified the academic provenance of a score of contributors to the Febvre festschrift, and as usual gave a critical reading to this study. Mrs. Florence Thomas prepared the charts and devised the ingenious maps. I received financial assistance for my work from the Concilium on International and Area Studies, Yale University.

In the final process of assembling, editing, and providing a title for *On Historians*, I have been blessed by the patience and help of Aida DiPace Donald and Camille Smith of the Harvard University Press and of my secretary, Ruth Kurzbauer.

J. H. Hexter

Washington University
Saint Louis, Missouri
July 1978

Contents

Introduction

This book is a collection of six essays on work by seven historians.

On the face of the evidence that opening sentence appears to exhaust the possibilities of common specification about the historians and the works treated except that the historians are all male and the works all in prose. Otherwise one no sooner sets out a general rule to cover all seven historians and all their relevant works than one notices that a particular work or a particular author breaks rank and, a truculent exception, goes sashaying down the road on its or his own. That is the best case; in the worst ones the exceptions seem to be the rule rather than to prove it. Thus:

The essays themselves all written within the past decade —except one.

The authors all of my generation—except one.[1]

The nativity of the authors: two Americans, two Englishmen, one New Zealander, one Canadian, one Frenchman.

The dimension of the works: four jumbo treatises; a stu-

1. Construing my generation to be those born within twelve years to either side of me. Carl Becker was born in 1873.

dy of considerable length; a collection of essays; a single essay of twenty-odd pages.

The time spans covered in the works: 1558-1660; c. 1550-c. 1950; 450 B.C.-A.D. 1800 with rather a bunching at 1513-1790; c. 1350-c. 1620; Eolithic to the present with rather a bunching at 1450-1650; any time at all.

The kinds of history: four, history of ideas; one, total history, minus politics, of a small but powerful sociolegal status group; one, global history of a vast and dimly bounded region; one, the writing of history.

Geographical locus: two, Europe; two, England; one, successively ancient Greece, imperial Rome, northern Italy, England, America; one, the Mediterranean basin and its adjacent lands; one, just about anywhere.

Reflections on Historians, then, does not appear to have been planned as a book. And indeed it was not. I was in the midst of writing the most recent essay it contains when for the first time the chance to gather the essays together for publication opened up to me.[2]

Yet among the several historians treated a significant similarity does happen to exist. Each in his way has committed himself to making sense of the matters he deals with, to ren-

---

2. As an instructor concerned with the writing of history I have often inveighed against historians who use the "irresponsible passive." For example, in the sentence, "Black slaves were bought from blacks in Africa," the identity of a responsible party vanishes into the abyss of the passive. Compare, "White slave traders bought black slaves from other blacks in Africa." That way we know who did it. The last clause in the text above demonstrates that with moderate craftiness one can bring off an "irresponsible active." The clause achieves the miracle of getting a book published without a publisher doing anything about it. Things do not happen that way. In the interest of responsibility the clause should read, "when Aida Donald of the Harvard University Press accepted from me the idea that a publisher might be willing to gather and issue my separate studies of several historians."

dering intelligible the doings and happenings that he confronts, the actors in the actions that concern him. None thinks that history is somehow going to make sense of itself without the historian's active intervention through interpretation. This similarity shows that in his essay of 1931, "Everyman His Own Historian" (see chapter 1) Carl Becker was no longer in dubious battle, but, despite his habitually elegiac manner, was celebrating a victory over the orthodox historians of his generation, the generation that had grown up before World War I. That generation was immersed in a particular conception of scientific history that held it the duty of the historian to establish the facts, which then would speak for themselves. It was this historical assumption that Becker castigated with such devastating mildness: "Hoping to find something without looking for it, expecting to find final answers to life's riddle by resolutely refusing to ask questions—it was surely the most romantic species of realism yet invented, the oddest attempt ever made to get something for nothing."

For the other six historians—Braudel, Ferguson, Hayden, Hill, Pocock, and Stone—scientific history in the pre-World War I sense is a dead issue, dead because their precursors of an earlier and pioneering generation have killed it. They owe their emancipation from its assumptions to Frederick W. Maitland and R. H. Tawney in England, Marc Bloch and Lucien Febvre in France, Charles Beard and Carl Becker himself in the United States, and looming behind them all, in this matter at least the Great Emancipator, Karl Marx. Hill and Hayden render their historical data coherent by imposing on them an external universal historical pattern or by selecting and interpreting their data to fit such a pattern, Marxian or Hegelian. With the fecundity of perception and conception for which he is rightfully noted,

Braudel confects his own general three-tiered scheme, ostensibly rigorous but in practice loose enough to let that incorrigible and ecumenical raconteur tell almost any tale he chooses. Pocock and Stone do not manifest any views on the universal form of the movement of history; perhaps they entertain no such views. Far from impeding their pursuit of clarification, explanation, interpretation, and pattern-finding, the lack of a metahistorical commitment allows them to see patterns that the blinkered vision imposed by such a commitment sometimes blocks out. With no metahistorical views, but with ravenous appetites for clarification and connection-making, Pocock and Stone are obsessive in their pursuit of explanation, intelligibility, and order in history.

With one exception these essays are quite recent, written or published within the past decade, so with that one exception major revisions have been unnecessary. Writing about historians is an activity arcane enough to generate relatively little published criticism, and therefore to provide small means for discovering one's errors and misjudgments. That has been true enough of the recent essays in this book to allow me to excuse myself from public penance for them in this introduction.[3] As for "The Renaissance Again—and Again," a quarter-century old, the passage of time has served it well and ill. Time has vindicated my suspicion that Hiram Hayden's gaudy conception of a counter-Renaissance was not going to make it in the big time. On the other hand, it has utterly obliterated my notion that the overworked idea of the Renaissance was not long for this world. Twenty-five years later the idea is in better shape

---

3. I will deal with what appears to be a summons to penance in the decent privacy of a footnote: chap. 5, n. 13.

than it has been since Burckhardt's day, slimmed down from the overblown, slovenly condition that it fell into about the turn of the century, capable now of efficiently giving coherent organization to a considerable body of historical evidence about cultural changes that began in Italy in the fifteenth century and spread through Western Europe in the sixteenth. The heroes of the rehabilitation of the hard-pressed Renaissance are two German-born scholars who came to the United States in their middle years—Hans Baron and Paul Oskar Kristeller. Although their views on the constituent elements of the Renaissance diverge on some issues, each has defined his position with care, precision, and great erudition. Thereby both have provided scholars with sensible, orderly ways to think about the emergence and diffusion of the phenomena of culture that Burckhardt first grasped as an ensemble more than a century ago. They have thus brought back to earth and firmly moored an idea in jeopardy. The idea of the Renaissance had become so inflated with the hot air exuded by generations of historians that there was a danger that it would take off for that great Beyond where sound concepts go after we ruin them.

The importance of historical work like that of Baron and Kristeller tends to be underestimated by the profession. From one point of view historical works of consequence may be roughly distinguished into three sorts of activity—construction, critique, and reconstruction. The intellectual atmospherics of Western and especially of American culture have been highly sympathetic with and favorable to practitioners of the first activity. The language is well supplied with adjectives of laudatory reverberation to describe those who devote themselves to elaborating new constructions in history: consider worn-out, old "innovation" and "seminal" as good examples of a bad genre. "Innovation" has wonderful ripple effects. It provides commentators who have never learned to appraise or understand the old with opportunities to display their own "with-it" credentials by puffing the new.

The critics who tumble some of the monsters that an excessive public appetite for innovation is sure to generate are never deemed so worthy as the architects of the monsters. Still, if they bash about hard enough to level a truly idiotic piece of innovative historical work and kick up enough dust in the process—an activity with which I have had some experience—they may attract a certain amount of attention. Enough to win labels like "brilliant," "fierce," "devastating," "acerbic" and so on, a type of attention that has its points if one does not too much mind being perceived as Attila the Hun in the throes of indigestion.

The reconstructors are unlikely to win either the inflated encomiums that the innovators receive or the more ambivalent ones awarded to the critics. Their work is hard. They have to pick through the rubble that the critic's devastation has wrought to find what is left of the structure the constructor built. Then they have to pick away at the baroque embellishments with which he burdened his own structure and at the still more baroque ones that his disciples added to it. After that they must rectify the deficiencies that made the structure vulnerable to the critics in the first place. Only then can they cautiously fill in the holes and add such sober improvements as make a fair fit with the repaired original and with what happened in the past. Their achievement is likely to receive the praise it merits only from the handful of experts who have previously spent time and effort at the site and thus can gauge with accuracy the extent and the quality of their efforts. Yet it is these reconstructors—the Barons and the Kristellers—who change the work of historians from a cyclical process of overbuilding and destruction to a discipline in which improvement of understanding is cumulative.

The studies of Braudel, Pocock, and Stone put the author in mind of how lucky he has been in the haphazard way this book has come together. The works of these three authors on which he concentrates—*The Crisis of the Aristocracy, The Mediterranean,* and *The Machiavellian Moment*—were and were intended to be *chefs d'oeuvre,* big productions on which the authors had spent two decades or more of their lives. Yet if I were to say "I was moved to reflect on these three books," only in the case of Pocock's *The Machiavellian Moment* would the correct French be "Je me mouvait." In the case of Braudel's *Mediterranean* and Stone's *Crisis of the Aristocracy* it would rather be "Quelqu'uns me mouvaient." The motion to have me reflect on the three books came from two discrete external shoves by editors of journals and from one death wish. Partly because I so little followed my own leading, was instead so much led, partly because the intervals between my systematic reflection on these works were so long—five years, then four—and so tightly packed with other work, I was never in the least tempted to take a comprehensive, inclusive view of the three books or to see them as "part of the broader, ongoing pattern of twentieth-century thought." (I cannot prove that anyone has ever used the phrase "broader, ongoing pattern of twentieth-century thought," but I would bet my shirt that people have. It is unfortunately the sort of thing people say.) If they had come at me all at once, I am sure that I would have been unable to resist the temptation to wrap them all up together in one gross historiographic fallacy or another and to read into them deep interconnections expressive of the zeitgeist. The temptation would have drawn additional force from the fact that the three books are the most powerful and significant works in the field of early modern history that appeared in English in the decade 1965-1975. They may be as important as any historical works in any field for the past half-century, members of a select club of perhaps two dozen, perhaps three dozen pieces of historical writing. Such a situation encourages the propensity in us all for emitting portentous pomposities.

I never did see Braudel, Pocock, and Stone together in my mind's eye. Therefore I was not in the least tempted to imagine that they were or should be minds marching together in exemplification of the Main Trends in Contemporary Historiography. I was able to start where I ought, reading each book for the great enjoyment that was in it, with no thought beyond finding what it was about so I could write about it. For an inveterate splitter like myself (see chapter 5 for the definition of a splitter), that is where coming to grips with a major historical work and a major historian should start. It seems to me that books like these three ought to be licensed to put on their covers in bold type *Pay attention! Listen to me! Follow along! Have fun!* Books as lively, as intelligent, as clever, as bubbling with ideas as these deserve to be read for themselves and for the intellectual excitement they generate, and the first obligation of one who writes about them, both to himself and to his readers, is to catch and convey some of that excitement. He may believe that he has other obligations, but that one he must fulfill first or he will fulfill any others meagerly and poorly. If one is hooked on using history writing as a clue to the zeitgeist, it is better to use the dull historians who reflect only the zeitgeist because they have nothing to reflect in themselves. To use historians of true stature for historiographic games before one has taken the trouble to grapple with and grasp their work is a cheap kind of exploitation, a seizure of labor that good men have put their hearts into, a rip-off of bits of powerful minds in the hope that the bits can be squeezed into a silly puzzle and that no one will notice that the minds themselves are missing. It is the same spirit that makes small-minded historians collapse universal individuals into "typical men"— St. Louis into "the feudal monarch," Thomas More into "the medieval saint" or "the protoliberal," Edward Coke into "the judicial herald of the triumphant middle class." It is not the sort of thing one wants to do to great books, once one has really got to know them, or through them to know the minds of their authors.

So much for the historians this book is about and the history they have written. So much, too, for general rules about writing about other historians, prescriptive rules in historiography. A general rule is implicit in the previous section: if you cannot get yourself, your prejudices and preconceptions, out of the way of the historians whose works *are* historiography completely enough to avoid throwing your shadow on them, if you will not see the few freestanding ones *as* freestanding, then stay out of historiography; you lack the first indispensable aptitude for it.

As for this book itself, I suppose its single unifying element is that it was written by one man who in the quarter-century in which it was all written remained in some respects the same from beginning to end, and who in the decade in which nine-tenths of it was written, 1967-1977, changed very little indeed.[4] So the book reflects my tastes, my preferences, my idiosyncrasies and, at a second remove, probably my character.

4. Rue at the diminished flexibility of mind that comes to most of us with advanced years is tempered by recollection of a shrewd observation of George Orwell's: people over fifty who drastically change their tastes and opinions could not have held them seriously in the first place.

Each piece in this book could have concentrated on the place of the historical writing under consideration in—so to speak—its historiographic milieu; they all might have spent more time than they do on the relation of the work in hand to similar or precursory works. Few of the studies wholly neglect such relationships, but with the usual exception or two they treat it rather casually. On the other hand, most of them look closely at the work studied for what it may reveal about the way a particular historian's mind works, the way he addresses himself to his data, what he looks at and what he overlooks and what his looking and overlooking tell us about the contours, habits, and style of his thinking. This is a sort of psychohistory, although not the sort that is currently chic. Whether in some grandiose sense of the phrase it is worth doing I have no idea. It certainly can produce personal gratification. It is fun to do, especially when the historian about whom it is done recognizes that it has been done effectively and certifies the verisimilitude of the result. Of the many pleasures in my chosen vocation, few have been greater than that given me by the letter I received from Ferdinand Braudel about my essay on the *monde braudelien.* "Comment vous est-il possible, ne me connaissant pas, de me voir avec exactitude, non pas l'historien, mais l'homme historien . . . C'est merveilleux. En tout cas, c'est absolument réussi." The small suspicion that the elegant French concealed a suggestion that I had not quite got Braudel the historian right was submerged in the flood of satisfaction that came from being told by one reasonably expert in the matter that I had absolutely succeeded in getting Braudel the man as historian right. Particularly since the portrait is not cheesecake but, as Oliver Cromwell preferred it, warts and all.

PART ONE

In General: Perplexities about Relativism

1.

Carl Becker and Historical Relativism

It appears that historical relativism in America came into being in the midst of one of those crises of confidence that seem recurrently to plague the historical discipline.[1] In the 1880s and 1890s, history, long the preserve of well-to-do amateurs, had been professionalized and centered in the academy. Academic history had created for itself a professional society, the American Historical Association, and a learned journal, the *American Historical Review*.

It had also created an ideology. History, the professional credo went, was a science, (1) because by applying the methods worked out in Germany to the critical study of sources, history established as objective truth what actually had happened in the past, and (2) because history also discovered the course of development by which mankind had progressed to the political, intellectual, economic, and moral heights

1. In what follows about history writing in the United States, I have relied heavily on Cushing Strout, *The Pragmatic Revolt in American History: Carl Becker and Charles Beard* (New Haven: Yale University Press, 1958), pp. 13-29; and on John Higham et al., *History* (Englewood Cliffs, N.J.: Prentice-Hall, 1965), pp. 87-131.

that it—or at any rate its successful white members—currently occupied. That the application of the scientific historical method might ever fail to point unambiguously to the onward and upward movement of mankind seems not to have bothered, and perhaps not even to have occurred to, the professors of the science of history. After all, most of them had as firm a faith in progress as in science.

The faith was challenged early in the twentieth century, however, by a cluster of historians marching under a banner inscribed "The New History." In general the New Historians alleged that the profession was neither scientific enough nor progressive enough. It was not scientific enough, they said, because most historians paid no attention to the social sciences or indeed to anything but the history of politics and political institutions. Moreover, its purported scientific character was simply a mask for conservatism. If history was to be of any use to men, if it was to contribute to progress, it should turn its attention to the social sciences, drop its claims to objectivity, and line up on the side of change. Since in the wider intellectual world of the day pragmatism was the new thing in philosophy, progressivism the new thing in politics, and reform the new thing in the social sciences, the New History was clearly on some sort of bandwagon. Today one may wonder what made the New Historians so sure that the social sciences were solidly on that bandwagon of progress and reform with them. In recent decades a good many social scientists have noisily or quietly renounced progress and all its works, and stepped down or sometimes across to other more chic bandwagons. In the 1910s, however, the New Historians did not doubt that the social sciences were on the bandwagon of progress because that was where they saw them. The evidence of their senses was gracious enough to confirm their prejudices.

The conflict between the scientific historians and the New Historians went on and on, the former writing more books, the latter more and livelier manifestos, for a couple of decades.[2] By 1930, however, twelve years after the end of World War I, ten years into the Republican hegemony, a year into an evidently serious collapse of the American economy, the ears of some American historians were no longer well tuned to paeans to progress. They were ready to hear music in a minor key.

In "Everyman His Own Historian," his presidential address at the meeting of the American Historical Association in 1931, Carl Becker gave them such music.[3] What he gave them has since been called historical relativism. Two years later in *his* presidential address, "Written History as an Act of Faith," Charles Beard picked up (or at least seemed to) where Becker had left off.[4] For almost two decades thereafter, relativism was perhaps the dominant way of thinking about history in the United States. At least it was the principal reference point with respect to which historians in the United States who had explicit views about their profession oriented their thinking.[5] In almost all discussions of the sub-

2. Carl Becker wrote a tongue-in-cheek critique of the propensity of the New Historians for manifestos *et praeterea nihil* in 1939, "What Is Historiography?" reprinted in *Detachment and the Writing of History: Essays and Letters of Carl L. Becker* (Ithaca: Cornell University Press, 1958), pp. 65-78.

3. Carl Becker, "Everyman His Own Historian," *American Historical Review* 37 (1932): 221-236, reprinted in Carl Becker, *Everyman His Own Historian* (Chicago: Quadrangle, 1966), pp. 233-255. Subsequent citations to Becker's presidential address will be to the reprinted version and will be given in parentheses in the text.

4. Charles Beard, "Written History as an Act of Faith," *American Historical Review* 39 (1934): 219-229.

5. I am not acquainted with any close study of the writing of history in the United States between 1930 and 1950. These dates coincide, however, with the first two decades of my own professional engagement with the dis-

ject, historical relativism in America is linked to the names of Becker and Beard and to their remarkable presidential addresses. Several analyses and criticisms of the thought structure of Becker and Beard as revealed in their historical relativism have already been performed with far greater skill and more learning than I possess.[6] The best I can do is try to deal with a few perplexities that continue to vex me after examining several accounts of historical relativism in America.

For example, what actually was it? If it made its way into the consciousness of American historians through the presidential addresses of Becker and Beard, one might reasonably expect to find it in some notion that those addresses had in common. They did have at least one idea in common. Here it is, as Becker put it: "Every generation, our own included, will, must, inevitably understand the past . . . in the light of its own experience" (p. 253). And as Beard put it: "Each historian who writes history is a product of his age, and . . . his work reflects the spirit of the times, of a nation, race,

cipline. I have a very strong impression that in those years relativism enjoyed a vogue that was not seriously diminished by a concurrent and partly symbiotic addiction of some "advanced" historians in the United States to a sort of Marxism. The terminal period of the early 1950s for the dominance of relativism is marked by two minor but symbolically significant events. In the last days of 1949, Conyers Read delivered his presidential address to the American Historical Association, "The Social Responsibilities of the Historian." *American Historical Review* 55 (1950): 275-285. His call on American historians, in the name of relativism, to dedicate their services to the Cold War was not enthusiastically received in the profession. On the other hand an article by myself, written in 1950, which aimed to outflank the relativist position, got a generally favorable welcome. J. H. Hexter, "The Historian and His Day," *Political Science Quarterly* 69 (1954): 219-233, reprinted in J. H. Hexter, *Reappraisals in History*, rev. ed. (Chicago: University of Chicago Press, 1978).

    6. Strout, *Pragmatic Revolt*, pp. 30-61.

group, class, or section . . . Every student of history knows that his colleagues have been influenced in their selection and ordering of materials by their biases, prejudices, beliefs, affections, general upbringing and experience."[7] Do these two succinct statements incorporate the kernel of historical relativism in America? Perhaps. At least it is hard to imagine that any historian who considered himself a relativist would reject the statements or deny that they expressed an idea that he as a relativist would assent to.

If, however, we accept this easy answer as adequate, if we point to those statements and say, "That is historical relativism," we encounter another vexing question: "When did historical relativism arise?" On the evidence the answer to that question must be, "A good while before the golden dawn of the presidential addresses of the early 1930s." For example,

There is in every age a certain response in the world of thought to dominant social forces. But the agreement is only for the particular age; the next age, or the next generation, will think very differently.

Some future Lord Morley will tell the world how the histories of the nineteenth century serve a useful social purpose . . . and if useful . . . then true — true in the only way that historical synthesis is ever likely to be true, true relatively to the needs of the age which fashioned it. At least, it is difficult to understand how the modern man so wedded to the doctrine of evolution can conceive of historical synthesis in any absolute sense.

Here we have historical relativism again. The truths of history are truths of a time and for a time; they serve the particular needs of a particular age. In this instance, in the classic form of a confrontation of opposites, the notion of the relative is explicitly set over against the notion of the absolute

7. Beard, "Written History," p. 220.

in what has to do with truth. And the writer is again Carl Becker. Not Becker the venerable and sage president of the American Historical Association, but Becker twenty-one years earlier, the bright young professor at the University of Kansas. Becker made his relativist point in an article entitled "Detachment and the Writing of History," published in 1910 in *The Atlantic Monthly*.[8] If it made any ripples in the stagnant puddle of historical orthodoxy, evidence of them has long since disappeared.

Those who have written on historical relativism in America have all recognized that the eccentric phenomenon named Carl Becker requires special treatment. He was, we are told, a lone voice, who lost his faith in the Methodism in which he had been reared and who remained skeptical both when he encountered the Germanic scientific, objective history that was the orthodoxy of his day and when at Columbia James Harvey Robinson introduced him to the New History. Nor, although his doctoral dissertation looked closely at the impact of the interests of economic groups in New York during the Revolutionary War, did he fall for the tempting "economic interpretation."

This special treatment of Becker seems appropriate. For a whole generation he was indeed an intellectually isolated figure among American historians. Was it his addiction to historical relativism, however, that isolated him? Did the formulations just quoted from two passages written two decades apart divide him from all his contemporaries? One may wonder. Let us consider another formulation of the same thesis: "History will not stay written. Every age demands a history

8. Carl Becker, "Detachment and the Writing of History," *Atlantic Monthly* 106 (1910): 524-536, reprinted in Becker, *Detachment*, pp. 3-28. In the reprinted version the passages quoted are on pp. 23 and 28.

written from its own standpoint—with reference to its own social conditions, its thought, its beliefs and its acquisitions—and thus comprehensible to the men who live in it."

Here we have another statement of the relativist argument about the historian's relation to his age and to the climate of opinion of that age. This one dates from fifteen years before Becker's "Detachment and the Writing of History." When this statement was made Becker was only twenty-two years old. But Becker did not make it. Professor William Sloane, who at the relevant moment was Seth Low Professor of History at Columbia University, did. In the present context, who William Sloane was is of less interest than where his statement appeared. It appeared in 1895 in the first article in the first number of the first volume of a brand new journal, the *American Historical Review*.[9] As far as one can make out, it evoked no more of an agitated response at that time than Becker's statement in the *Atlantic* did a decade and a half later. This absence of outcry may give us pause. How could the scientific historians have taken the relativist heresy so calmly, when an eminent pillar of orthodoxy slipped it into the first number of what was intended to be the serially issued Holy Writ of that orthodoxy? This perplexity, however, need not hold us up for long. What Charles Beard said in "Written History as an Act of Faith" resolves most of the difficulties. The version of Beard's observations quoted earlier was slightly edited. In full, the first sentence actually read *"Has it not been said for a century or more that* each historian who writes history is the product of his age, and that his work reflects the spirit of his times."[10]

9. William M. Sloane, "History and Democracy," *American Historical Review* 1 (1895): 5.

10. Beard, "Written History," p. 220. Italics added.

What was so obvious to Beard in 1933 had after all been obvious to a good many people for a long time, not only to Carl Becker. Historians write history, all men write what they write, say what they say, do what they do, on the basis of their own experience, because in fact there is no other possible basis for writing, or saying, or doing anything. And the experience of each man is inescapably of his own day or age or time. Thus all men, including historians (perhaps especially historians), mirror, in the phrase Becker borrowed from Whitehead, the climate of opinion of their age.[11] Long before Becker and Whitehead, Hegel had taken note that every age had its *Geist*, its mind or spirit, an entity not all that different from a climate of opinion. Indeed I would not be surprised if animadversions on "the spirit of the age" were a commonplace of political oratory in Europe and the United States in the nineteenth century. And Karl Marx, of course, did not exorcise the spirit of the age. He rather provided it with a material habitation and thus made the zeitgeist plausible to people who found the self-realization of universal reason a somewhat ethereal base to build history on. So if we stop at Hegel (and perhaps we could go further back), it does indeed appear that, as Beard said, historical relativism had been around in one guise or another "for a century or more" when Becker wrote his presidential address.

If we have identified historical relativism correctly, then, it was a centenarian commonplace in 1931. The tentative resolution of our perplexity about what and when relativism was has only landed us in another perplexity: how could a relativism so old and so commonplace have made a turning point

11. Alfred N. Whitehead, *Origins of Modern Science* (Cambridge, England: Cambridge University Press, 1926), pp. 4-5.

in the self-perception and craft-perception of American historians when Becker trotted it out in 1931?

This new perplexity resolves itself rather easily: it could not have and it did not. Yet those who write about such matters do assign "Everyman His Own Historian" a literally epoch-making place in the history of historical thought in America, and in this they are probably correct. So—another perplexity—what beyond the commonplace happened in Becker's presidential address? And—yet another—when did it happen? As is often the case in the study of history, it is easier to say when something happened than to say what the something was; so we will follow the path of least resistance, and ask, "When did something particularly noteworthy happen in Becker's presidential address?" Becker himself has given us clues as to when whatever happened did happen. Sometime in August 1931 he wrote to his friend and former student, Leo Gershoy, "I will have to get to work again . . . the completion of that blasted presidential address. I had it ⅔ finished in June and there it stuck. I don't know how to end it."[12] Well before October 20 Becker had got the address unstuck. That day he wrote to Frederick Jackson Turner, "I have just finished my Pres. Address—blast the thing."[13] But exactly where had it got stuck before? And how had it got stuck?

Internal evidence suggests an answer to the first question, at least. As published in the book of the same title, *Everyman His Own Historian,* Becker's presidential address is divided into three sections. The first two sections take up fourteen

12. *What Is the Good of History? Selected Letters of Carl L. Becker, 1900-1945,* ed. Michael Kammen (Ithaca, N.Y.: Cornell University Press, 1973), p. 145.

13. Ibid., p. 148.

pages, the third section nine. It is reasonable to assume on this evidence that it was around the end of section II that Becker ground to a stop in June, and that section III was the one-third of the address that he completed between August and late October. And here we have a small new perplexity. Why did Becker's work on his address get stuck just as he got to the third section? Are there any clues on this matter in the address itself?

In quest of such clues let us first consider the two earlier sections of "Everyman His Own Historian," the parts Becker had written before he ran into trouble in June. He starts by trying to define history in a way that will, as he says, present "its essential nature, . . . to reduce it . . . to its lowest terms." The history he is talking about, he says, is not the happenings of the past, which are no longer directly accessible to anyone, but rather what is now remembered about that past. He concludes that the definition, " 'History is the *memory* of things said and done' . . . includes everything that is essential to understanding what it really is." But if this is so, Becker continues, it is evident that Mr. Everyman—that is, each human being—is a historian. Each day Mr. Everyman orients himself to his world by summoning up from memory what he needs to know—who he has been, where he has been living, who his wife has been, where his toothbrush has been kept. Sometimes, to recapture a lost memory of something he needs to know about, Mr. Everyman resorts to a written record, perhaps a memorandum book. There he may find a note to himself indicating, for example, that the due date has come for the payment of a coal bill. Here, in consulting and interpreting a document, and elsewhere in his dealings with the past for his own purposes, time and again Mr. Everyman will perform "all the essential operations involved in historical research" (pp. 233-239).

In any present moment, Becker says, "Mr. Everyman cannot do what he needs or desires to do without recalling past events; he cannot recall past events without in some subtle fashion relating them to what he needs or desires to do . . . In this sense all *living* history . . . is contemporaneous (p. 242)," at once past, present, and future. For Mr. Everyman it is not necessary that his history be a true or complete picture of the past, only that it be useful to him; so he rarely has need or time to question or meticulously verify the exact truth of a remembered event (pp. 245-246). Each event "will have for him significance and magic, much or little or none at all, as it fits well or ill into his little world of interests and aspirations and emotional comforts" (p. 246). In the printed version it is here that the second section of "Everyman His Own Historian" ends. And it was at about this point, I have a hunch, that the "⅔ of the blasted Pres. Address" that Becker had finished by June 1931 ended. It is delightful and witty and thoughtful—and to those who have read Becker's earlier utterances, it is not very new. In one place or another, he had said it all or almost all before, though not as elegantly or persuasively.

I have just suggested that Becker got stuck about at the end of the second section of "Everyman His Own Historian." Actually I suspect that by June he also had finished the first sentence of the third section: "What then of us, the historians by profession?" (p. 246). Somehow through veils of time and ignorance I seem to see the good professor on a pleasant spring day writing down that sentence almost without thinking about it, then pausing to contemplate its essential rightness. As he did so, his pleasure may have turned to perplexity and then to discomfort. "What then of us, the historians by profession?" What indeed? Perhaps after pondering that question Professor Becker put down his pen and decided that he had better drive around Ithaca a while in his car and think things over. At this point in his discourse, "What then of us, the historians by profession?" was clearly the right question. Custom dictates that somewhere in his address the president of the American Historical Association, out of his years of wisdom, exude portentous observations on the condition of the profession or emit some wholesome admonition to the assembled congregation on the way in which they should walk. Now Becker had to decide what observations to make, what admonition to deliver. And he had to figure out how to link them with Mr. Everyman.

In the summer of 1931, Becker was up against it; indeed, he had put himself up against it. He had spent two-thirds of his address with Mr. Everyman and his kind of history; he could not just drop him and his history for the final third. On the other hand he had not yet written the mandatory sermon to his fellow professionals. Somehow that sermon had to talk about the link, if any, between Mr. Everyman's history and professional history, perhaps to consider what the work of professional historians had to do with the historian who is Everyman. So although the first sentence of the third section probably flowed from Becker's pen with an easy inevitability, the next sentence may have been harder, and may have come as much as two or three months later. But in this case Becker's passion for coherence, his sense of proper order, and his honest inability to avoid thinking about what he was committed to think about demanded the next sentence of him, so he set it down. It was "What have we to do with Mr. Everyman, or he with us?" (p. 246). There it was, on the table. Only the label, "What, if any, are the social responsibilities of the historian?" was left off. The question of what professional historians have to do with the public, with society, with Mr. Everyman, and vice versa, is a tantalizing one. For a historian who thinks his lifework should not be just to make a living, or for fun, for one who thinks that history is in some sense a calling, this question may be acute like an exposed nerve or chronic like a nagging backache. In any case it is susceptible to a large number of different answers. Becker spent the third section of his address wrestling with this awkward question. It is my impression that he gave several answers or fragments of answers to it, not all of them consistent with each other. To one of the answers, however, we need to give close attention.

Berate him as we will for not reading our books, Mr. Everyman is stronger than we are, and sooner or later we must adapt our knowledge to his necessities. Otherwise he will leave us to our own devices, leave us it may be to cultivate a species of dry professional arrogance growing out of the thin soil of antiquarian research. Such research, valuable not in itself but for some ulterior purpose, will be of little import except in so far as it is transmuted into common knowledge. The history that lies inert in unread books does no work in the world. The history that does work in the world, the history that influences the course of history, is living history, that pattern of remembered events, whether true or false, that enlarges and enriches the collective specious present, the specious present of Mr. Everyman . . . If we remain too long recalcitrant Mr. Everyman will ignore us, shelving our recondite works behind glass doors rarely opened. Our proper function is not to repeat the past but to make use of it, to correct and rationalize for common use Mr. Everyman's mythological adaptation of what actually happened. (pp. 252-253)

Becker had done his duty. In a sense, after years of reflection on history and what professional historians in America were doing about it, as president of their professional association he told them what they ought to be doing about it. They ought to be correcting and rationalizing for common use Mr. Everyman's mythological adaption of what actually happened. The option was to do that or "to cultivate a species of dry professional arrogance growing out of the thin soil of antiquarian research." Note that antiquarianism was not an evil alternative to "scientific" history; it was the consequence of "scientific" history. It was the natural yield of the pseudo-scientific detachment that Becker had seen through a quarter of a century earlier, of the illusion that the historian merely had to assemble the facts and they would speak for themselves.[14] There was no longer room for the kind of scientific historian who imagined that "by *not* taking thought a cubit would be added to his stature" (p. 250). That kind of scientific historian wrung from Becker a mildly exasperated exclamation of wonder. "Hoping to find something without looking for it, expecting to find final answers to life's riddle by resolutely refusing to ask questions—it was surely the most romantic species of realism yet invented, the oddest attempt ever made to get something for nothing" (p. 250). There was no longer room, either, for the kind of scientific historian who derived spiritual consolation from the belief that his dry-as-dust biography of a minor New Jersey abolitionist was a contribution to the history of human progress.

Finally, there was no room for the New Historian, who, equipped with the social sciences, laid bare the ignorance and superstition of the past in the name of progress. In "Everyman His Own Historian" Becker had broken the link between relativism and the idea of progress. As far as he was concerned, the history written anew in every age need not celebrate the myth of progress, need not rearrange the past in the semblance of a staircase with mankind on it, ever ascending. If that semblance is pleasing to Everyman at a given moment, let the historian celebrate it. If not, let him not.

14. Becker, "Detachment," pp. 20-25.

After all, in the fifth century, in an age that despaired of earthly good, St. Augustine's *City of God* was probably doing a better job enlarging and enriching Mr. Everyman's specious present than James Harvey Robinson's *The Mind in the Making* was to do in the 1920s.

Most generally, the historian must do for Mr. Everyman in a small way what Mr. Everyman as historian daily does for himself in a large way: reinforce and enrich "his immediate perceptions to the end that he may live in a world of semblance more spacious and satisfying than is to be found within the narrow confines of the fleeting present moment" (p. 240). It was precisely the link with progress that had made historical relativism not only tolerable but attractive to scientific historians for a century. Ever since Condorcet, with the help of Hegel, Spencer, and the Darwinists, historians had seen man as on the march onward and upward. Each new age had indeed produced a new history, different from that of the preceding age. But each age also deemed its new history better than that of the preceding age, better because it belonged to a better age, one generational step up the ladder of improvement and progress.

For most of Becker's predecessors among the historians in the United States the idea of progress embodied the ultimate truth about the human race, a truth that was also a law of history. To write history that changed with each age was to show each age the line along which it had advanced and to offer it intimations of how it could advance still further in its progressive march. Becker, however, had scarcely any faith in the idea of progress, much less in the idea that historians were its chosen handmaidens. As far as he could make out, the idea of progress was just one of Mr. Everyman's current mythological adaptations of what actually happened, his current way of living in a world of semblance more spacious and satisfying than was to be found within the narrow confines of the fleeting present moment. As historians during the past century had helped make Everyman's dim perception of progress more spacious and satisfying, they must be ready to do the like again for whatever mythological adaptation Mr. Everyman wrapped himself in next time around.

At the end of Becker's presidential address at the Minneapolis meeting of the Association in 1931 his audience gave him the standing ovation he had well earned. But just what were they applauding? We can never be sure. "Everyman His Own Historian" is a piece rich in ideas, elegantly phrased, beautifully structured. Even historians who disagreed with most of what Becker said must have admired the panache with which he said it. And surely not everyone realized what Becker was up to. One man at least did know something about what Becker was doing, and had made a detour to Minneapolis to applaud him when he did it. That man was Charles Beard.[15]

15. Becker to Conyers Read, [May 10, 1933], Becker, *What Is the Good of History?* pp. 182-183. The four following paragraphs are almost entirely based on this letter and on one from Beard to Becker, May 14, 1933, ibid., p. 351. These letters are part of a three-cornered exchange among Beard, Read, and Becker, which must have involved at least one earlier letter from Read to Becker, a still earlier exchange between Beard and Read, and a second communication between Beard and Read between May 10 and May 14. One or more of the last three communications may survive. What happened is easy enough to infer from the two published letters. The date of May 10, ascribed by the editor of the Becker letters to Becker's letter to Read, is perhaps the consequence of a conception of the early virtues of the United States mail service at once nostalgic and oversanguine. Even in the heroic 1930s, if Becker had written on May 10 from Ithaca, I doubt that his letter would have reached Read in Philadelphia and Read's (missing) letter would have reached Beard in New Milford in time for the latter to have written Becker on May 14. Nor was long-distance telephoning likely to have taken

At that very meeting Beard was elected vice president of the American Historical Association. This meant that according to the ordinary rules of succession he himself would be delivering the presidential address in 1933. Being the inveterate showman that he was, from the moment he knew of his election as vice president, Beard doubtless began planning to drop a bombshell when he addressed the association two years later. Being the sly fox that he was and given the nature of the bombshell he intended to drop, he also doubtless conceived the idea of conning his friend Becker into arranging the fuse for him shortly after he heard "Everyman His Own Historian."

Early in May 1933 Becker received a letter from the brand new executive secretary of the American Historical Association, Conyers Read. It had to do with the planning for the December meeting in Urbana. Would Becker help? Would he organize and act as chairman of a session on historiography? Surely he would want to come to hear Beard in Urbana, as Beard had gone out of his way to hear Becker in Minneapolis? Then Read unfortunately let the cat out of the bag: revolutionary changes, he said, were being planned for the association, and the session on historiography in December was an essential part of the scheme.

It did not take Becker long to figure out that in this letter the hand was the hand of Conyers Read but the voice was the voice of Charles A. Beard. The notion of the executive secretary of the stodgy old American Historical Association acting as front and cover man for a revolutionary plot hatched by its president was too much for someone with Becker's fine-honed sense of the ridiculous. He answered Read,

up the slack. Such telephoning was not often in the academic repertoire in the early 1930s.

Your letter startled me like a fire bell in the night . . . so you are "planning," . . . actually planning "revolutionary changes." I can't believe it. I remember a slight insurrection in the Association a number of years ago, but it was not planned by those in high office. It is incredible. What is the Association coming to? . . . There are so many things to say that I hardly know where to begin. I might as well begin with Beard. Since he is capable of being up to anything, I suppose he is at the bottom of the whole affair. At all events he is trying to drag me in, to lead me astray as it were; and with the worst sort of Jesuitism — the sort that is perfectly transparent. He knows perfectly well, and he knows that I know, and that I know that he knows, that he did not go all the way to Minneapolis to hear me spout. He was on his way . . . to California to deliver some lectures . . . and merely stopped off at Minneapolis on his way.[16]

As Becker no doubt foresaw, Read finessed answering this letter, turning the task over to Beard. Beard piously pointed out to his old friend Becker that there were shorter routes to California from southern New England than via Minneapolis. Then he imperiously commanded Becker to "help Read out by outlining a program on historiography . . . on pain of expulsion from the heavenly city."[17] Beard got what he asked for, or at least part of it. Becker obeyed the command. Although he was too ill to take part in it, there was indeed a session on historiography at the American Historical Association meeting of 1933, the first trickle of what in later years swelled to a flood, and at Beard's behest, Becker had helped Read get it going. Moreover, that session provided a suitable fuse for Beard's bombshell, his presidential address. With the singular felicity of a professional practicing a long-cultivated skill, Beard, the venerable would-be revolutionary, gave the address a title well calculated to raise the

16. Ibid.
17. Ibid., p. 351.

maximum number of available conservative hackles: "Written History as an Act of Faith"—faith, of all things!

Here we will have to decide which way to go, since we have come to a fork in the road. At first the choice looks easy. One of the forks starts with Beard's presidential address. In its very first paragraph this address continues along the road of relativism that Becker had opened in 1931. "The philosopher . . . sometimes pretends to expound the inner secret of history, but the historian turns upon him and expounds the secret of the philosopher by placing him in relation to the movement of ideas and interests . . . by giving to his scheme of thought its appropriate relativity.[18]

That is one way to go. The other is a mere meandering byway; it follows the mind of Carl Becker in the years after his formulation of historical relativism in "Everyman His Own Historian."

Naturally we choose to follow Beard. Having made our choice, however, we shortly begin to wonder where the hell he is leading. Beard's relativism lasts for two or three pages of his address. Then characteristically he issues his "supreme command" to historians. They must "cast off" their "servitude to the assumptions of natural science and return to [their] own subject matter—to history as actuality."[19] Very good, very good, and given the inclination of some historians to tame the friskiness of the past by jamming it into the straitjacket of mechanistic or organismic assumptions, well worth saying. But the three or four pages that follow, which Beard devotes to excoriating scientific history, do not really have much to do with relativism. At last he comes back to it. And —as we said in my youth—and how! Here is what he says:

18. Beard, "Written History," p. 219.
19. Ibid., p. 222.

Having broken the tyranny of physics and biology, contemporary thought in historiography turns its engines of verification upon the formula of historical relativity . . . Contemporary criticism shows that the apostle of relativity is destined to be destroyed by the child of his own brain . . . As the actuality of history moves forward into the future, the conception of relativity will also pass, as previous conceptions and interpretations of events have passed. Hence, according to the very doctrine of relativity, the skeptic of relativity will disappear in due course, beneath the ever-tossing waves of changing relativities . . . The historian . . . sees the doctrine of relativity crumble in the cold light of historical knowledge.[20]

Having left relativism in ruins amid the relativity of relativity, Beard goes on to tell historians what they should do about it. In conformity to the prescription of Leviticus 18:7, with proper filial concern for the reverence due to a father of the historical profession in America, I will draw the veil of silence over Beard's prescriptions, saying only, with relief, that very few historians followed them. The odd but characteristic procedure of Beard's presidential address—the issuance of "supreme commands," the running up of the flag of relativism, and the running of it down again, and the running up of another flag or two, all in ten pages—reminds us of what we ought to have known all along: Beard's quick, casual wink at relativism could not be the beginning of a serious affair. Beard was a crusader all his life, a man with a cause, whole hosts of causes from workers' education in his twenties to isolationism in his seventies.[21] Historical relativism does not work very well as a cause. If the heart of the matter is that in their writing historians inevitably mirror their times, well, that's that; they do it willy-nilly. It is hard

20. Ibid., p. 225.
21. Richard Hofstadter, *The Progressive Historians: Turner, Beard, Parrington* (New York: Knopf, 1969), pp. 167-346.

to sustain enthusiasm for a crusade whose aim, if any, would be to convince the profession that it ought to do what it is sure to do in any case.

I do not wish to suggest that Beard's address was inconsequential in the history of history-writing in America, or even that the crusade he launched in 1933 was unsuccessful. Quite to the contrary. I would maintain, however, that it was only tangentially related to historical relativism. Beard's successful crusade took off from a passage of "Everyman His Own Historian" that in the furor over relativism received little attention. In that passage Becker reflected on what he took to be a dominant trait of the orthodox doctrine among historians in the United States in his day.

The scientific historian deliberately renounced philosophy only to submit to it without being aware. His philosophy was just this, that by not taking thought a cubit would be added to his stature ... Hoping to find something without looking for it, expecting to obtain final answers to life's riddle by resolutely refusing to ask questions — it was surely the most romantic species of realism yet invented, the oddest attempt ever made to get something for nothing. (P. 250)

On this idiosyncrasy of his peers Becker had been reflecting for a quarter of a century, and he had in a fragmentary way expressed to his fellow historians the bewilderment his reflections engendered—but nothing much had come of it. He had not induced many historians to take thought about what they were doing, about the discipline they were practicing, about what history was about.[22]

When Beard took up a cause, something came of it. In the instance at hand Beard wrought mightily for the cause for a decade. The early result was two further pieces by him in

22. See especially Becker's "What are Historical Facts?" in *Detachment,* p. 54.

the *American Historical Review*. The most consequential result was a bulletin of the Social Science Research Council. In that bulletin, at Beard's instigation and under his direction, the professional historians of the United States undertook something like an official inquest into their own activities, into how they had written history and how they should write it. Since that time only a few aborigines in the historical hinterlands have been able consistently to shove into the back of their minds the question, "What the devil are we, am I, up to? And why?" We may be doubtful how to evaluate the heightened self-consciousness of historians in the United States. We may wonder how to balance the benefit to historians of professional self-awareness against the cost to them of the profession's confusion, inhibition, and time spent in dealing incompetently with arcane matters. Both self-awareness and confusion were consequences of Beard's campaign. Nevertheless, the evidence that Beard did rechannel the intellectual habits of a whole profession is there to see. For more than a decade now a specialized journal, *History and Theory,* has undertaken custody of historical navel-watching in the United States.[23]

So? So, c'est magnifique, mais ce n'est pas le relativisme.

23. Charles A. Beard, "That Noble Dream," *American Historical Review* 41 (1935): 74-87; Charles A. Beard and Alfred Vogts, "Currents of Thought in Historiography," ibid. 42 (1937): 460-483; Social Science Research Council, Committee on Historiography, *Theory and Practice in Historical Study*, Bulletin 54 (New York, 1946). I doubt that any other historian has enjoyed hospitality of the columns of the *AHR* for articles in three years out of four for any purpose whatever, much less for proposing and propagandizing for "revolutionary changes" in the profession. Where Beard picked up this new cause is not clear. It may have had something to do with his association with the German refugee Alfred Vagts, who married Beard's daughter Miriam. So far as I know Beard had not displayed an appetite for "sermons by mystical Germans" before the 1930s.

And since relativism is what this essay is about we had better go back to that meandering byway where relativism is or was—to the mind of Carl Becker.

How irrevocably attached was Becker to the radical historical relativism that was one of the central themes of his presidential address? We may make a safer if not a faster way through this question if we come up to it indirectly instead of head on. Let us start with the most trivial perplexity of all—who was Everyman? Trivial, indeed apparently silly, since in his presidential address Professor Becker tells us who Everyman is. He is, says Becker, "every normal person . . . just an ordinary citizen without excess knowledge" (p. 236). Normal, ordinary, without excess: these are the terms a prudent man uses when he wants to avoid or to put off being pinned to saying something precise and definite. We cannot afford to be shuffled off that way just now. Such bits of identification are so vague and casual that we need to investigate the identity and personality of Mr. Everyman a little further. We will find that Becker referred to him before 1931, poorly concealing him under an implausible alias. Everyman first shows up in 1922 in Becker's review of Benedetto Croce's *History: Its Theory and Practice*. There he is identified as "you."[24]

How do we know Everyman and "you" are the same fellow? Well, according to the record—the presidential address and the review of Croce—they do the same things. They wake up in the morning and recapture their identity by relying on memory to provide them with a past, a history, and a place in the world of today. Moreover, in orienting them-

24. Carl Becker, "History as the Intellectual Adventure of Mankind," *New Republic* 30 (5 April 1922): 174-176.

selves they both consult their memorandum books, and, behold, those books contain almost identical entries, reminders to pay a coal bill. Not only that, but the payment noted is due to the same coal dealer, Smith. In 1922 the reminder goes "Pay Smith's coal bill today"; in 1931 it goes "December 29, pay Smith's coal bill, 20 tons, $1017.20." Any lingering doubt that "you" of 1922 and "Everyman" of 1931 are the same fellow must surely be resolved when we note that their memoranda contain an identical error: they both name Smith as the payee for the coal bill; but on further investigation they both find out they have bought the coal from someone else; both "you" and Everyman have actually bought the coal, Becker tells us, from Brown, the same someone else. Here, as far as historical research can yield a QED, it seems to me we have achieved one: Everyman (1931) = you (1922).

Perhaps we can arrive at a more concrete image of Everyman if we check on what he thought about as he tried to pull himself together to face the day in 1922 and 1931. Here is a composite list drawn from the review of Croce and the presidential address:

    my room
    house
    furnace in the cellar
    ashes
    coffee
    office
    affair of John Doe
    Rotary Club lunch
    Washington conference
    Debs
    starving Russians
    Bolsheviks
    General Motors dropped three points
    a conference for ten o'clock in the morning

nine holes at four-thirty in the afternoon
a coal bill to be paid someone.

A glance at the list informs us that Mr. Everyman is not, as Becker alleged he was, "every normal person." He is almost certainly well informed (he knows about Debs, Bolsheviks, and the Washington Conference). He is urban (he goes to conferences himself and has an office). He is probably a shareholder (he follows stock-market prices). A homeowner (surely that recurrent coal bill is for heating his own house). Male, middle-class, middle-aged (he is a Rotarian), and white (golf-club membership in 1931 taken with all the rest just about guarantees a white Anglo-Saxon Protestant). In short, Mr. Everyman was a classic WASP.

So, Mr. Everyman was not every normal person, not really; rather five percent or less of normal persons in the United States in 1931. After all, once out of high school or grade school, 95 percent of those normal persons never had read anything a professional historian, even Carl Becker, had written, and were not about to be conned into doing so. The likelihood of a professional historian correcting and rationalizing whatever myths they were addicted to was minimal. With informed, urban, share-owning, home-owning, male, middle-class, middle-aged WASPS the chances might have been appreciably, though not immeasurably, better.

More interesting than what Becker's shrunk-to-size Mr. Everyman was is what he was not. Of course he was not a lot of things that are in vogue today in the United States— not a woman, not poor or deprived, not young, not black or Chicano. But those negations are anachronisms. Most importantly in 1931, Becker's Everyman was not a hard-eyed, jackbooted young ruffian, parading, Jew-hating, street-fighting, and committing assault, wearing a brown shirt with a

Hakenkreuz emblem on it, and shouting "Heil Hitler" in unison with his fellow German Everymen. For this German version of Everyman, issued in an edition far larger than Becker's American middle-aged, middle-class, male, WASP version, many German professional historians were shortly to perform the service that Becker had prescribed. Those historians did not "cultivate a species of dry professional arrogance growing out of the thin soil of antiquarian research." The history they wrote was intended to do work in the world, to be living history that influences the course of history, to enlarge and enrich the collective specious present of the Nazi Everyman, to encourage him to embrace the thousand-year Reich. When the time came, they took care "not to repeat the past but to make use of it, to correct and rationalize for common use Mr. Everyman's mythological adaptation of what actually happened" (p. 253). If the corrections were few, the rationalizations made up the balance. And those German historians who did their work well were doubly rewarded. They enjoyed the spiritual profit that comes from writing living history. They also enjoyed the material profit of taking over the places of those inhibited by impediment of blood or by moral queasiness from writing the kind of living history then in demand in the Third Reich.

How did such exponents of living history that did its (or perhaps Dr. Goebbels's) work in the world suit Carl Becker? What did Becker make of the generous services that, following his prescription without being aware of it, so many professional historians in Germany rendered to Mr. Everyman, when he appeared in the guise of Herr Stürmer? He does not tell us directly; and he did not directly pass judgment on the historians in Nazi Germany, who along with the idea of blood and race gladly accepted from the Nazis the jobs of Jews and liberals who were displaced from university positions. In the Becker oeuvre, Mr. Everyman makes his last appearance in the presidential address of 1931. That address was, I think, Becker's last published effort to reflect systematically on the business of being a professional historian. After the Nazi-Soviet pact of 1939, however, Becker did reflect on the intellectual genealogy of some of the actualities of the preceding decade. In doing so he reflected, quite indirectly, on the education and the intellectual milieu of the young Carl Becker. In 1940 in an article for the *Yale Review*, "Some Generalities That Still Glitter," he defined the suppositions, "the 'anti-intellectual' assumptions," that were the context from which Nazism, Stalinism, and Professor Carl Becker had emerged, the common climate of opinion in which those diverse plants had flourished. Here are the common assumptions, and what men made of them:

If reason was an instrument biologically developed to serve the interests of the organism, its pronouncements could never be disinterested; . . . if truth was relative, nothing could be really true; . . . if morals varied with the customs of time and place, any custom that got itself established was moral, and one system of morality as good as another; . . . if ideas were inspired by individual or class interest, the success of an idea in promoting individual or class interest was the only test of its validity . . . The existence and pressure of the fact carry their own justification; the assumption that ideas are weapons was itself a weapon which could be put to use in the world of practical affairs.[25]

These ideas, here stated, as Becker remarked, "in their crudest and least defensible form" (p. 136), were the "assumptions as to the nature of man and the mind of man [that] were the chief contribution of scientific investigation and disinterested critical analysis to the social thinking" of his own

25. Carl Becker, "Some Generalities That Still Glitter," in Becker, *New Liberties for Old* (New Haven: Yale University Press, 1941), p. 137.

adult years. Had he himself succumbed to these assumptions? Probably not, at any rate not "in their crudest and least defensible form." But in the arid climate of American historical thought in the 1900s, like a modern St. Anthony, he had been sorely tempted. By 1940, however, with the accidental aid of Germany's young brown-shirted version of Mr. Everyman, he had returned to grace. By then "the trend of thought variously known as anti-intellectualism, relativism, activism" had lost much of whatever savor it had once had for him; it had reached "a final fantastic form [in which] truth and morality turn out to be relative to the purpose of any egocentric somnambulist who can succeed . . . in creating the power to impose his unrestrained will upon the world," in short, the form of Adolf Hitler.[26]

In 1940 Becker firmly rejected the fallacious supposition "that reason cannot transcend its lowly animal origin . . . that because it . . . can be and is employed in the service of purely egotistical and brutal impulses, it cannot serve purposes of a more humane and impersonal import." In 1940 Becker also produced a sort of counter-creed to "anti-intellectualism, relativism, activism," a creed that included

faith in the dignity and worth of the individual man as an end in himself, [belief] that it is better to be governed by persuasion than coercion . . . that fraternal good will is more worthy than a selfish and contentious spirit . . . that in the long run all values are inseparable from the love of truth and the disinterested search for it . . . that knowledge and the power it confers should be used to promote the welfare and happiness of men.

We may be a little dubious that the values expressed in this creed were, as Becker alleged, established by "Buddha and Confucius, Solomon and Zoroaster, Plato and Aristotle, Soc-

26. Ibid., pp. 144, 145.

rates and Jesus." What we cannot doubt at all is that they were the values of Carl Becker, his creed, in 1940.[27]

In an America that took these values seriously, what could the task of the historian by profession, no longer Mr. Everyman's manservant, be? What should history be? To that question Becker had an answer. Unlike scientific knowledge,

knowledge of history cannot be . . . practically applied, and is therefore worthless except to those who have made it, in greater or less degree, a personal possession. The value of history is, indeed, not scientific but moral: by liberalizing the mind, by deepening the sympathies, by fortifying the will, it enables us to control not society, but ourselves — a much more important thing.[28]

These views of what history was for and might be able to do appeared in 1915 in a book review by the young Carl Becker. They seem to be wholly compatible with his creed in 1940, as that creed is revealed in "Some Generalities That Still Glitter." But can they be reconciled with the historical relativism of "Everyman His Own Historian"? That is my last perplexity, and I leave it with you.

1974

27. Ibid., pp. 148, 149.
28. Carl Becker, "A New Philosophy of History," *The Dial* 59 (1915): 148.

PART TWO

In Particular: Early Modern Europe

2.

Wallace K. Ferguson and Hiram Hayden: The Renaissance Again – and Again

"The Renaissance" has proved a protean term, multiform in its uses, capable of embracing divergent, even incompatible historical phenomena. Only a variety of approaches to the entities, varied in content and time-scope, that the term has been used to encompass, can do justice to its almost infinite variety. This essay will consider two somewhat eccentric ways of coming to grips with the Renaissance, that of Wallace K. Ferguson in *The Renaissance in Historical Thought* and that of Hiram Hayden in *The Counter-Renaissance*.[1] In his study Ferguson keeps an impenetrable buckler between himself and the fundamental question: what was it about that age, whenever it began, that justifies us in characterizing it as the age of the Renaissance? He escapes that awkward question by focusing unwaveringly on another: on what historical traits, actual or illusory, of that dimly delimited age have historians over the centuries bestowed the name Renaissance, and why? Or more broadly, in what as-

1. Wallace K. Ferguson, *The Renaissance in Historical Thought: Five Centuries of Interpretation* (Boston: Houghton Mifflin, 1948); Hiram Hayden, *The Counter-Renaissance* (New York: Charles Scribner's Sons, 1950).

pects of what time spans have historians believed that they discerned traits to which the notion of renaissance or rebirth is germane, and on what grounds have other historians greeted each discerning with cries of "Fiddlesticks," in the belief that such discerning missed the real point of the Renaissance or in the more devastating belief that there was no Renaissance to miss the point of? When one has finished Ferguson's book, one no longer wonders that so many historians of the Renaissance appear to be exhausted by a struggle against a suffocating mass of preconceptions or misconceptions. For purposes of comment the pairing of *The Renaissance in Historical Thought* with *The Counter-Renaissance* conveniently exemplifies the difficulties that those who put the Renaissance in the center of their historical thinking encounter, since the latter book is a resolute attempt to meet problems in historical writing whose complexity and urgency the former reveals.

Under the appearance of simplicity that results from the clarity of Ferguson's style, *The Renaissance in Historical Thought* is an intricate book. At its least integrated level it is a fine critical bibliography of most of the important works that have dealt with the Renaissance concept for a matter of five hundred years. Ferguson analyzes and comments on an appalling mass of historical studies in a manner that conceals both art and years of patient study. Each separate comment is shrewd, judicious, and charitable, although the author occasionally with a mild grin exposes and thrusts aside the balderdash in his path. He has a special aptitude and predilection for demolishing German scholars of a romantic and nationalistic bent, whom he felicitously describes as *begriff-stricken*. This work of critical comment is enough to render *The Renaissance in Historical Thought* indispensable to specialists in the field.

At another level Ferguson uses the Renaissance concept as a sort of focusing mirror, which reflects the main lines of development of intellectual sentiment for half a millennium. He shows how in every age the notions of intellectuals at large about the world at large left a distinct impress on what historians of each age thought about the Renaissance. The broad and general conceptions of our ancestors, the assumptions, sometimes obscure or covert, that directed and limited their thought, these mental habits that often lurk so vaguely on the periphery of history suddenly become intelligible, clear, and distinct, when (thanks to Ferguson) we see them, as it were, standing for the last five hundred years at the elbow of the historians of the Renaissance, pouring ideas, prejudices, and preconceptions into their heads, almost palpably guiding their hands as they wrote. We may indeed become a little suspicious of the intellectual stability of our profession, when through Ferguson's eyes we watch our brethren spinning like weathercocks at each shift of the winds of doctrine; but then as historians we are glad to know that in each age our predecessors have unconsciously provided us with so reliable an indicator of which way those winds were blowing.

Finally and primarily, *The Renaissance in Historical Thought* is the biography of an idea—the story of the Renaissance concept from its beginnings up to the year before last. As Ferguson skillfully unfolds that story, he makes clear his belief that it is dominated by one man and one book—Jacob Burckhardt and *The Civilization of the Renaissance in Italy*. To that man and book all lines of the growth of the concept lead, and away from them all lines of disintegration of the concept wander—each along its peculiar course.

The Renaissance concept certainly, the thing in itself perhaps, according to Ferguson, began in Italy with the notion that the fifteenth century saw a revival of antique learning and letters, which had been allowed to lie dormant for centuries. To the idea of an Italian revival of classical literature Giorgio Vasari added the idea of a simultaneous revival of classical art. North of the Alps the influence of Erasmus led to the coupling of the idea of religious with the idea of literary renovation; and the Reformation, in a backhanded way, accentuated the contrast between the fifteenth Christian century and the preceding ten by painting the latter a uniform black comprised of ignorance, idolatry, and superstition. These vague beginnings were accepted and made more precise but not much developed or altered in the seventeenth century. The Renaissance concept was decisively advanced toward maturity during the Enlightenment by Voltaire's elaboration of the principles of the history of culture. He sought to define the distinctive traits of each great historical epoch. The Protestant tradition provided him with a characterization of the Middle Ages altogether to his taste, an epoch red in tooth and claw and clerical black in every other respect. By way of contrast, the dawn of the modern era came in Italy with the emergence of a new way of life compounded of anti-papalism, civilized manners, cultivated tastes, and rationalism in religion and mode of living. Against the Enlightenment the succeeding romantic movement created a new representation of the medieval period, transforming the darkness of the age of ignorance into the dim religious light of the age of faith. By transvaluating the eighteenth century's valuation of the age of the Renaissance in an inverse sense, however, turning it from an era of illumination to one rather of confused dark glare, the romantics maintained the element of sharp contrast between the Middle Ages and what followed.

So, by the 1830s most of the ingredients of the Burckhardtian concept of the Renaissance, including the name, were available to historians, and the period was beginning to be viewed as something distinct in itself, not merely as the first modern age. The idea that such a period must have sharp traits that distinguish it from all other ages and constitute its special *Geist* took hold in the minds of many historians through the influence of Friedrich Hegel.

In 1860 the climactic work, *The Civilization of the Renaissance in Italy,* was published. It created the orthodox historical tradition in the image of Jacob Burckhardt. Burckhardt's Renaissance was Italian, and it ran from the fourteenth to the early sixteenth centuries. It was modern, and its basis was the unique position of the Italian city-states. It was rationalist and individualist, nourished but not created by a new understanding of classical antiquity. Its distinctive mark, in contrast with the preceding age, was its discovery of man's this-worldly capacities and personality. Burckhardt documented his view of the Renaissance from a rich knowledge of the literature of the age in Italy and presented it with the finesse of a skilled artist.

Burckhardt's conception of the Renaissance was not seriously challenged or modified for forty years; but for the past half-century it has been beaten about unmercifully. Ferguson offers a patient and systematic account of its recent vicissitudes, and, after reading his narrative, one is not sure whether the concept has suffered worse at the hands of its enemies who detest it, of its friends who in the process of saving it have modified it beyond recognition, or of the Boojum school who make it softly and silently vanish away. It is impossible here even to mention the vast variety of modifications, alterations, and revisions that Ferguson describes. What emerges from his narrative, however, is the sense that positive knowledge about the period between 1200 and 1600 has vastly increased in the last fifty years, while the relation and even the relevance of the concept "Renaissance" to the events of that period has become increasingly confused, obscure, and uncertain.

The chaos made palpable in the later chapters of *The Renaissance in Historical Thought* has long been a standing invitation for the intellectually intrepid or rash to leap in and get things straightened out. Hiram Hayden has accepted the invitation. His *The Counter-Renaissance* is an "attempt to characterize" the Renaissance, roughly defined as the three centuries between "the crowning of Petrarch with laurel" and the death of Francis Bacon, and described as "the transition from the medieval to the modern world" (p. xi). What characterizes this transition period, according to Hayden, is "three large distinct *intellectual* movements" (p. xi, italics added). A quick look at the index confirms what the phrase suggests. Among the forty-five leading characters in the book there is not a prince or a chief minister, not a pope or a bishop (except St. Augustine), not a warrior or an explorer or a financier. The numerous references to two statesmen (Machiavelli and More) and two religious revolutionaries (Luther and Calvin) are deceptive, since all four are discussed not in connection with their active careers but solely as theologians and philosophers. With such a cerebral cast we can hardly expect much action in the drama Hayden unfolds for us, and indeed we get very little. We hear nothing of the overseas expansion of the Atlantic powers, nothing of the new dynasties of international finance, nothing of the establishment of standing armies, nothing of the consolidation of dynastic territorial states, nothing of the religious revolutions that shook great princes in their shoes. In fact, we hear nothing of any changes in social, economic, political, or religious arrangements. In some respects this is all to the good. My own first semiintimate contact with the Renaissance took place in a graduate course in which the instructors were committed to the notion that the Renaissance was at once an era and a spirit. This dual and incongruous commitment produced some wondrous historiographic monsters when it was applied to everything that happened in Europe west of the Elbe from sometime early in the fourteenth century to sometime late in the sixteenth. It was not easy to envisage the nature and boundaries of a spirit that could entertain as joint tenants—among others—William of Occam, Pizarro, Richard II, Nicholas of Cusa, Jakob Fugger, Cardinal Ximenes, and Thomas à Kempis, along with the Medici and the Italian artists and men of letters whom one thinks of as holding squatters' rights over that spirit. Hayden, of course, is under no enforceable obligation to deal with mundane matters, and he is probably prudent not to do so. He should realize, however, that in completely disregarding them he is leaving out a great deal of what was involved in the transition from the medieval to the modern world. His reconceptualization of the Renaissance almost by definition can give us but a very partial and one-sided glimpse of that process of transition.

If, however, the intellectual changes between Petrarch and Bacon are a good deal less than the whole of the transition from the Middle Ages to modern times, still they are an important part of that transition—a part, moreover, concerning the precise character of which there have been extreme and almost violent differences of opinion among historians. If *The Counter-Renaissance* really succeeded in bringing some order out of this chaos, we should surely pardon Hayden's tendency to exaggerate the import of his own work, a weakness which after all he shares with all of us. What, then, is the pattern that Hayden discerns in the intellectual changes between Petrarch and Bacon? There are, he says, "three large

distinct intellectual movements discernible between the mid-
fourteenth and the early seventeenth century" (p. xi) : the
classical Renaissance, the counter-Renaissance, and the scientific revolution. Although the three movements overlapped,
the above listing follows "the order in time of their strongest
maturities" (p. xii). The classical Renaissance slightly modified but "did not challenge the synthetic vision of Thomas
Aquinas" (p. xiii). Its protagonists are marked by a belief
in reason, in the essential goodness of nature, especially human nature, and in the consonance of the real with the ideal.
They are preoccupied with "universal law and order, with
design and purpose and unity, . . . with the idea of limit . . .
There are three basic concepts implying, or related to, 'limit,'
which color almost all of their thought about reality and
value: that of 'degree' or inequality or gradation; that of fi-
nality or completeness or finiteness; and that of harmony or
moderation or balance" (pp. 293-294).

The succeeding counter-Renaissance is characterized by
its rejection of all Renaissance standards. Its religionists turn
to faith and repudiate reason; its scientists are radical empiri-
cists. Its historical, political, and ethical writers reject natural law and innate justice and give an almost exclusive value
to the evidence of fact. "What unites these otherwise dissimi-
lar thinkers . . . is that they share completely an anti-intel-
lectualistic, anti-moralistic, anti-synthetic, anti-authoritarian
bias" (p. xiii). With the scientific revolution, about which
Hayden has not a great deal to say, there is a "return to confidence in reason-and-nature" but not to the Renaissance "re-
conciliation between theology and science" (p. xvi).

The first thing about Hayden's schema to catch our eye is
his conception of the first or "Renaissance" movement. According to Hayden, it was practically unchallenged from
Petrarch to the beginning of the sixteenth century; but, if

we investigate the fifteen principal writers to whom he ascribes an essentially Renaissance world view, we run into a curious chronological dilemma. Six of them had been dead from twenty-five to fifteen hundred years before Petrarch was crowned with laurel. Four of them were contemporaries of Francis Bacon, the last great exemplar of the counter-Renaissance, and four more—Ficino, Pico, Erasmus, and More—are clustered in the half-century that preceded the Reformation. The only major representative of the Renaissance movement, as Hayden conceives it, in its first century and a quarter is Petrarch himself, who stands at its beginning. This vacuum is a little perplexing, since it coincides exactly with what has traditionally been described as the age of the Renaissance in Italy, *the* Renaissance par excellence for most historians since Burckhardt. Hayden, however, explains the omission: "Italian humanism concerned itself vastly more with other aspects of man's life on earth than with the dutiful exercise of reason in pursuit of virtue" (p. 66); and elsewhere, "the humanism of the Renaissance (except in fifteenth century Italy) was basically Christian" (p. 14).

The implicit conclusion is that Italian intellectual history from Petrarch to Ficino, because its humanism was not Christian, is outside the Renaissance movement. Hayden's method here has a touching though somewhat naive forthrightness. The history of ideas for almost half of the Renaissance period must be omitted because it is recalcitrant to the author's reconceptualization of that period. Historians who have had the shattering experience of seeing a big beautiful iridescent idea blow up in their faces on contact with dull cold data are certain to sympathize with the feeling that informs Hayden's method. Yet, they are likely to feel that the orthodox procedure, which in such circumstances requires not the omission of the facts but the reconstruction of the theory to conform with them, has, after all, considerable to be said for it. They are also likely to feel that an attempt to revivify the Renaissance concept that begins by cutting its heart out will perhaps fall somewhat short of complete success.

Actually, the situation is rather worse than has been indicated. Although Pico and Ficino are set down as exemplars of Renaissance humanism, the citations to the latter are, to say the least, ambiguous on this point (pp. 332, 335, 344, 348, 353, and 525), while practically all the subsequent mentions of and citations to the former align him with the counter-Renaissance. Indeed, Hayden himself ultimately gives up the Count of Mirandola as a whited sepulcher, and characterizes him as a "romanticist of the Counter-Renaissance" (p. 465). The cases of Petrarch and Erasmus are scarcely better. Hayden first pastes the Renaissance label on them and later rather consistently cites them as exemplars of counter-Renaissance tendencies. Thomas More comes through the ordeal unscathed; but that is the consequence of Hayden's rather selective choices of quotations. Any amateur reader of the *Utopia* could quickly come up with dozens of quotations to exemplify what Hayden describes as counter-Renaissance ideas. Alas, as a Renaissance thinker St. Thomas More is not without blemish.

St. Thomas Aquinas is without blemish, and thereby, of course, hangs the tale. By a rather complex ideological maneuver Hayden makes the author of the *Summa theologica* provide the standard by which men and ideas are judged orthodoxly Renaissance or heretically counter-Renaissance. The argument seems to go something like this. The Renaissance was a humanist movement. The humanists (with certain exceptions whom Hayden prefers to disregard) were Christian humanists. They drew their ethical ideas from the tradition of classical antiquity. Aquinas drew not only his ethics but his physics, metaphysics, and politics from the classical tradition. He was also very Christian. Therefore, he was the best Christian humanist of all; and by the same token the only truly Renaissance thought is that which does not deviate much from his ethics, metaphysics, physics, and politics. This explains Hayden's difficulty in coming up with reliable exemplars during the Renaissance period of the Renaissance movement as he conceives it. There just were not many good Thomists around at that time. But then very few people have ever alleged that there were.

Thus, Hayden's conception of the Renaissance suffers from malnutrition of historical content. His new conception—the counter-Renaissance—does not. All the rich intellectual diet that he has refused to the Renaissance has to be crammed into it, and the result is a rather obese disorganized notion. To bind so invertebrate a concept together and thus avoid a case of acute pterodactylism,[2] Hayden devotes the larger part of his big book to establishing what he believes to be connections among the various sixteenth-century writers who deviate from the classical, traditional, middle-course, humanist way of thinking. He somewhat simplifies his problem and gives a slightly specious appearance of absolute novelty to the counter-Renaissance by disregarding or brushing aside as atypical all medieval writing that possesses any trait that he ascribes to the counter-Renaissance. Augustinian theology; Ockhamism; Bernardine, Victorine, and Germanic mysticism; goliardic poetry; the code of chivalry and courtly love; the fabliaux; medieval satire; Franciscan simplicity—counter-

2. The pterodactyl is an extinct bird or reptile with highly individual traits. Pterodactylism is the assertion that all other creatures are alike in that they are not pterodactyls. This assertion is perhaps true but not interesting.

Renaissance citadels right in the midst of the Aquinas country —are simply bypassed, and perhaps it is just as well. Anyone who undertakes to make Calvin and Luther, Paracelsus and Cornelius Agrippa, Machiavelli and Montaigne and Bacon, Bruno, Bodin, Raleigh, Rabelais, and Guicciardini march together like an army with banners has quite enough of a mission on his hands without worrying about anything else.

Some of the links that putatively bind these diverse men together are fragile at best. The case of Calvin illustrates the length to which Hayden has to go to make the facts fit his theory. There is, he claims, a "startling parallel" between Machiavelli's Fortuna and Calvin's God. This parallel disregards the differences between the blind Dame who controls men only halfway, leaving the rest to their *virtù*, and the omnipotent ruler of the universe whose eternal decrees are immutable; but Hayden says it links Calvin with Machiavelli, a naturalist who denied limit. But Bodin denied limit, too, by rejecting on historical grounds the medieval idea that the number of monarchies since the creation was *limited* to four, and Montaigne denied it too by doubting whether in their daily lives men acted as if they were limited by a natural moral law. So by associating Calvin, as well as Machiavelli, Bodin, and Montaigne, with denial of limit, the author has stuffed them into the same bag, although it has taken something rather like punning to do it. Besides being a naturalist, Calvin is a romantic, which is the opposite of a naturalist but is also counter-Renaissance. He is a romantic because "his insistence upon God's inscrutable will and omnipotence and man's wretched helplessness . . . as surely splits the whole working principle of the relatedness of the ideal to the actual as does the defiant nihilism of some nineteenth-century Romantics" (p. 19). The man who spent boundless energy in making the actual commercial town of Geneva conform to his ideal of the *regnum Christi* might object to this characterization, but it suffices, in Hayden's opinion, to bind him to such counter-Renaissance romantics as Pico, Paracelsus, and Bruno. Through a series of such almost miraculous transformations the author of the *Institutes of the Christian Religion* and of the government and discipline of the Reformed churches comes out with a "completely . . . anti-synthetic, anti-authoritarian bias."

This peculiar straining of analogies and stretching of the meanings of words is epidemic in *The Counter-Renaissance*. It is most unfortunate, because it smothers much that is excellent in the book. In the sixteenth century certain ways of thinking and feeling about life and the world touched and colored with a like hue the views of men who in other respects were very different from one another. Hayden has discovered some of these common traits and revealed some remarkable and viable connections in the process. Indeed, he has discovered enough of them to fill a book—a much shorter and better book than *The Counter-Renaissance,* and with a different title. What drove him beyond the excellent small book, for which he had ample material, to the unsatisfactory large one he wrote? I think he was driven by the form of explanation that lay behind his conception. This form of explanation is not made explicit in the book itself. Why the three phases of thought—Renaissance, counter-Renaissance, and scientific revolution—should follow one another seems not to preoccupy Hayden much. Yet he does have an explanation, so little emphasized that the reader is likely to overlook it. The counter-Renaissance was a reaction to and denial of the values of the Renaissance. The scientific revolution brought together the vital elements of both Renaissance and counter-Renaissance into a new way of thought, and the dialectical development of ideas coincides roughly with the historical passage of time. In other words, we have here the Hegelian triad of thesis, antithesis, and synthesis; Renaissance, counter-Renaissance, and scientific revolution are zeitgeists following the proper Hegelian pattern. Hayden's book illustrates perfectly how a conception scarcely adverted to can dominate an elaborate intellectual work. Only under the spell of the Hegelian dialectic or its Marxian inversion would a writer dedicate himself to the foredoomed task of demonstrating a basic similarity among Vives, Calvin, Montaigne, Luther, Bruno, Rabelais, and Machiavelli. Only by emphasizing much that is trivial and casual in their way of thought, misinterpreting much that is not, and disregarding the rest can such spiritual incompatibles be made to appear as comrades in the same movement of thought. The idea of the absolute does not perhaps dominate history, but it almost always dominates Hegelians, self-conscious or otherwise, who write history. Both the major weaknesses and the minor aberrations of *The Counter-Renaissance*—strained analogies, irrelevant or dubious examples, mystifying chronology—thus become intelligible. They are the cinders and ashes left behind when common sense and ordinary perspicacity are offered up in an auto-da-fé to the Hegelian dialectic.

So Hayden's study fails to lead us out of the historiographic muddle that the late chapters of *The Renaissance in Historical Thought* reveal. It is one entry added to a long list of previous failures, failures so numerous that some historians seek to avoid the perplexities of the Renaissance concept by dropping the term "Renaissance" altogether. Against such a renunciation Ferguson quotes with approval a remark Henri Hauser made in this connection: "It seems to me that, save in case of absolute necessity, it is a grave matter to renew in the scientific domain the miracle of the confusion of tongues" (p. 394). Yet we may wonder whether we are not near such absolute necessity with respect to the Renaissance. For though a renewal of the confusion of tongues is hardly a desideratum, the confusion caused by dropping a term would be no more stultifying than the employment by different authors of the same term to signify two entirely separate historical periods, or, what is worse, to signify two simultaneous, opposite, and mutually exclusive cultural constellations. Indeed, the confusion of tongues has already been renewed, since when a historian uses the term "Renaissance," we are forced to stop and determine which of the numerous current meanings of the term he has in mind. As to "the essential question of the nature of Renaissance civilization, viewed in its entirety as a European phenomenon" (p. 397), there is simply no agreement among historians.[3]

1951

3. On this point see my second thoughts in the Introduction to this volume, pp. 4-5.

3.

Fernand Braudel and the Monde Braudellien . . .

In 1949 a *thèse* in fulfillment of the requirement for the degree of *Docteur ès Lettres* at the Sorbonne was published in Paris. It was 1,175 pages long. It had no illustrations, maps, or graphs. Its author was a French scholar, then forty-seven years old, named Fernand Braudel. The title of the work was *La Méditerranée et le monde méditerranéen à l'époque de Philippe II*. Seventeen years later, in 1966, a revised and corrected two-volume edition of *La Méditerranée* appeared, replete with tables, maps, graphs, and handsome illustrations, its length 1,218 pages. Now an English translation of the revised edition of *La Méditerranée* has been published in both England and the United States.

The preface to the second edition begins as follows.

It was with much hesitation that I undertook a new edition of *The Mediterranean*. Some of my friends advised me to change nothing, not a word, not a comma, arguing that a work that had become a classic should not be altered. But how could I decently listen to them? With the increase in knowledge and the advances made in our neighboring disciplines, the social sciences, history books age more quickly now than in the past. A moment passes, and their vocabulary has become dated, the new ground they broke is familiar territory, and the explanations they offered are challenged.

And so we have a historical problem, one of those problems with which, according to Professor Braudel, historical investigation should start: what made *La Méditerranée* a classic in 1949? What makes its second edition a classic in 1972? For it stretches credulity to the breaking point to believe that an English commercial publishing house would undertake the translation and issue of a 1,200-page history book unless it were a classic.

In terms of the view of history set forth in *La Méditerranée* and propagated by Braudel ever since, however, the historical problem just raised is badly posed. Or better, perhaps, it is raised out of order, too soon. It is a question that has to do with a mere event, and in Braudel's tiered or three-layered image of the past and of the way historians should deal with it, what has to do with events, the *événementielle*, is the least important layer, and the one to be dealt with last. The study of events gains whatever value it has (not much, in Braudel's view) only insofar as it rests on the two more substantial layers that underlie it. The base layer is what Braudel calls *structures*, and it is with them that we should begin.

In the case in point the *structures* are the *mentalités*, sets of mind, points of view, paradigms imbedded in institutions, durable organisms, that give French historical scholarship its particular posture and quality. Of its quality we may think it is the best and must think it is the most ecumenical in the world today. Of its posture we must say that it has been more successful than historical scholarship in any other nation in achieving favorable and fruitful relations with the social sciences. In France those relations enrich the study of history and continuously confront the social sciences not only with the existence of history as a discipline but with its importance both intellectual and institutional for them. No need to point to the contrast between France and the United States in this respect. In this country the social scientists have been able to turn their backs on history, and without vigorous challenge have tended to define their central problems in ways that spare them from thinking about history at all. Of this gulf nothing is more symptomatic than a phenomenon Braudel himself observed. After World War II programs of "area studies" began to proliferate in American universities. An "area" is a large territorial and population group marked by major significant interrelations of some of its parts—shared economic level, political tradition, language, historical experience, religious outlook, social institutions, and so on. The purpose of area studies is to investigate such regions— Latin America, the Middle East, black Africa—in the round, "globally," bringing to bear on each the joint expertise of specialized social scientists. What Braudel noticed was that initially in the United States such clusters of experts often did not include historians. In France such an institutional expression of an ahistorical view of the proper study of man would not have passed, as it did in the United States, without serious challenge. It would have had to deal with and confront two powerful institutions. One is a journal, *Annales: Economies, sociétés, civilisations.* Its chief directors have been successively two historians, Lucien Febvre and Fernand Braudel. The other is the now famous VIe section, the sixth section or division of the Ecole pratique des hautes études: Sciences économiques et sociales. Its presidents, unthinkably from an American perspective, have been successively two historians, Lucien Febvre and Fernand Braudel. Any inquiry into the structural relation of history to the social sciences in France must start with the *Annales* and the VIe section.[1]

_____

1. I had neither the materials nor the time to do adequate research on

Structures

In 1929 Lucien Febvre and Marc Bloch, history professors at the University of Strasbourg, founded the *Annales d'histoire sociale et économique*. They did not claim that their journal was an innovation. They believed that the study of history in France was in the doldrums, lagging far behind such study in Germany, England, and the United States. What they saw as the retardation of historical work in France

the history of the *structures* under investigation. What follows in this first section should be considered rather as a sounding, subject to all the limitations that inadequate documentation involves and all the modification that further investigation may require. The main documents available to me have been the following: (1) *Annales* from 1929 to 1972. Beginning in 1939, *Annales* underwent a number of changes of title until 1946, when it first appeared under its present title, *Annales: Economies, sociétés, civilisations* (hereafter cited as *Annales E.S.C.*). (2) *Vingt-cinq ans de recherche historique en France (1940-1965)* (n.p.: *Comité français des sciences historiques,* n.d.). (3) *Rapport d'activité 1969-1970 et programme scientifique 1971-1974* of the Laboratoire associé no. 93 of the Centre nationale de la recherche scientifique (hereafter CNRS): the Centre de recherches historiques of the Ecole pratique des hautes études. (4) Ecole pratique des hautes études (EPHE), VIe section: Sciences économiques et sociales, *Programme d'enseignement 1971-1972.* (5) Publication catalogs: (a) *Collection: Civilisations et sociétés* (Paris: Mouton and Cie); (b) *Publications de l'Ecole pratique des hautes études, VIe section: Centre de recherches historiques, 1972-1973* (Paris: S.E.V.P.E.N.). (6) *Eventails de l'histoire vivante: Hommage à Lucien Febvre,* 2 vols. (Paris: A. Colin, 1953); announcement of *Mélanges en honneur de Fernand Braudel* (Paris, Privat, 1972). (7) The *Annuaires* of the VIe section, 1965-1971.

Throughout this essay citations to Fernand Braudel's *La Méditerranée et le monde méditerranéen à l'époque de Philippe II* will be to the second edition, 2 vols. (Paris: A. Colin, 1966), cited *Méditerranée.* Volume and page numbers given in parentheses in the text or the notes refer to this edition. Since to do so would in no way affect my argument, I have not altered the statements as to dates in the following section, or revised the graphs to bring them up to date. They stand as of 1972, when this essay was written.

they ascribed to an institution, an attitude, and a deficiency. The institution was the Faculty of Letters of the University of Paris, or more precisely the dominant historians of that faculty. Febvre called them *les Sorbonnistes*. For him the word became an epithet equivalent to *l'infâme*. In the interest of the advance of historical studies he felt that the *Sorbonnistes* must be crushed. He regarded their attitude as a symptom of the shrinking timidity of the France that had emerged in spiritual disarray both from the debacle of 1870 and from the pyrrhic victory of 1914-1918. The professors of the Sorbonne immersed themselves not only in political and diplomatic history, but in the empty minutiae of those branches of history. They produced very large tomes on very small matters. Worse, as the trainers of succeeding generations of French historians they produced a progeny in their own image. For practical purposes the history faculty at the Sorbonne owned French history. It turned its back on all the new and exciting horizons that, so Febvre and Bloch believed, historians in other lands were discovering and exploring. This was the deplorable deficiency, the thinness, the malnutrition that the historical establishment, forgetting the great tradition of an earlier day, forgetting Guizot, Thierry, and Michelet, imposed on the study of history in France.

The goal of the *Annales* from the outset, therefore, was to undo the work of the *Sorbonnistes*, to turn French historians away from the narrowly political and the narrowly diplomatic and toward the new vistas in history, especially toward social and economic history. This was the *mentalité* of what came to be known as the *Annales* school of French historians, or the *Annalistes*. In a sense of the term that we will explore more deeply later, this *mentalité* became a *structure*, a controlling habit of thought so deeply imbedded in the minds of the believers that they scarcely subjected it to critical examination.

This *structure*, conceived by Febvre and Bloch, has taken over historical studies in France against considerable odds, at the same time winning for those studies worldwide admiration, something like a consensus that in history France is indeed Number One. The marks of the "new history" in France have been an indifference to political, constitutional, and diplomatic history approaching outright rejection and a wide open hospitality to all other kinds of history, actual or imaginable. Thus for more than forty years the most powerful voices in the French historical profession have called on historians to keep abreast of advances in the social sciences, or, as they would insist, in the *other* social sciences, or better still, because wider open, in *les sciences de l'homme*.

In the 1930s Febvre and Bloch moved from Strasbourg to Paris, Febvre as professor at the Collège de France, Bloch as *maître de conférence* and finally professor of economic history at the Sorbonne itself. The *Annales* moved with them. The war years brought many vicissitudes. Bloch went underground to work for the Resistance, and the Germans captured and shot him. Febvre somehow kept the journal going, assembling and publishing issues on an occasional rather than a regular basis. After the war, still under Febvre's direction, the *Annales* was reborn and rebaptized as *Annales: Economies, sociétés, civilisations*. Fernand Braudel succeeded Febvre as editorial director of the journal in 1957 and remained in control until 1968.

The Ecole pratique des hautes études is funded by the Ministry of Education, outside the framework of the French universities. "Its teaching program, resting on the results of the researches" of its teaching staff, "is oriented to the training of researchers."[2] Its structure, rules, and methods of re-

2. EPHE, VIe section, *Programme d'enseignement 1971-1972*, p. 5.

cruitment are flexible, free from the French university system's regulations and obligations to undergraduate instruction. The plan of the Ecole included six sections, three in the natural sciences, three in the *sciences humaines*. Before World War II a number of distinguished historians taught in the Ecole, among them Lucien Febvre and, in 1937, Fernand Braudel.

The seed for the VIe section of the Ecole pratique des hautes études, the section called Sciences économiques et sociales, was planted in 1869, one year after the school itself. It was a long time taking root. In 1947, more than seventy-five years after it had got into the plans, the VIe section was finally inaugurated as a teaching and research organism. Its first head, the *président*, was not an economist or a sociologist or an anthropologist but the historian Lucien Febvre. On Febvre's death in 1956, Fernand Braudel succeeded him as *président*; he still holds that position in 1972.

Part of the credo of the *Annalistes* was that as a science history would benefit by having some of its needs met by a laboratory. In pursuit of that purpose, within a year of its own establishment the VIe section established the Centre de recherches historiques. Fernand Braudel was its first director. A little later the CNRS (Centre nationale de la recherche scientifique), the approximate equivalent of our National Science Foundation, began to provide funding for French research centers in the social sciences. That funding now assists about a dozen research teams and laboratories attached to the VIe section. Among them is Laboratoire associé no. 93, an alias for the Centre de recherches historiques. Its director is Fernand Braudel.

No doubt, then, that the *structure* of history that forty-three years ago began to develop in the hands of Marc Bloch and Lucien Febvre has imbedded itself in institutions to all appearance solid and durable—the *Annales*, the VIe section, the Centre de recherches historiques. Still, to some American scholars these institutions may be little more than names; and above all other people, Americans are skeptical of the extent to which a name is a clue to what lies beneath the name. They usually want some evidence of substance, best a few confirming figures. Some figures are available. First the *Annales*. In a sense the *Annales* represents the *conjonctural* periodical embodiment and expression of the *structures*, the durable paradigms about the nature of the historical enterprise, that were the program of Bloch and Febvre, inherited and continued by Braudel. Since 1929 some learned journals have expanded, some have shrunk, some have died, some have been born. Starting with the first year of the *Annales*, let us compare its growth with that of several leading French historical journals (see figure 3.1).[3]

For a new journal the *Annales* started large, larger than the *Revue d'histoire moderne* or the *Revue d'histoire économique et sociale*. It was, however, less than half the size of the old established *Revue historique*. It did not grow, it even shrank a little, in the years before World War II. After the war it returned to its previous dimensions, as the *Revue historique* did not. The *Annales* did not begin to grow again until after the mid-1950s. By 1960 it had almost doubled its original size, and ten years later it had nearly trebled it. Far outstripping the *Revue d'histoire économique et sociale* and the *Revue d'histoire moderne et contemporaine* (refounded in 1954), in 1960 it passed the *Revue historique* in size, becoming the largest historical journal in France. It remains so today.

3. Gaps in the graphs of some publications during the period of World War II simply indicate that the volumes for those years are not currently in the Yale University Library.

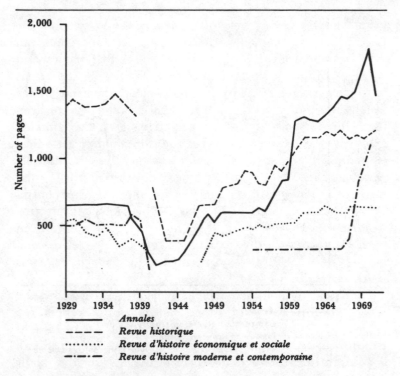

Figure 3.1. Growth of four French historical journals, 1929-1971.

Now let us compare the growth of the *Annales* with that of journals published outside France, whose field of concern coincides with or overlaps the concerns of the *Annales*. I have chosen one German, one English, and two American journals for comparison (see figure 3.2).

Again the *Annales* was larger at its start in 1929 than the older German *Vierteljahrschrift für Sozial- und Wirtschaftsgeschichte*, almost three times the size of the English *Economic History Review*. After its postwar refounding it was once, in 1954, overtaken in size by the American *Journal of Eco-*

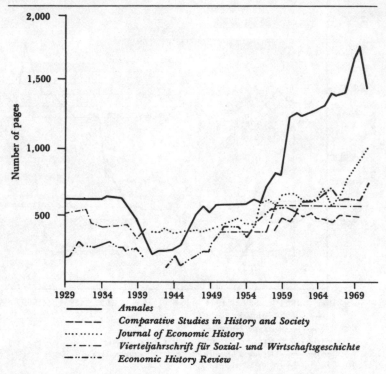

Figure 3.2. Growth of five journals of social and/or economic history, 1929-1971.

nomic History, founded in 1941, but that was before its period of rapid growth. Both the English and the American journals enjoy over the *Annales* the advantage of being the publications of professional societies. The advantage has had its compensatory drawback. The range of the *Journal of Economic History* has shrunk in recent years until it threatens to become the house organ of the sect of the econometrists, capable of continued growth only because in the boom years subscribers were too affluent and indolent to drop their sub-

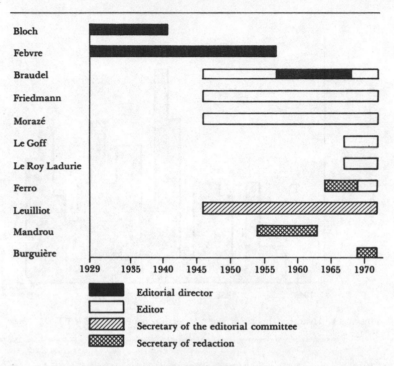

Figure 3.3. Staff history of *Annales*, 1929-1972.

scriptions. A second American journal, *Comparative Studies in History and Society*, appeared in 1958. Its program has some of the spaciousness of the *Annales*, but since 1961 it has consistently remained one-third the size of the French review. The dominance of the *Annales* in its chosen field is unchallenged anywhere.

Granted what is evident, that the *Annales* has enjoyed a truly luxuriant growth since its foundation, another question will rise to perplex American historians: what has given that journal its continuity? What gives every reader of the *Annales* over the span of its years the sense that it has grown not by

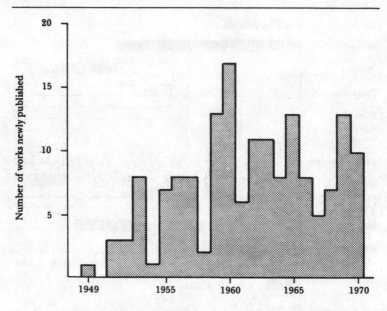

Figure 3.4. Historical books of the VI[e] section issued by S.E.V.P.E.N., 1948-1971.

abandoning the path of the founders but rather by widening it? In the United States, where historical journals shed their editors and editorial boards the way a snake sheds his skin,[4] if not quite so often, continuity of specific purpose in editorial direction is just about impossible. Not so with the *Annales* (see figure 3.3).

For the forty-three years of its existence the *Annales* has been under the editorial direction first of both, then of one, of its founders, and then of the successor of that founder. For the past twenty-five years two historians—Braudel and Morazé—have continuously served on the editorial board of

4. Always excepting the *Journal of the History of Ideas*.

the *Annales*, and one historian, Leuilliot, has served as the secretary of the board. The continuity of outlook, the *structure mentale*, of that journal has been maintained by a truly amazing continuity of personnel in its editorial management. There is no better way to put a revolution in the *structure* of history on a sound footing than to keep it under a continuing management for half a century.

The *Annales* may be thought of as the regular rhythmic pulsation of the "new history" in France. Irregularly but with remarkable frequency and with the aid of the Centre de recherches historiques, the VI[e] section has published the books of historians who work within the bounds of the *Annales* paradigm. Many of these books, though by no means all, are issued by that publisher of mysterious but convenient name, S.E.V.P.E.N. The categories under which these works are published are a sort of guide to the preoccupations of the founders of the *Annales* and of its current editor: Affaires et gens d'affaires; Archéologie et civilisation; Démographie et sociétés; Les hommes et la terre; Monnaie-prix-conjoncture; Ports-routes-trafics. The bar graph in figure 3.4 does not do justice to the full range of support that the VIe section has provided for the publications of historians. It indicates only those works issued by the section and currently in print in the S.E.V.P.E.N. catalog.[5]

The total volume of VI[e] section historical works in print at S.E.V.P.E.N. is impressive: 164 titles. If the publisher has been moderately assiduous in keeping the books in print, the increase in output in the twelve years to 1970 over the previous eleven has been more impressive, an average of ten per annum as against four. Unfortunately, data on VIe section

5. S.E.V.P.E.N. stands for Service d'Edition et de Vente des Publications de l'Education Nationale. Mouton and Cie publishes the VIe section series, Civilisations et sociétés, and Armand Colin publishes the *Cahiers des Annales*.

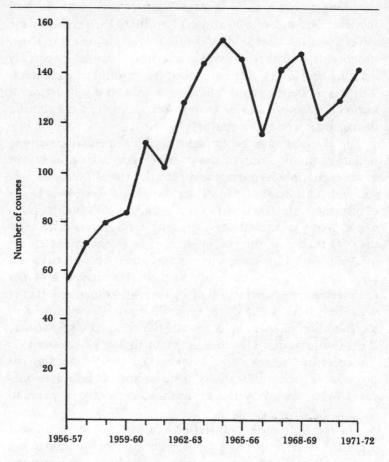

Figure 3.5. Number of courses offered by the VIᵉ section, 1956-1972.

history books no longer in print at S.E.V.P.E.N. are not readily available.

Regardless of its political outlook, the academic world is internally one of the most conservative of human institutions, a granitic *structure*, indeed. And of its many provinces the

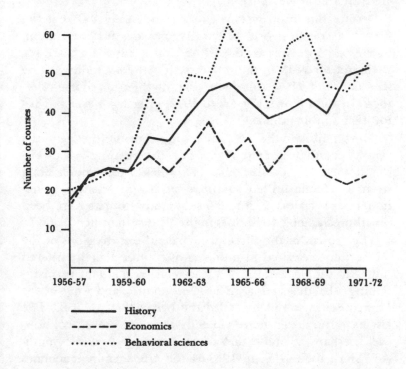

Figure 3.6. Fluctuation of courses offered by the VIᵉ section, 1956-1972.

French academy has been among the most conservative of the conservative. Injected into that rigid body about a quarter of a century ago, how has that odd organism, the VIᵉ section, Sciences économiques et sociales of the Ecole pratique des hautes études, fared under the successive presidencies of two historians? Unfortunately the publication of the *Annuaire* of the VIᵉ section did not begin until 1956-57. From that date to 1971-72, annual figures on courses offered by the section are available (see figure 3.5).

Despite the unpropitious climate and stony soil that the French academic world ordinarily provides for innovation, in the past fifteen years the VIᵉ section has made a place for itself and thrived. In the six years after the beginning of the *Annuaire* the VIᵉ section more than doubled its course offerings. In the following years to 1972, offerings never fell below that doubled figure.

The teaching in the VIᵉ section should exemplify one of the central paradigms of the *Annalistes*, the opening out of history to the other social sciences. How has history gotten along in an academic milieu specified by law as sciences économiques et sociales? Figure 3.6 shows how courses have been distributed among disciplines in the VIᵉ section since 1956-57.[6]

The growth of the three principal subject divisions of the VIᵉ section measured in numbers of courses actually offered indicates the good faith of the *directeurs d'études* in maintaining a balance among history, economics, and what in the United States would be called the behavioral sciences. The last have fluctuated more violently than the other two, however, perhaps an indication of exuberant but erratic youth. And since their peak in 1963-64 the offerings in economics have irregularly declined in number. A clearer picture of the quantitative relations among the subjects emerges if we plot their offerings as percentages of the total offerings of the VIᵉ section in each year since 1956-57 (figure 3.7).

From 1956-57 to 1969-70 the offerings in history remained a highly stable percentage of the course offerings of the VIᵉ section, never dropping below 29 percent or rising above 34

6. The classification of courses is mine, as is the title "behavioral sciences" to describe a cluster of disciplines (sociology, anthropology, social psychology, linguistics, and so forth) that would be so described in the United States.

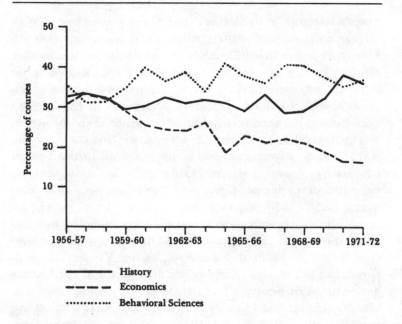

Figure 3.7. Fluctuation of percentages of courses offered by the VIᵉ section, 1956-1972.

percent. In its share of instruction in the VIᵉ section, economics has declined fairly steadily from 30 percent in 1956-57 to 17 percent in 1971-72. Whether in the VIᵉ section Febvre and Braudel have succeeded in historicizing economics and the behavioral sciences it is hard to say. They certainly have succeeded in economicizing and especially in sociologizing history. History offers the most courses of any particular discipline, thirty-four in 1972-73 compared with eighteen in economics, the next largest offering. The persistent outreach of history to the economic and social sciences, a central paradigm of the *Annales* school, is firmly implanted in the history offerings of the VIe section. Six seminars have *économie* or *économique* in their titles; sixteen *société* or *social*. Five more are entitled "histoire et sociologie" of this or that area, and there are two history offerings on "sociologie de la Grèce ancienne." However the social and economic sciences have fared under Braudel's presidency of the VIe section, history has certainly held itself open to their influence.

The embodiment of the paradigms, the *structure,* of the *Annales* in a major section of a major school in the French educational system is a remarkable feat. By having an *Annales* historian (himself) put in charge of the Section of Economic and Social Sciences at the Ecole pratique, Febvre accomplished that maneuver so warmly recommended by military experts—seizure of the strategic heights (well, one strategic height). From that time on, as the VIe section prospered, two notions still more or less alive in the United States were buried in France. The first is strong among American historians: interdisciplinary studies in the social sciences are unprofitable. The second thrives among social scientists engaged in interdisciplinary studies: history has no place in such studies. In France those notions would have come up against the hard reality of the VIe section, dedicated to interdisciplinary studies and prospering under the direction of a historian.

Finally, the Centre de recherches historiques of the VIe section. What does it do? Many things. To an elderly American like me, a handicraft historian, still capable of being astonished by historical enterprises on a colossal scale, the systematic inventories of information from large archival aggregations undertaken by the Centre are dazzling. For example, from the Florentine *catasto* of 1427 the Centre is reconstituting 80,000 families at the beginning of the fifteenth century. The *registres de contrôle* of the troops of the era of the French Revolution will provide information on "a *million* soldiers sociologically defined."[7] From a fiscal series of 1810 comes a census for each *arrondissement* of 600 notables of the Napoleonic empire, 150,000 individuals, from which can be ascertained their professions, civil status, wealth, and number of children. The military archives of the nineteenth century will make possible horizontal studies of each annual class of conscripts and, of course, vertical studies of changes in their health, height, weight, place of origin, status, and trade. Among the inquiries on the way to completion in 1970 were one on the history of agricultural production in France from the fifteenth to the eighteenth century, one on French climate from 1775 to 1792, and one on buildings in Normandy and Paris from the fifteenth century to the French Revolution. Studies based on the 40,000 titles published in eighteenth-century France are providing statistics on the diffusion of culture and on historical semantics. An atlas will soon be published tracing the historical geography of the distribution of cereals, roots, fruits, and sugar cane over the face of the earth. Currently some thirty-five major projects are in progress at the centre or with its aid. Its resources are put at the disposal of many scholars not permanently attached to it. Currently there are fifty-six scholars and researchers and twelve engineers and technicians from the CNRS on the centre's permanent staff.

More convincingly than statements of corporate self-praise made by representatives of the *Annales* school of history (subject to suspicion of self-interest), the figures and graphs above

7. I assume the Centre is following the method of family reconstitution worked by Fleury and Henry, although it is not clear to me how that method can be applied to a *catasto*. The study of a million soldiers is described on p. 2 of the *Rapport d'activité 1969-1970 et programme scientifique 1971-1974* of the Laboratoire associé no. 93.

provide evidence of the triumph of the *mentalité* of the *Annalistes*, of Bloch, Febvre, and Fernand Braudel. They warrant Jean Glénisson's summary of the current situation: "Today—need one say it again—the historical conception of which the *Annales* is the most active champion scarcely leaves room for hostile or merely different trends." On the other hand the extraordinary range of instruction offered by the VIe section, as well as the openness of the *Annales*, justifies Glénisson's apologia. "The ecumenical care that the successors of Lucien Febvre take to be fully aware of every point of view, whether revolutionary or merely innovative, has the consequence that every innovation is immediately sucked into the dominant current."[8]

"The successors of Lucien Febvre," says Glénisson; but who are they? Although Febvre has many heirs, many who enjoy the fruit of his thought and his academic statesmanship, he has only one successor—Fernand Braudel. On Febvre's death Braudel became the directing force at the two nerve centers of the "new history" in France—editorial director of the *Annales, président* of the VIe section of the Ecole pratique des hautes études. And from the start in 1949, first jointly with Febvre and then alone, Braudel was director of the Centre de recherches historiques. In the establishment of the dominance of the *structure* of the *Annales* over the historians of France, there are three crucial moments: 1929, the founding of the *Annales*; 1946-1947, its refounding by Febvre and the acquisition by that indomitable *frondeur* of the *présidence* of the new VIe section; and finally, 1956-1957, the succession of Fernand Braudel.

8. Jean Glénisson, "L'historiographie française contemporaine: Tendances et réalisations," *Vingt-cinq ans de recherche historique en France (1940-1965)*, p. lxiii.

Niccolo Machiavelli, speculating in the *Discorsi* on the conditions for the well-being and survival of a commonwealth, observed that Rome prospered because its founder Romulus was followed by two successive leaders who directed it along the course it needed to follow. The intermeshed institutions we have been examining—a compact commonwealth under a single guiding chief and embodying a unitary *mentalité*—was fortunate in the succession of Fernand Braudel. Febvre was indeed a bit like Machiavelli's image of Romulus, powerful, domineering, fierce, pugnacious, a warrior, almost a brawler, at heart, who even set aside a section of the *Annales* for *Combats,* a man of ecumenical intellect but not of irenic spirit. Braudel was an academic statesman of more judicious temper. What were the consequences of Braudel's succession for the institutions that Lucien Febvre entrusted to his care? Precise data for the Centre de recherches historiques are not available to me. However, none of the enormous projects currently under way at the centre seems to date from before 1957. The well-known works of Baehrel, the Chaunus, and Goubert may have owed something to the facilities of the centre. The impression, however, is one of growth under Braudel both in the number and the dimension of the centre's undertakings. As to the VIe section, my accurate information starts at the moment of Braudel's accession to the *présidence*. Of its pattern of growth in earlier years under Febvre's guidance no evidence is at hand. We can say that the growth of the section's teaching function has been spectacular under Braudel's administration. It is harder to double the size of a considerable operation than to double a small one. In the year Braudel took over, the VIe section offered 56 seminars. Sixteen years later it offered 142. The evidence of Braudel's influence shows most clearly in the expansion of the *Annales*. Twenty-seven years after Bloch and Febvre founded it, and still in the latter's hands, the *Annales* in 1956 was almost exactly the same size as it had been in 1929. Three years later under Braudel its size had doubled. Lucien Febvre and Fernand Braudel have at one time or another unabashedly proclaimed themselves imperialists. Febvre's imperialism was mainly of the mind. Braudel also operates with extraordinary success in another sphere, one about which he has written a book: the *civilisation matériel*.

Braudel did more than nurture the institutions that he succeeded to. He spread their influence beyond the bounds of France. Of this the qualitative evidence is abundant: the international fame of the *Annales* and of the VIe section; the hospitality that both extend to foreign scholars, the former in its pages, the latter in its seminars. Consider the issue of the American journal *Daedalus,* published in 1971, devoted to "historical studies today." Articles by eleven contributors. Three from members of one American department of history, the one most closely associated with the VIe section. One by a Cambridge University historian who has researches in progress at the Centre de recherches historiques. Three from *directeurs d'études* of the VIe section itself.[9]

An adventitious source yields yet more impressive evidence of the internationalization of the *Annales structure.* In 1953 two volumes were published, *Eventails de l'histoire vivante: Hommage à Lucien Febvre*, with eighty-five contributors, one of them Fernand Braudel, who, one imagines, had a larger hand in the project than his introductory essay indicates. Figure 3.8 shows how those contributors were distributed geographically. One contributor, if even one, behind a curtain

9. *Daedalus* (Winter 1971). The articles mentioned are by Robert Darnton, Lawrence Stone, and Jack Talbott of Princeton University; M. I. Finley of Cambridge University; and François Furet, Pierre Goubert, and Jacques Le Goff of the VIe section.

effectively iron in the last days of Stalin. One from the United States, none from Germany, a cluster from bordering neighbors; from France, 80 percent.[10]

In 1972 a two-volume *Mélanges en honneur de Fernand Braudel* was announced, 93 contributors. Figure 3.9 shows how they were distributed geographically. From France, 43 percent; none, oddly, from Brazil, where Braudel taught for two years; none, even more oddly, from the North African shore of the Mediterranean that he loved so well, not even from Algeria where he taught for more than a decade; but 57 percent, fifty-three scholars, from sixteen other lands, with large clusters from Hungary, Poland, and the United States. It is hard to look at the two maps without getting the eerie feeling that with a solid base in France and with Fernand Braudel in command, the *Annalistes* are on a march that by friendly persuasion is about to conquer the historical world.

Why, an American tends to ask, why France? Why not the United States, with its enormous resources, with the traditional collective outlook on history of its professional historians far less rigidly confined to national boundaries than any other equivalent group? Among certain American historians in the United States in the 1930s and 1940s there prevailed a view similar in many respects to that of the *Annalistes*. And there were historians with the qualities of Febvre and Braudel. At least one such historian existed in my generation—Oscar Handlin of Harvard University. A historian of the broadest learning, deeply and early concerned to draw on the achievements of the social sciences. A historian who need not and would not shrink from a comparison of his scholarly work

---

10. I am not certain whether Constantin Marinesco lived in Rumania in 1953. His degree was from Paris.

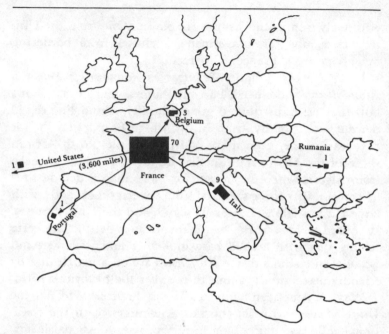

Figure 3.8. Geographical distribution of contributors to *Eventails de l'histoire vivante: Hommage à Lucien Febvre.*

with that of Braudel. A historian, moreover, with an extraordinary command of languages and with personal ties to historians of what may be called the historical "international set." A historian, finally, with enormous energy and high administrative skills, an imperial vision, and a proper ambition. Why, we may well ask, does Braudel serenely preside over a great school of historians, firmly based in Paris but spread throughout the world, while Handlin attends meetings of the American Historical Association to deliver public threnodies on the decay of history as a humane science and a profession in the United States?

In one of the most engaging chapters of *The Prince*, Ma-

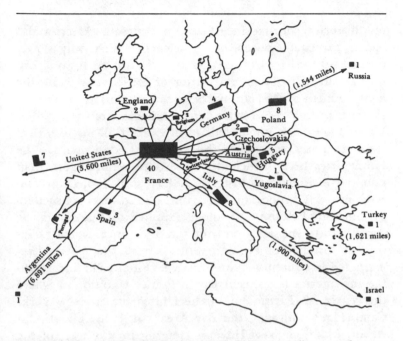

Figure 3.9. Geographical distribution of contributors to *Mélanges en honneur de Fernand Braudel.*

chiavelli ponders the role of *necessità* and Fortuna in human affairs. Fortuna is a bitch goddess who is likely to capitulate to an ardent assault. But not always. For *necessità,* the solid order of things, may not be favorable. It was favorable in France for the *Annalistes,* for Febvre and Braudel; there circumstances came to the aid of the vigorous. Consider by contrast what was lacking in the United States. First, the United States had no tradition of historical journals that reflected the historical outlook of their editors, a tradition already created in France before 1900 by Henri Berr's *Revue de synthèse.* Indeed, the United States had had no great editorial tradition at all for a long while, no truly outstanding editor of a historical journal since Franklin Jameson. America also had a parochial conception of science, which only slowly opened up to the social sciences and did not open up to history at all. This became a matter of consequence with the establishment of the National Science Foundation. Up to the present, history receives no direct support from the NSF.[11] Up to 1966 there was no federal support at all for historical research. Only recently has the National Endowment for the Humanities been sufficiently funded to render more than nominal assistance to history. A historical project or two rode into NSF support on the coattails, so to speak, of sociology, but only because a sociologist applied for the assistance. Again a different situation from that in France, where exclusion of history (or even literature) from the *sciences humaines* was structurally improbable. Finally, higher learning in America is polycentric. In France who doubts where the center is? Paris. But in the United States—New York? Cambridge? Chicago? the Bay Area? but what about Ann Arbor, Madison, New Haven? Here again the heart of the matter was to concentrate in a capital of learning a critical mass of historians with a shared point of view or set of paradigms. The Programme d'enseignement of the VI[e] section for 1972-73 offers forty-nine research seminars in history, all inclined in the *Annaliste* direction. Where in the United States would one find an advanced history faculty of such dimension, not to speak of such shared inclination? Indeed where in the United States would one find a university ready to concern itself with the care and feeding of such a gaggle of advanced historical scholars? To achieve in the United States what Febvre and Braudel achieved in France was beyond the capacity of Handlin, beyond the capacity of any historian in

11. Support is confined to the history of science.

the United States. It would, I believe, have been beyond the capacities of Febvre and Braudel. All the *structures* of the scholarly and educational enterprise that favored the *Annales* school in France were lacking in the United States. No bold historians seized Fortuna here, because here there was no Fortuna to seize.

So the unique and successful intermeshing of history with the social sciences that Febvre and Braudel achieved in France was just not in the cards in the United States. The loss to history has been serious. The loss to the social sciences has not been negligible. Let that stony, sterile barrens, the *International Encyclopedia of the Social Sciences*, bear witness. It should not have happened anywhere. It would not have happened in the France of the *Annales*, the VIe section, and Fernand Braudel.

Conjonctures

In historical studies conceptual apparatus, guidelines, general theories, *idées maîtresses* about the past and about the proper relation of historians to it tend to be far less lasting than institutions. They are phenomena of *moyenne durée*, middling length, and thus in Braudel's own historical schema belong in the second layer or tier of history, that of *conjonctures*. They even conform sometimes to Braudel's notion that noneconomic phenomena have a rhythmic pattern similar to economic *conjonctures* or cyclical movements. Such was the implication of a remark of that merry skeptic Herbert Heaton: "Big ideas in history have a half-life of about five years." Without wholly committing ourselves to Heaton's Law we may note that while the popularity curves of what, when they emerge, are called generative or seminal ideas in history have varying lengths, they have similar shapes: a rapid rise, around the peak a slow leveling of rate of ascent and beginning of descent, a more rapid falling off, and finally a fast downward plunge toward oblivion.

The first *idée maîtresse* of Braudel concerns the relation of history to the social sciences. In its protean forms he shared it with and inherited it from the founders of the *Annales*, Marc Bloch and Lucien Febvre, especially the latter. Our previous examination of *structures* has shown how effectively he maintained, expanded, and strengthened the institutions designed to realize that idea. *La Méditerranée*, which launched him on his career as a central figure in French historical studies, also exemplified his wish to bring history into close relations with social sciences, especially human geography, economics, and sociology. In 1951, generalizing his outlook, he wrote, "For us there are no bounded human sciences. Each of them is a door open on to the entirety of the social, each leads to all the rooms, to every floor of the house, on the condition that on his march the investigator does not draw back out of reverence for neighboring specialists. If we need to, let us use their doors and their stairways." No science of man must cut itself off from the other sciences of man, for in so doing it creates the falsifications economic man, social man, geographic man. No, students of the *sciences humaines* must deal not with such ghosts but "rather with Man living, complex, confused, as he is, . . . Man whom all the social sciences must avoid slicing up, however skillful and artistic the carving."[12]

In the years following 1951, and particularly after his succession to the strategic positions held by Lucien Febvre in the *Annales* school, Braudel had to give further thought to the relation of history to the social sciences. By then two real-

12. *Annales E.S.C.* 6 (1951): 491.

ities had commanded his attention. First, some practitioners of most of the other sciences of man did not share his appetite for roaming through the house of the social sciences. Although that house, like God's, had many mansions, most social scientists were satisfied to stay in their own rooms. Or in his other metaphor, they went right on carving man up. The other reality was the opposite but also the consequence of the first, a propensity of each of the social sciences to enlarge its room. "Without the explicit will to do so, the social sciences encroach on each other; each tends to seize upon the social in its entirety. While believing that it stays at home each moves in on its neighbors."[13]

Such inner contradictions and confusions required resolution. Braudel was ready to propose, indeed even to impose, such a resolution. For the moment he wanted "a unification, even a dictatorial one, of the diverse sciences of man to subject them less to a common market than to a common *problématique*, which would free them from many illusory problems and useless acquirements, and after the necessary pruning and *mise au point*, would open the way for a future and new divergence, capable at that point of being fruitful and creative. For a new forward thrust of the sciences of man is in order."[14]

In this process of confluence and reflux what will be the place of history? On this point, no doubts or hesitations. History is the science of the sciences of man. Mingling with them, lending them its own impetus and its dialectic, it feeds itself on their multiple and indispensable movement. Such is Braudel's view; such, he adds, is the view of those eager imperial-

13. Ibid. 13 (1958): 726.
14. Fernand Braudel, "Histoire et sociologie," in *Traité de sociologie*, ed. G. Gurvitch, 2 vols. (Paris: Presses Universitaires de France, 1958-1960), I, 88.

ists of the mind and the academy, "the young French historians, taking great pains to keep their craft at the junction of all the sciences of man," in short, of the *Annalistes*.[15]

The issue is not whether history is a science. On this matter Braudel and the *Annalistes* saw matters no differently from their scapegoats, the *Sorbonnistes* of the 1920s, who were equally firm in the conviction that history, as they practiced it, was *scientifique*. Here perhaps French historians were beneficiaries of a shade of linguistic divergence between their language and English. There appears to be a structural difference between the two tongues, well worth further investigation, that has made French *science* a more inclusive term than English "science." *Science* extends in the direction of organized knowledge in general. "Science" tends to restrict its application to disciplines that take physics as a model. The trouble with the *sciences historiques* as they were practiced in France in the 1920s was their isolation, a consequence of their isolationism. Fortunately the French had two phrases that might be used to break through history's isolation—*sciences humaines* and *sciences de l'homme*. It was harder in France to doubt that history was one of these than it was in the English-speaking world to deny that it was a social science. So Braudel's view was not merely that history must place itself among the *sciences de l'homme*, but that it should be at their head or at least at their center.

If history is to take this place, it must not hang back and refuse to make use of the laboratory, the instrument that has been indispensable to the advance of the other sciences. And it must be ready to engage in "team projects," which have so much accelerated the forward movement of other

15. *Annales E.S.C.* 16 (1961): 423.

sciences. Braudel, therefore, is ready and happy to toll the bell for the passing of *l'histoire artisanal*,[16] the history that is the work of individual craftsmanship, of the scholar working alone in his study with the books he has collected and the notes he has taken to deal with the problem that has captured his attention. Such craftsman-style history Braudel regards as a mode outmoded, no longer adequate for coping with the issues to which history must address itself, insufficient to *capter l'histoire du monde*.[17] For the new history a new sort of equipment is necessary, and a new organization of research, a scientific organization of cooperative research. The kinds of questions historians now want to ask are unanswerable by the traditional methods of the craft; the materials available for answering such questions are beyond the reach of traditional methods. Who can doubt it? For a great span of the nineteenth century there exist registers of induction into the army for every *département* of France. The registers yield information on the height, weight, and vocation of every man who was taken into the service. They also offer clues to the health of the conscripts. Such a resource promises to enlighten us not only on the geographical cadres of French economic life but on the transformation of those cadres over time, and to provide materials for a biological history of the male Frenchman in the nineteenth century. So much was offered, but who would, who could accept the offer. Not the traditional historian with his traditional methods, surely. His tools were too simple, his life too short. Yet the offer has been accepted, and many offers like it are being accepted not only in France but in England, the United States, Scandinavia, Russia, wherever the material and human resources to cope with such

16. For an early *Braudellisme* on this matter, see ibid. 4 (1949): 192.
17. Ibid.

problems can be mobilized—and paid for. Problems of such dimension, materials of such extent and density, require a corresponding concentration and organization of resources— maps and computers; data-banks, laboratories, and research centers; programmers, cartographers, typists, consultants, researchers, and directors of research. This kind of history is work for organized, cooperative, directed investigations.

Surely this is true, and only a grumpy skeptic would deny the importance and the desirability of such organized research efforts. Yet to infer from their necessity and their success the total obsolescence of the artisan-historian equipped only with pen, ink, industry, patience, curiosity, truculent individualism, and such brains as God gave him is perhaps premature. An old friend once told me how during World War II the physicists of the General Electric Atomic Research Laboratory were stymied by a problem the government had assigned them. For consultation they called in Enrico Fermi. He took a few instrument readings here and there and sat down with pen and paper. In two hours he had cracked the problem, which had blocked the progress of the laboratory for two months. "Now," said my friend, "we would have solved that problem eventually. But it would have taken us three more months and two million dollars." History, of course, has no Enrico Fermi and never will have. It is not built like physics, and its necessary structure is a permanent constraint on the production of Fermis. On the other hand, compensatorily it tends to produce a considerable number of little Fermis, *fermetti*, so to speak, men who in their small way have the knowledge and the knack for keeping the historical operations that concern them from getting stuck on dead center and for a long time marching in place. H. J. Habakkuk has offered a succinct, sensible explanation why this should be so.

In the past most historians . . . absorbed a large number of miscellaneous facts relating to the period in which they were interested or to problems very loosely defined. Their tastes were catholic and they did not accept or reject on any rigorous test of relevance to a hypothesis. They retained in their minds an accumulating stock of information, as it were a compost heap, on which in due course ideas and generalizations burgeoned, as a result of reflection, flair, and intuition. This process is very haphazard, . . . but it has produced a great many penetrating insights, and it keeps the mind open to a wide range of considerations.[18]

This view cannot be written off as mere romantic and obscurantist individualism, certainly not by Braudel and the *Annalistes*. At the top of their historical honor roll stand two works: Marc Bloch's *La société féodale* and Lucien Febvre's *Le problème de l'incroyance*. These works were produced by methods wholly artisanal. Nor is it clear that a large cooperative apparatus would have eased their production or improved them. It might rather have got in the way or made the books gratuitously long—which they are not, as some of the recent products of the VIe section certainly are.

Braudel's vision of the place of history in relation to the social sciences gives us a link with Braudel's second *idée maîtresse*—the conception of *durée*. Among the sciences of man history distinguishes itself by being *globale*, "susceptible to extending its curiosity to any aspect whatever of the social." But it does not have a monopoly on this distinction; it shares it with sociology. What then justifies Braudel's unrepentant imperial claims for his discipline? He justifies them by relating them to history as the sole study linked to *la durée*. *Durée* does not mean time, but rather unit of time, duration. In practice most sociologists, Braudel says, assume one of two

18. H. J. Habakkuk, "Economic History and Economic Theory," *Daedalus* (Spring 1971): 318.

postures toward *durée*, both in different ways stultifying. Some, intensely concerned with that convenient fiction "the present," are trapped in a unit of time too brief to afford them anything but ephemeral perceptions about man. They are prisoners of the *durée trop courte*. They miss the historical experience, so valuable for understanding the present, of displacement into an unfamiliar past that enables a man to know "those most profound and original traits of the present that he was unfamiliar with before, as a consequence of being too familiar with them."[19] Other sociologist-ethnographers, Lévi-Strauss, for example, are preoccupied with microunits of social behavior—the phoneme, the marital structure, the raw and the cooked—that endure multimillennially. They are prisoners of the *durée trop longue*. Between the instantaneously present and the perennially immobile of the two sociologies lie the effective *durées* that are the constant preoccupation of historians and that are history's unique and indispensable contribution to the sciences of man.

Braudel assimilates (although not explicitly) the *durées* that are the historian's business to the wave phenomena of physics. Thus radio transmission can be analyzed into waves of considerable length, carrier waves, bearing waves of lesser length, bearing waves of yet lesser length. In Braudel's view the past can be analyzed into the interrelation of waves of three lengths, and it can be written about most effectively that way. The first set of waves are short ones, those of *durée courte*. These short waves are the most readily observed ones because they embody the experience "of daily life, of our illusions, of our immediate awareness." Because of their immediacy, they are the substance of the individual conscious-

---

19. "Traits les plus profonds et originaux . . . que vous ne connaissiez pas à force de les connaître," *Annales E.S.C.* 13 (1958): 737.

ness. Braudel, following the philosopher-economist Simiand (1873-1935), also calls them *événementielle*, having to do with events. "Events are explosive, 'resounding news,' as they said in the sixteenth century. With their deceptive vapors they fill the consciousness of contemporaries but they do not last at all." Although the most conspicuous, "the *temps court* is the most capricious, the most deceptive of the *durées*."[20] It is the subject and the substance of the newspaper and in ages past of the chronicler. By preference the *durée courte*, the *événementielle*, is also the past that historians of politics, traditional historians, bury themselves in.

Economists and economic historians, on the other hand, frolic in waves of intermediate length—price curves, demographic progressions, movements of wages, changes in interest rates, *conjonctures*, which follow cycles of ten, twenty-five, or at the limit fifty years. The notion of cyclical movements or rhythms can be extended from economic to social phenomena, and even beyond. Braudel presses for the investigation of *conjonctures* in the realm of culture, "if one may extend to this domain, as I would gladly do, the expression which up to the present passes current only for economic life."[21] Although such waves of change exist and profoundly

20. Ibid., p. 728.

21. *Encyclopédie française* (Paris: Société de gestion de l'Encyclopedie française, 1935-1966), vol. 20: *Le monde en devenir*, fasc. 12, p. 9. There is no satisfactory English equivalent for *conjoncture*. Its English homologue "conjuncture" does not bear a similar sense. The difficulty can be illustrated from the choices the English translator made when he found the term in a chapter heading. Thus he translated "Navigation: tonnage et conjoncture" (I, 271) as "Shipping and Changing Circumstances"; "Les responsabilités de la conjoncture" (I, 429) as "The Gold Trade and the General Economic Situation"; and "La conjoncture italienne" (I, 538) as "Italy's Situation." Braudel seems to use *conjoncture* fairly consistently to signify cyclical economic transformations or, less precisely, changes in society, sciences, or technology,

affect human affairs, men are not always aware of them. Their very length often conceals them from their victims. Recurring only a few times, sometimes only once in the lifetime of an individual, they often escape the consciousness of those who nevertheless live in and have to learn to live with them.[22]

The history of *conjoncture*, of historical rhythms of *moyenne durée*, fascinates Braudel. But instead of turning him back to a search for the linkages between medium-wave and short-wave or *événementielle* history, it projects him forward on a search for historical waves of even vaster length. And he finds them. Before him, economists had spoken of secular (that is, centuries-long) trends, but they had not investigated them much. Braudel, however, identifies in the past (and present) such "extremely slow patterns of oscillation, . . . movements [that] require hundreds of years to complete." (I, 92).[23]

Or again, in greater detail, beneath the waves of *conjoncture*, "phenomena of trends with imperceptible slopes appear, a history of very long periods, a history slow to take on curvature and for that reason slow to reveal itself to our observation. It is this that in our imperfect language we designate

to all of which he ascribes cyclic changes (undefined) over times (not clearly specified). I shall try to use the term *conjoncture* to label phenomena that conform to or at least do not lie beyond the phenomena that Braudel so identifies.

22. In France the effective application of the economic conception of cycles to history was the work of Ernest Labrousse, who investigated the cyclical movement of prices in eighteenth-century France in *Esquisse du mouvement des prix* (Paris: Dalloz, 1933), and then in *La crise de l'économie française à la veille de la Revolution* (Paris: Presses Universitaires, 1944) associated the economic crisis of the 1780s with the onset of the French Revolution.

23. I am not sure that Braudel uses the term *moyenne*. He may, however. In the context of his views on *durée* it seems so apt as to be irresistible.

by the name of *histoire structurale*."[24] Historical waves of great length constitute the *longue durée*. They belong not to the recurrent crises of *conjonctures* but to *structures*. Sociologists see *structures* as "fixed relations between realities and social masses," historians (or at least Braudel) as "a reality that time has a hard job wearing down, and carries a long while." Some *structures* "encumber history in impeding, and therefore commanding, its course."[25] They mark bounds, limitations that for centuries men cannot conquer or control. Such for example are the slow transformation from nomadism to transhumance and the movement of men out of the mountains to settle in the plain (I, 92). The history of the *longue durée* is the history of the constraints that *structure* imposed on human movement in the broadest sense of the word "movement"—not only migration but intellectual thrust and spiritual transformation.

As he loves the Mediterranean, Braudel loves the *longue durée*. It is the land where his heart lies, and the very last lines of his arduous revision of *La Méditerranée* are at once a confession of faith and a declaration of love.

Thus confronted by man, I am always tempted to see him as enclosed in a destiny which he scarcely made, in a landscape which shows before and behind him the infinite perspectives of the *longue durée*. In historical explanation as I see it, at my own risk and peril, it is always the *temps long* that ends up by winning out. Annihilating masses of events, all those that it does not end up by pulling along in its own current, surely it limits the liberty of men and the role of chance itself. By temperament I am a structuralist, little attracted by events and only partly by *conjoncture*, that grouping of events carrying the same sign. (II, 520)

Still, faith and love aside, Braudel knows that the *longue*

24. *Revue économique* 9 (1960): 41.
25. *Annales E.S.C.* 13 (1958): 731.

durée is not the sole proper concern of the historian. "This almost motionless framework, these slow-furling waves do not act in isolation. These variations of the general relations between man and his environment combine with other fluctuations, the sometimes lasting but usually short-lived movements of the economy. All these movements are superimposed on one another." Superimposed, not separated. Rather, interpenetrating. The function of the historian, aware of the three *durées*, is to discern and set forth the dialectic that takes place among them.

Such, then, is Braudel's perception of the past: *événement —courte durée; conjoncture—moyenne durée; structure—longue durée*; and collisions, tensions, and interchanges of each with the others.

In calling the perspective of these superimposed *durées* to the attention of historians, Braudel was also setting forth a program, if not for adoption at any rate for serious consideration. It surely was not an accident that his fullest systematic exposition of his views on the matter was set forth in "La longue durée," the first systematic article he published in the *Annales*, after he had assumed direction of that journal and of the *Annales* school on the death of Lucien Febvre.[26] In some measure the program was successful. The language of *structure* and *conjoncture* has become the fashion among younger French historians of the *Annales* school—Baehrel, Deyon, Gascon, Le Roy Ladurie. The language received its most colossal if not its most elegant application in the three volumes (following eight volumes of statistical tables) of Pierre and Huguette Chaunu's *Séville et l'Atlantique*.[27]

26. "Histoire et sciences sociales: La longue durée," ibid. 13 (1958): 725-753.
27. See Braudel's review, ibid. 18 (1963): 541-553.

Braudel's conception of the *longue durée* is touched (if not tainted) by a measure of personalism. In his view *structures*, not only geographic but also technical, social, and administrative, act as obstacles. In this view there seems to be latent a trace of teleological thinking, a notion that history has a predestined path to follow, and that certain entities literally superhuman, *personnages,* block the way. The conception that history has a preordained path is an analytical instrument not free of philosophical flaw. It is, however, far less alarming in Braudel's generous ecumenical hands than it was when the direction of history was toward the thousand-year Reich and the structures in the way were the inferior civilization of the Slavs and the perverse one of the Jews.

Yet even as his conceptions of *structures* and the *longue durée* won adherents, Braudel began occasionally to distance himself from them. As early as 1958 he wrote a little deprecatingly of two words "victorious *just at the moment,* structures and models," and in a footnote he quoted Febvre's devastating evaluation of the term: "And then '*structures*.' A fashionable word, I know; it even sprawls through the *Annales* occasionally, a little too much to suit my taste."[28]

Indeed, when it comes to the crunch Braudel is not satisfied with the image of the past that his metaphor of wee little waves on middle-sized waves on great big waves yields. After all, the terms *courte, moyenne,* and *longue* conceal a series of lengths of the waves of *durée* that may, for all one knows, stretch in a continuum from the instantaneous to the multimillennially *trop longue.* At one point he recognizes this difficulty and, embracing it with characteristic hospitality, speaks of "three, ten, a hundred diverse *durées.*" Unfortunately in

28. Gurvitch, *Traité de sociologie,* I, 90; italics added. See also *Annales E.S.C.* 12 (1957): 180.

this massive bear hug the *dialectique des durées* gets irretrievably fragmented. History as a dialectic between two, even among three, *durées* is at any rate conceivable. But among a hundred? Babel and bedlam. This is not said merely to make a debating point; it will come up again later. Let us, however, postpone further pursuit of this issue to consider two further *idées maîtresses* of Braudel—the idiocy of the *événementielle* and the pursuit of *histoire totale* (or *globale*) as a goal.

About *histoire événementielle* Braudel writes with a passionate and at times unreasonable antipathy. The problem is to identify what he so detests and to try sympathetically to understand his detestation. This is not easy, because in diatribes he drops clues in a random way that leads the reader astray. What is *histoire événementielle?* Political history, says Braudel. But surely not the political history, for example, of Edmund Morgan's *The Stamp Act Crisis*, or C. Vann Woodward's *Reunion and Reaction*, or Robert R. Palmer's *The Age of the Democratic Revolution?* Diplomatic history, says Braudel. But surely not the diplomatic history of Garrett Mattingly's *Renaissance Diplomacy?* Administrative history. But surely not Geoffrey Elton's *The Tudor Revolution in Government?* Biography. But surely not Woodward's *Tom Watson*, or Mattingly's *Catherine of Aragon*, or H. R. Trevor-Roper's *Archbishop Laud?* No, this is obviously a false trail, even though Braudel has liberally left his footprints on it. Note, however, that all these counter-examples come from English and American writers and from the years since 1940.[29]

29. For a small sample of Braudel's adverse remarks on *histoire événementielle* and its practitioners, the *historiens traditionalistes*, see *Annales E.S.C.* 2 (1947): 226; 13 (1958): 728-729; 15 (1960): 51, 511; 16 (1961): 727; 18 (1963): 119; and Gurvitch, *Traité de sociologie*, I, 86.

Fernand Braudel was marching to the beat of a different drummer, to the drumming of Marc Bloch and of Lucien Febvre in the birth years of the *Annales*. Their summons to attack, as we have seen, was directed against a particular kind of biography, a particular kind of political and diplomatic history—a kind, let it be said, not wholly unknown in the favored Anglo-American sector. And once one has known history of that kind, it is easy to believe that the purpose of its perpetrators is not so much to write history as to kill it. But whereas in England and America, Maitland, Vinogradoff, Robinson, Beard, Becker, and Turner—historians who did not write that kind of history—enjoyed eminence and admiration before the mid-1920s, in 1929, at the age of fifty-one, Lucien Febvre, who had defended a superb *thèse* in 1911, was still at Strasbourg. Meantime in happy possession at the Sorbonne were historians who from Strasbourg, and perhaps on even closer inspection, looked like fuddy-duddies, men sunk up to their ears in the German tradition of historical pedantry and kept sunk by a misreading, derived from Comte, of the nature of scientific investigation. These historians, who could scarcely see beyond such subjects as "the policy of Francis I toward Mantua in the third Italian war," set the tone and pace for French historians in the half-century from 1875 to 1925, or so it seemed to Lucien Febvre.

These facts—or better, perhaps, the conviction of Lucien Febvre that these were the facts—account for the stridency of the attacks of the first *Annales* on the rulers of the academy in France and on the sort of history those rulers wrote. It accounts for Lucien Febvre. But after all, Febvre won his battle and lived to enjoy the rout of his enemies. So how does it account for Braudel and his hostility to that *histoire événementielle*, which by a process of invidious selection turns out to be the very worst history written by the dullest Sorbonnistes of the first quarter of the twentieth century? Well, for one thing, Braudel is above all the heir of Lucien Febvre, attractively and utterly devoted and faithful to the man he succeeded. The enemies of Lucien Febvre are the enemies of Braudel—even when they have fallen from power and are mostly dead.

More than that, however. The *Sorbonnistes*, the proponents of *histoire événementielle*, were not only the not-so-*chers maîtres* of Febvre. They still held the strategic heights when Braudel was a student at the Sorbonne. In the early days of his researches he was ready to scale the Sorbonnic heights by producing one of those *thèses* which at that time so conveniently opened the way to the cushiest berths that French academia could offer to historians. It was to be on the mediterranean policy of Philip II, a pure exercise in *histoire événementielle*. Since Febvre had taken as the subject of his thesis Philip II and the Franche Comté, it was natural for Braudel to write him about his own project. Febvre replied: "*Philip II and the Mediterranean*, a good subject. But why not *The Mediterranean and Philip II*? A subject far greater still? For between those protagonists, Philip and the inland sea, it is not an equal match." These "imprudent remarks" were to strengthen in Braudel "hesitations and scruples" the implications of which hitherto "he had not dared to draw." The power of his scruples and of Febvre's advice launched him "on a magnificent and exhausting campaign of documentation through all the archives of the Mediterranean world." So besides all else, Febvre stood at the beginning of Braudel's disaffection with the career of *historien événementielliste*, on which he was preparing to launch himself, turning him in the direction of the vast work, not to appear for nearly two decades, *La Méditerranée et le monde méditerranéen.* Such is Febvre's account.[30]

Enough? Enough to account for that occasionally myopic disaffection with *histoire événementielle* that marks both Braudel's *idées maîtresses* and his own historical work? Perhaps. Yet there may be more. At least I think there is more. It concerns the particular form that a common bitter experience öf all Frenchmen took for a French army officer nearing middle age, Fernand Braudel. The experience was the *étrange défaite* that Marc Bloch wrote about with such insight, the collapse of France in the summer of 1940, and the consequences that followed from it.

In his systematic reflection on his view of history, "La longue durée," Braudel goes somewhat out of his way to take Jean-Paul Sartre to task for "the intelligent and dangerous game" he had played in some of his recent reflections.[31] What was this game? It was the assertion that at the heart of history lie the act and the event, which gather into themselves the whole meaning of the life of the person who makes himself what he is by his way of participating in them. Moreover, their unfolding is a true mirror of the society in which they are played out. What do Sartre's involvement in the *événementielle* and Braudel's aversion tell us? Something, perhaps, about the impact of the strange defeat of 1940 on two remarkable Frenchmen. Where was Jean-Paul Sartre in the years that followed that defeat? He was teaching in the Lycée Condorcet. He was acting in the organized Resistance to the Nazi conquerors. He was living with daily risk of life and daily decision. And he was sitting in onë café in Paris or another re-

---

30. Febvre's review of Braudel's *La Méditerranée, Revue historique* 203 (1950): 217. Braudel has not, as far as I know, validated it.
31. *Annales E.S.C.* 13 (1958): 737.

flecting on the meaning of his experience. For him the daily
string of events and his way of dealing with them made him
the person he was and required him to remake himself each
day in the face of them. The daily event was the test of his
very being. So Sartre lived in Paris under the German occupation. And Braudel? Where was Fernand Braudel in those
days and what was he doing? He was held in a German prison camp. He was the *recteur* of the camp, leader of and responsible for the French prisoners. There, helpless to do anything but live from day to day and help his fellow prisoners
survive, there without a single document, a single note, a single book, "he achieved the incredible feat of writing from
memory one after another, the successive chapters" of the first
draft of *La Méditerranée*, that colossal study, so enamored of
the *longue durée*, so hostile to *temps court*, although devoting
hundreds of grudging pages to it.[32] Of his state of mind at the
time, Braudel tells us something:

In the course of a gloomy captivity I fought hard to escape from
the chronicle of those difficult years. To reject the events and the
time of events was to put one's self beyond them, in a shelter, to
look at them from a little distance, to judge them better and *not
too much to believe in them*. From *temps court* to pass to *temps*
less *court* and *temps* very long; . . . then having arrived at this
destination, to stop, to consider everything anew, and to recon-
struct it, to see everything in reverse order: such an operation has
something in it to tempt a historian.[33]

For Fernand Braudel in a German prison camp, the *événementielle*, the short view, the immediate present, was despair,
a powerful enemy not to be faced head on, to be defeated
only by ruse, to be put at a distance, to be escaped. For Fer-

---

32. Febvre, *Revue historique* 203 (1950): 217.
33. *Annales E.S.C.* 13 (1958): 748-749; italics of English words added.

nand Braudel, not trapped like Sartre in a maelstrom of decision and action in Paris but trapped more helplessly in a prison camp, on an island in time where no action could matter much, for such a man, in such a place, at such a moment to reject the merely momentary, the very short view, the *événementielle*—may it not have meant more than a move in an intellectual game, may it not have been a necessary act of faith, the narrow path to salvation?

When a historian takes a position sheltered from events, very far from them, his act of distancing leads him, at any rate led Braudel, to see vast panoramas of the past. Ultimately he is confronted with the problem of transforming a sweeping vision to truculently linear word-by-word prose. In such circumstances what is he to do and how is he to do it? On this matter Braudel had two *idées maîtresses*, and to the question he returned two answers: *histoire problème* and *histoire totale*. In the year of publication of *La Méditerranée*, in a review of a geographical study of Martinique, Braudel firmly stated the "problematic imperative." "The region is not the framework of research. The framework of research is the problem, selected with full independence and responsibility of mind, beyond all those plans, so comfortable and so tempting, that carry with them as an extra dividend, the warranty and blessing of the University."[34] If the geographer is to take the problem rather than the region as the unit of research, the historian is to take the problem rather than the event or string of events. *Histoire problème* provides the route of escape from *histoire événementielle*. Charles André Julien, author of *Les voyages de découvertes*, had, said Braudel, "the taste for that *histoire-problème* which goes far beyond events and men, history grasped within the framework of a living

34. Ibid. 8 (1949): 496.

problem or a series of living problems, clearly posed, to which everything is thereafter subordinated—even the joy of describing or rediscovering real lives, the delights of restoring to life the great shadows of the great."[35] And fourteen years later, by then the unchallengeable oracle of historians in France, Braudel reiterated his warning of 1949: "I do not want young French historians to throw themselves futilely into enterprises analogous to those of the prestigious disciples of Vidal de la Blache, studying the various regions of the French mosaic one after another. Neither the *bailliage*, nor the *pays*, nor the region provides the true bounds of research. But rather the problem."[36] "Lucien Febvre never ceased saying it," Braudel concluded. And indeed Febvre never did. More than that: Febvre himself wrote *histoire problème*. In articles: "An Ill-stated Question." In books: *The Problem of Unbelief.* And without so frequently stating it, needing no incantations to keep him on the road he was predisposed to follow, so did Marc Bloch write it. Among historians of England, of course and supremely, Frederic William Maitland wrote it, lighting the dusty corridors of medieval English law as he passed through them with one lively question after another.

Histoire problème, then. Yes, but not entirely, not always. Fernand Braudel has another love—*histoire globale, histoire totale.* In *histoire globale* we must "remerge each observation, each measurement, into the totality of the field of social force."[37] "Faithful to the teaching of Lucien Febvre and

35. Ibid. 5 (1950): 453.
36. Ibid. 18 (1963): 778.
37. Ibid. 8 (1953): 359. At times the term *globale*, drawn from the sociology of Georges Gurvitch, makes Braudel a little uneasy (see *Traité de sociologie*, I, 88, 74).

Marcel Mauss, the historian will always want to seize the whole, the *totality* of the social."[38] It is in the interest of a totality that allows varied possibilities of slippage, uncertainties, explanations which are "daughters of the moment," that historians must part company with sociologists. It is not easy to be sure what Braudel means by *histoire totale*. It comes more frequently to the lips of younger historians. But the impulse is there; who can doubt it? Who can doubt it, when after reading the 653 packed pages of *Beauvais et les Beauvaisis*, Braudel remarks that its author, Pierre Goubert, might have done well to consider other areas of northern France as well?[39] When, after three fat volumes of *Séville et l'Atlantique*, he observes that the Chaunus had taken in only the Antilles, not the whole Atlantic, as he had taken in the whole Mediterranean[40]—and (he might have added) a good bit more? *Histoire totale*—but what are its bounds? And is "total history" the correct translation? Should it not rather be "endless history," "interminable history"?

Between these two *idées maîtresses*, these two conceptions of history, *problème* and *totale*, there lies not just the possibility of conflict but the reality, and with this conflict, in another context, we will have to concern ourselves. That Braudel himself is aware of the conflict with its implication of mutually exclusive aspirations is not clear. In any event, it is not among the many issues he has dealt with. Faced with that issue, which would he choose, *histoire problème* or *histoire totale?* One can almost see an adult and a small boy. The adult asks, "What do you want?" Properly and promptly the small boy replies, "I would like a marshmallow cookie

38. *Traité de sociologie*, I, 94.
39. *Annales E.S.C.* 17 (1962): 778.
40. Ibid. p. 542.

heavily coated with dark chocolate." A little doubtful, the adult asks again, "What do you really want?" This time the boy pauses. Then his eyes light up. "I really want—everything in the world!"

Evénements

And now to turn to that pregnant event, *The Mediterranean and the Mediterranean World,* that classic whose first utterance is, "I have passionately loved the Mediterranean." Where does one begin to deal with an event 1,100 pages long? Perhaps, bowing to circumstance, with an *histoire événementielle,* a chronicle, superficial and perforce inexact, of its genesis drawn from the bits of evidence at hand. So . . . Born in 1902, Fernand Braudel, a student of history at the Sorbonne, decided to write his doctoral thesis on the Mediterranean policy of Philip II, king of Spain (1556-1598). In 1923 Braudel went to teach in Algiers. At some point in his stay there, having made good progress on his thesis, he wrote the eminent French historian Lucien Febvre about it.[41] Following both the advice he received from Febvre and his own inclination, he radically reoriented his thesis topic and embarked on a further round of archival research. In 1937 he became a *directeur d'études* at the Ecole pratique des hautes études. By 1939 he had finished his research; he had in mind the structure of his thesis.[42] In 1940 he was taken

---

41. The evidence at hand does not permit me to state the date.
42. In one sense he had clearly finished his research. He certainly did no research during his imprisonment, from 1940 to 1944 or 1945, and revision of his first draft including the footnoting must have carried him nearly to the date of his defense of his thesis. In another sense I am not so sure. Did Braudel finish his research, or did the Germans call an abrupt halt to it? Had it not been for the Germans would the flow of chapters have started when it did? One cannot be certain.

prisoner by the Nazis. In the prison camp he wrote the first draft of his thesis. On his release from captivity, he prepared the final draft of his work, including the massive scholarly apparatus. In 1947 he successfully defended his thesis and was awarded his doctorate, and in 1949 the thesis was published, *La Méditerranée et le monde méditerranéen à l'époque de Philippe II*. The text is exactly 1,100 pages long, followed by a bibliography of twenty-eight pages detailing among other matters intensive research in archives located in nineteen repositories in eleven cities in four countries.[43] The work is divided into three major parts. Part I, "La part du milieu," 304 pages, deals with mountains, plateaux, and plains; the seas of the Mediterranean and its shores and islands; the outreaches of the Mediterranean into Europe and into the encroaching deserts. The first part also includes consideration of the physical unity of the Mediterranean—its climate —and of the human unity created by its sea and land routes and its towns. Part II, 414 pages, bears the title, "Destins collectifs et mouvements d'ensemble." It first concerns itself with Mediterranean economies in the sixteenth century, especially the role of distances and population densities, precious metals and prices, commerce and transportation. Second, it deals with Mediterranean empires, civilizations, societies, and forms of warfare in the time of Philip II. Part III, "Les événements, la politique, et les hommes," 366 pages, is a detailed account of the struggles between the Spanish and the Turkish empires for mastery in the Mediterranean between 1551 and the death of Philip II in 1598. Roughly, then, the architecture of Braudel's book follows the scheme expressed in one of his *idées maîtresses:* Part I—*structures* and the *longue durée*;

43. Five countries since the independence of Algeria.

Part II—*conjonctures* and the *moyenne durée*; Part III—
événements and the *courte durée*.[44]

In a review the year after the publication of *La Méditerranée,* Lucien Febvre described it as "this perfect historical
work . . . more than a professional masterpiece. A revolution
in the way of conceiving history. An overthrow of our old
practices. A 'historic mutation' of capital importance . . . a
great progress, a salutary renewal. The dawn of a new time,
I am sure of it."[45] Some fifteen years later, as I started by
saying many pages back, some of Braudel's friends advised
him not to revise the book, not to "modify a text that had become classic" (I, II). Does this mean that *La Méditerranée*
is a flawless work? Certainly not. To the examination of
some of its flaws I shall devote the first part of my critique.

An early reviewer of *La Méditerranée* noted that on three
occasions Braudel refers to the castilianization of Aragon during the sixteenth century. Each time reference is made to
only one piece of evidence; each time it is the same piece, a
book by an Aragonese nobleman written in Castilian. But,
asked the reviewer, "What language would Braudel expect
an Aragonese nobleman to write, at any time?"[46] This multiple use of the same document to prove a point that it did
not actually prove alerts the critical reader to the possibility
that Braudel is not a meticulous weigher and deployer of evidence and documentation. Thus alerted, one finds clues that
the case of the Aragonese nobleman does not stand alone. For
a point on English social history under Elizabeth I, Braudel
relies on Lytton Strachey, perhaps not the most reliable authority on such matters (II, 72 and n. 3). For "the tradition"

---

44. Just roughly, however: it is not clear whether *sociétés* and *civilisations*
in Part II are *conjoncturelles* or *structurelles.*

45. *Revue historique* 203 (1950): 215, 224.

46. *American Historical Review* 55 (1949-50): 350.

that "the Duke of Medina Sidonia, the unfortunate hero of the Armada, founded the Cabaret of the Seven Devils in Madrid," he refers us to Victor Hugo's *William Shakespeare* (II, 57 and n. 8), and we begin to wonder about the evidential value of the tradition.

A man "as well-informed as the Duke of Feria" reports that in 1595 "Naples, Sicily and Milan flourish as never before under their present government." For Braudel this is evidence of the prosperity of those places. The purpose of the report, it turns out, is to persuade Philip that the best he can do for England is to bring it under that same government, that is, his own (I, 449-450). Given such a context how highly ought we to value the well-informed duke's observation? It is my question, not Braudel's. Again, so great a city was Constantinople, that "in March 1581 eight ships loaded with grain provisioned it for a single day only." Who says so? Salazar (I, 320 and n. 8). Who is he? Presumably Cristobal Salazar, the Spanish ambassador to Venice (I, 507).[47] Writing from Venice on March 5, 1581, how does he know how many grain boats arrived in Constantinople in March? And how much grain is eight boatloads? Some Mediterranean ships carried 1,000 or even 2,000 tons. Braudel estimates the mean tonnage of Mediterranean shipping at seventy-five tons, and there were many craft that could handle no more than fifty tons, some even less (I, 272). At the unbelievable maximum eight shiploads means bread in Constantinople beyond a glutton's dream; at the minimum it means mass starvation (except, of course, that the city had sources of grain supply besides the Nile valley). Constantinople was indeed a great city, a metropolis, which is the point Braudel intended to

47. He fits the specification of the letter-writer better than two other Salazars in the index.

document. But Salazar's letter does not document it.

When nature fails to bear the particular witness Braudel wants it to bear, it receives the same flexible treatment that more formal documents occasionally get. The mountains, for example, are places of "a partial and incomplete form of civilization." What of the Alps? Of course, not them. "The Alps are after all the Alps, an exceptional range of mountains." The Andes? No mention of them. The Apennines then? No mention of them, either, perhaps out of deference to the late (in sixteenth-century terms) Duke of Urbino. The Pyrenees? Yes and no. But Aures, the Rif, and Kabylias —there are real mountains (I, 29-30). In sum, on the face of the evidence, mountains that house incomplete forms of civilization house them, and mountains that don't, don't.

Socioeconomic generalizations are as pliable as sociogeographical ones, as little subordinate to rigorous demonstration. "Was it a coincidence that Genoa . . . ? Was Barcelona's misfortune . . . not a consequence of . . . ? By stretching the argument to its limit might it not be possible to say . . . ? Is it possible to go even further and say . . . ?" All these interrogative hypotheticals are in pursuit of a cyclical theory of urban regression from trade to industry to banking, with banking surviving and impelling the decline of the first two (I, 295-296). Readers may entertain themselves by thinking up instances to which the theory does not apply.

We have already seen one instance of Braudel's casual way with figures. Here is another. Speaking of the effects of flooding in Venice, he tells of a disaster in 1443 in which the loss was said to be "quasi mezzo million di ducati" and of another "identical catastrophe" in 1600 "con dano di un million d'oro . . . which is also evidence that prices had risen in the meantime" (I, 213). Of course prices *had* risen in the meantime, but the diluvial misadventures of Venice are hardly to the point. Even in our age, more attuned to statistical precision, we tend to discount quick estimates of damage from material disasters; and is there any conceivable way to know that two such disasters a century and a half apart, the more recent almost four centuries back, were identical?

Actually such a light-hearted attitude toward statistics is not Braudel's customary one. Yet he does not treat them the way Anglo-American economic historians do, or the way his associates Goubert, Le Roy Ladurie, and Meuvret do. These other historians deal with number the way a jealous husband treats a wife on whom he is wholly dependent, ever examining her behavior with an anxious eye. Braudel treats number like a loose but charming mistress. He only half believes his statistics, but he is enchanted with them and loves to play with them, so he refrains from scrutinizing too closely what they are up to. Thus the calculation of the annual havoc wrought by corsairs in the Mediterranean. The only figures are for Venice, 250-300 ships lost to corsairs from 1592 to 1609. Given that Venice had one-tenth of the shipping in the Mediterranean, 2,500-3,000 ships were lost during the eighteen-year period, 138-166 per year, a modest number. Only, however, "if one accepts for a moment, *without believing it too seriously*, that the trade of Venice was a tenth of that of the sea . . . *Let us not put too much faith in the reasonableness of the uncertain figures* (II, 209; italics added)." Indeed not!

A richer example of Braudel's way with number is offered by his effort to discover the volume of commercial transactions in the Mediterranean. "Let us attempt our estimate," he begins (I, 419). The *alcabala* in Castile was a 10 percent transaction tax. In 1598 it raised 1 billion maravedis. Therefore, volume of transaction in Castile in 1598 was 10 billion maravedis, or 1,500 maravedis (4 ducats) per capita. As for foreign trade, 363 million maravedis of import duties figured at one-tenth ad valorem gives 3,630 million maravedis as the value of imports. Double it to take in exports: 7,260 million. Add 700 million for precious metals brought in, and the total port and border transaction comes to about 8 billion, total transaction to 18 billion maravedis for Castile, nine ducats per inhabitant—a ratio of one to three between imports and internal trade.

What of France? During 1551-1556, 36 million livres of imports. At two livres, six sols per écu, that equals 15.7 million écus. Double to count exports: 31.4 million. Apply to France the one-to-three ratio of Castile between imports and internal trade, and France's internal trade comes to 47.1 million écus; total transactions to 78.5 million. Sixteen million Frenchmen and therefore a total transaction average of five écus (or 5.6 ducats) per head. Round the numbers and extend the French rate to the whole Mediterranean population, estimated at 60 million, and the volume of mercantile transactions for the area comes to "300 *millions d'or*" (I, 419-420). So there it is!

What are we to make of it? A few questions. How do we judge the worth of the statistical base, the amounts given for the *alcabala*, the Spanish import duties, and the value of French imports? We look to the footnotes for guidance. For the French figure, reference to an article in the *Revue de géographie* of 1894, not a vintage year for statistical scrupulosity. For the Spanish figures, no references at all in the footnotes. One becomes a little uneasy. Then what about the assumptions? To compute the internal trade of Castile, 1,500 maravedis per capita in 1598, a population of six and two-thirds million in 1598 must have been assumed. But in calculating total trade per capita, "Castile 5 million inhabitants" —a 25 percent slice off the population, a veritable statistical

Black Death. The frightful mortality may account for another curious statistical anomaly: although the ratio of gross internal to gross external trade is five to four, the rate of per capita internal to per capita external trade is four to five, a very unusual thing actually to happen. What of the one-to-three ratio of imports to internal trade boldly carried over from Castile to France? Somehow it is not perfectly persuasive. It is built into the same set of calculations that give a four-to-five (or five-to-four) ratio of foreign to domestic trade. How credible is the one-to-three ratio? At the ports there is one transaction only, either import or export. But what about internal trade? How many transactions to get the wheat from the stalk to the townsman's or the herdsman's table as bread? How many to get the wool off the sheep's back onto the townsman's or peasant's or herdsman's back as clothing? The one-to-three ratio one way or another is incredible. Either the Castilians were evading the *alcabala* by doing an inordinate amount of trading by barter, or in a great many cash transactions they were just not giving the king's government its cut. To transfer a ratio, implausible in the first place, derived from the *alcabala* in Castile, to France where there was no *alcabala* is not statistical analysis; it is legerdemain. As for the assumption that the volume of trade in France can be extrapolated to the whole Mediterranean basin, its boldness is exceeded only by its improbability. So we really do not believe Braudel's estimate of the volume of trade in the Mediterranean. We are in good company; neither does Braudel. The fiscal documents of Castile: "I need hardly indicate their shortcomings." The figure for the *alcabala*, "alas, also includes the *tercia*," another tax. The relation between import duties and value of imports, "*arbitrarily* on the basis of 1 to 10." The population of France accepted as 16,000,000 by all historians "but without proof." As to the

300 *millions d'or* for the trade of the whole Mediterranean area: "This figure is surely not firm." Even from the outset he did not believe there would be a solid outcome. "The results will certainly be false but the operation will be instructive." A dark view of the practices of historians, owing its tone to past experience, leads one to foresee generations of scholars entering into investigations of the sixteenth-century economy with the Mediterranean's 300 millions of Braudelian gold taken at face value, the way chroniclers' figures on the size of medieval armies used to be.

Braudel is candid and specific about his disaffection with history that concerns itself with people as persons. Such persons are *individus*; they belong to the ephemeral realm of the *événementielle*; and they have little impact on history in the *longue durée* or even in the *moyenne durée*. The *longue durée*, however, he populates with nonpeople persons—geographical entities, features of the terrain. Thus in the Mediterranean, peninsulas "are key actors . . . have played leading roles . . . They are almost persons . . . who may or may not be conscious of themselves" (I, 48). Towns are vested with intentions, Constantinople, for example, with "the determination to impose settlement, organization and planning" on the Ottomans. It "triumphed over and betrayed" them, luring them into the wrong wars with the wrong goals (I, 171-172).

The protagonist of this somewhat peculiarly cast historical drama, of course, is the Mediterranean itself, or rather herself. She has designs or purposes of her own, which she sometimes succeeds in fulfilling. She "contributed . . . to preventing the unity of Europe, which she attracted toward her shores and then divided to her own advantage (I, 460). And in the sixteenth century, through Genoa, she "long allocated the world's wealth."[48]

Times, too, get personalized. "The sixteenth century had neither the courage nor the strength" to eradicate the ancient evils of the great cities, and "Modern Times [la Modernité] suddenly projected the territorial state to the center of the stage" (I, 300).

One geographical phenomenon, the big city, is subjected to a veritable trial, with Braudel serving as historical juge d'instruction. First the evils for which big cities were responsible in the sixteenth century are laid out. They were "parasites"; they "gave virtually nothing" and consumed a great deal. Then, on the other hand, "one cannot launch inconsiderately into a prolonged indictment of huge cities . . . There are perfectly good reasons for them," and "a plea of not guilty" might be entered "on behalf of these admirable political and intellectual instruments" (I, 316-321). I am not at all sure that our historical perceptions are sharpened by the depersonalization of men or by the personification of the inanimate features of geography.

So far, I have criticized defects in details, significant only because their repetition gives them a patterned quality that mirrors certain consistent traits of Braudel as a historian. Two other difficulties are of serious concern. The first, and less important, makes it hard to follow intelligently the large section of La Méditerranée devoted to economic activities. Braudel refers to a vast number of weights, measures of vol-

48. In fact "she" did not allocate the world's wealth, even metaphorically. On the contrary, by working out the means of transfer payments from Spain via Italy to the Netherlands, the Genoese bankers at the behest of Philip II drained money out of the Mediterranean to fuel the wars of the Netherlands (I, 435). Philip allocated the money; the Genoese executed his orders. Braudel's implicit identification of wealth with silver and gold is odd.

ume, and moneys, both coined moneys and moneys of account from all over the Mediterranean. For example, a few minutes' search turned up the following names for moneys: ducats, écus d'or, sequins, lire, soldi, zeanars, dobles, soltaninis, livres, sous, écus d'argent, doblones, escudos de oro, reales, aspri, tourrones, escus pistolets, courrones, tallieri, quattrini, bajocci, kronenthäler, marchetti, pesos, reali ad 8, 6, and 4, maravedis, pfennigs, drachmas, reales, déniers, thalers, maidin. Occasionally, either by an explicit statement or by providing means for an inference, Braudel enables the reader to make an equation for two different moneys: for example 375 maravedis equal one ducat. Nowhere in *La Méditerranée*, however, is there a table of coins and moneys of account. Or of weights and measures. For such guides in the morass of moneys, weights, and measures, a reader, at least this reader, feels a pressing need.

The second difficulty is more serious, since it speaks to a nearly blind spot in Braudel's historical vision. Perhaps in self-defense in dealing with *structures*, he attends almost entirely to material structures—peninsulas, islands, mountains, plateaus and plains, seas and oceans, climate and seasons, routes, shipping, and towns. Routines imbedded in custom and law receive less attention or none. The Mediterranean world is the world of grain, the olive tree, the vine, and the sheep. As to the shepherds, we hear only of those involved in the migration from high summer pasture to low winter pasture. Of the daily, scarcely changing life and practices of the vineyard, the olive grove, and the wheat field we hear too little. Nor do we learn much about how small communities —guilds, villages and towns—or large ones—provinces, principalities, city states, realms, or empires—actually ordered their affairs or of what held them together in durable structures. In the age of Philip II two great empires, that of the king of

Spain and that of the Ottoman sultan, divided and fought over the Mediterranean. Of the bonds that held each of those unwieldy conglomerates more or less together we catch only fleeting glimpses. Of the religious structures, Christianity and Islam, that at once united and divided each empire, we see nothing from the inside.[49] They are recurrent names, but what gave them life—their interlaced institutions, practices, and beliefs—is nowhere to be found.

So *La Méditerranée* is in some ways a flawed book. But here we need to pause. To judge a great work like *La Méditerranée* by its flaws is like judging an economy during a boom solely on the record of concurrent proceedings in bankruptcy. There is much more to the book than casual mistakes or even than systematic ones. Indeed all the remarks so far in this critique might rightly be condemned as myopic. They are certainly the work of a historian more exclusively admiring than he need be or should be of tightly built historical works, works that in all their lineaments, articulation, and composition bear the marks of fine, delicate, and patient craftsmanship. His first instinct, and not a very ingratiating one, is to pry away at the places in a historical work that show haste or careless handiwork. It is the wrong instinct for approaching *La Méditerranée*, for to such an approach that book is bound to be vulnerable; indeed, its vulnerability to the above criticism is, I think, an inevitable concomitant of the two qualities in continuous tension with each other that make it a classic.

The first of these great qualities is Braudel's vast appetite for extending the boundaries of his undertaking, the perime-

---

49. The religious structures divided the empire of Philip because of the Reformation; that of the Ottomans, because of the tension between ruling ex-Christian slaves and Moslem subjects.

ter of his vision. We become aware of it when we ask what the book is about. The Mediterranean in the age of Philip II—that is, a bounded body of water between A.D. 1556 and 1598? Of course not. As to time, Philip II begins being king in 1556 and stops in 1598—two events; but the Mediterranean, a structure of geohistory, does not begin and end like that; it goes back to man's settlement on its shores, and to the ways of life that such settlement mandated. And it goes forward to today, when some of those ways of life still survive. Other ways of Mediterranean life, born long before Philip, continue long after he was laid to rest. Philip was not the master of structural time, the *longue durée*; the creations of that time were silent constraints on all he did. Nor does the time of *moyenne durée*, of *conjoncture*, accommodate itself to the ephemeral span of his reign. The discernible rhythms of economies, societies, and civilizations lie to both sides of him, before he began, after he ended—the whole sixteenth century at least. But not the sixteenth century of traditional historians, bewitched by the sign of the double zero. With respect to the cycles of the Mediterranean economy, according to Braudel, there are two sixteenth centuries. One ran roughly from about 1450 to about 1550, an economic upswing in the Mediterranean followed by an economic downswing. A second ran from about 1550 to 1630 or 1650, a revival of the Mediterranean economy and then its final plunge and departure from stage center, thrust out by the Atlantic and the powers of the Atlantic rim of Europe.

And the space of the Mediterranean: is it the blue waters of the inland sea and the men who sailed them or lived on their shores? Of course, but far more than that. *La Méditerranée* starts in the mountains, the Alps, the Pyrenees, the Apennines, the Dinaric Alps, the Caucasus, the mountains of Anatolia and Lebanon, the Atlas, the Spanish Cordilleras, the interior massifs of Sicily, Sardinia, Corsica. Then it moves down from the mountains to the plateaus, to the hills, to the plains, and at last to the sea or the several seas of the Mediterranean basin. But Braudel does not stop there. There is a "Greater Mediterranean" to consider. The desert touches the inland sea, and by caravan routes Braudel takes us through the hot deserts to the Africa of the blacks, whence gold came to the Mediterranean; by caravan again through the cold deserts of Asia to China, whence came silk and fine fabrics and to which the Mediterranean sent gold and silver. By four "isthmuses," combined land and water routes, Braudel stretches the Mediterranean to Russia, Poland, Germany, France; and along those routes he takes us junketing to Moscow, Lublin, Lvov, Nuremburg, Augsburg, Ulm, Lyon, Paris, Rouen. So the terrestrial Mediterranean stretches out. Much more, the watery Mediterranean, through the Strait of Gibraltar, first to Bruges, Antwerp, London, Hamburg, Danzig —the route of wool and wheat southward, cloth and alum and oriental goods northward. Then several more great bounds to the islands of the Atlantic, to Mexico and Lima, and at last by the way of Acapulco to Manila and to China. There by this vast extension of the Mediterranean of the seas westward, we meet ourselves coming east by caravan train across the Mediterranean of the deserts.

Let us not deceive ourselves. No doubt there is a reason or a rationale for some of these flights through time and space, and more or less plausible excuses for others. But we fail fully to understand the historian behind *La Méditerranée* if we pause to quibble over this journey or that one. They may be a piece of Braudel's historical design; they are surely a piece of something more insistent and consistent than any design—his temperament, his feel for history. The countervailing manifestation of that feel is Braudel's inexhaustible delight in piling up concrete detail—detail for detail's sake.

A few examples. The Mediterranean was a sea of small ships: "barques, *saëtes, laudi, luiti,* tartans, frigates, *polaccas*" (I, 112). Among writers who described caravans are not only Tavernier but also "Gobineau, G. Schweinfurth, René Caillé, Brugnon and Flachat" (I, 165). The transhumance routes that the Mediterranean sheep and their shepherds followed had different names in different places: "*cañadas* in Castile, *camis ramadas* in the Eastern Pyrenees, *drayes* or *drailles* in Languedoc, *carraires* in Provence, *traturi* in Italy, *trazzere* in Sicily, *drumul oilor* in Rumania" (I, 86). The hungry camel driver lives on "famine foods." "The Taureg of the Air use . . . the seeds of the *drinn,* the *mrokba,* wild *fonio, cram-cram, tawit,* the rhizomes and young shoots of the *berdi.* Their neighbors the Tibu . . . get their bread from the fruit of the *dûm*" (I, 159). The commerce between Spain and North Africa brought to the African shore "textiles—broadcloths, silks, velours, taffetas, rough village cloths—cochineal, salt, perfumes, gum, coral, saffron, tens of thousands of caps," and brought back "sugar, wax, tallow, cowhides and goat skins, even gold" (II, 186). It is a tragedy that the Spanish did not pursue their enterprise in North Africa "after the occupation of Melilla in 1497, of Mers-el-Kebir in 1505, of the Peñon de Velez in 1508, of Oran in 1509, of Mastaganem, Tlemcen, Ténès, and the Peñon of Algiers in 1510" (I, 108). The Tyrrhean almost lived off its own resources: "grain from Sicily . . . ; salt . . . from Trapiani; cheese from Sardinia; wine . . . from Naples; salt meat from Corsica; silk from Corsica or Calabria; fruit, almonds, walnuts as well as barrels of anchovies and tuna from Provence; iron from the isle of Elba; . . . capital from Florence or Genoa" (I, 112). And then there is the mind-boggling six-page census of the shipping of Atlantic powers in the Mediterranean before 1550—the shipping of the Basques, the Biscayans, and the Galicians; the Portuguese; the Normans and the Bretons; the Dutch and the English—compiled out of the archives of Mantua, Simancas, Venice, Paris, Florence, and Ragusa; out of the contemporary writings of Sanudo, Forquevaux, Hakluyt, and Argenté; out of the books edited by Gosselin and Charrière; out of the modern studies of Heers, Almeida d'Eça, Gioffrée, Billioud, Mollat, Collier, Delumeau, Douais, Doëhaerd, Carus-Wilson, Amman, Capmany, Cunningham, Williamson, Wood, Lubimenko (I, 549-556).

And Alpharbar's ship was laden with "gold, silver, rings, jewels, spices, drugs and aromatic perfumes, parrots, pelicans, civet cats, monkeys, black-spotted weasels, porcupines."

This last list is not from *La Méditerranée* by Fernand Braudel but from *Gargantua* by François Rabelais. It suggests that when we first started to think about *La Méditerranée*, we began with the wrong image of a classic in our mind. The image of Racine, perhaps, with his "classical" unities of time, place, and persons, tightly interlocked by an event that forced each person into momentary yet absolute self-revelation, a "moment of truth." Racine, the "classical" dramatist of the "classical" seventeenth century. Nothing of this in Rabelais, the man of the sixteenth century, or in Braudel, the historian of a sixteenth century which, in his spreading Rabelaisian embrace in *La Méditerranée*, becomes two, many centuries—a different kind of classic. Braudel's way with the past is Gargantuan; he has an enormous delight in it, its largest lineaments and its most intimate details, an irrepressible appetite for going everywhere, seeing everything, and telling all about it. Thus he pursues the flow of gold from the Sudan into the Mahgreb, which was open to all the

Mediterranean traders of Europe. Eleven ports of the Mahgreb to which the Europeans came—Ceuta, Tangiers, Fez, Oran, Tlemcen, Bougie, Constantine, Tunis, Tripoli, Algiers, Hone. The nine kinds of Europeans who came—Aragonese, Castilians, Catalans, Marseillais, Provençals, Ragusans, Sicilians, Venetians. And the Genoese. About them a lovely useless piece of information. At Tunis in 1573, "the Spanish found not the [Genoese] quarter, but its old cisterns" (I, 425). Another flow, the irresistible flow of the mountain people of the Mediterranean into its plains—Corsicans, Albanians, Bergamasques, Armenians. Armenians? A bit off the Mediterranean really; still, they did go to the Mediterranean, to Constantinople and "to Tiflis, Odessa, Paris, the Americas" (I, 45). That very great "Greater Mediterranean"!

Braudel is not padding; no need to pad a book of 1,100 pages; he just cannot resist all the lovely irrelevant or quasi-relevant details that his researches brought into his net. Many, many had to be discarded, but not all. For several pages he sets out that solemn and methodical catalog of every recorded voyage that northern sailors made into the Mediterranean in the early sixteenth century. Finally he comes to the last account of such a voyage in Hakluyt, the voyage of the *Aucher* in 1551. And for a page he sails us merrily around the sea with its commander, Captain Bodenham, and tells us that aboard the *Aucher* was "Richard Chancellor, who ten years later, in 1553, was to reach the mouth of the Duna in northern Russia" (I, 555-556).

Pursuing one of his favorite topics, "the route," the paths that men and news and goods moved on, Braudel deals with sea routes and roads on land, and comes to the navigable rivers, to the Adige, the Po, the Adda, the Oglio, the Mincio, the Guadalquivir, the Nile, the Ebro, the Arno, and last to the Tiber, "the home of curious river boats with lateral rudder and two raised ends that served as steps for disembarking on the steep banks of the river" (I, 258). After he dropped this charming bit of random information, perhaps an awareness of one of his own traits lodged in Braudel's subconscious. At any rate a few pages later he writes appreciatively of Rabelais, "who took an interest in everything" (I, 261).

As with Rabelais, Braudel's bursts of arcane information rise off the solid rock of an erudition enormous in scope. He examines "the weaknesses of the maritime sectors" of the Mediterranean. Part of those weaknesses was the result of shortages of the various kinds of wood for ships. Braudel tells us of the timber for the Ragusan boats, of the kinds of wood the Ragusans used and where it came from, of the kinds the Turks used, of the best wood for oars and where it came from, of the buyers of ship timber, Ragusa, Spain, Genoa, Barcelona, and the sellers, Tuscany, Naples, the Catalan Pyrenees, the Calabria with its forests of "Nerticaro, Ursomarso, Altomonte, Sandonato, Policastrello." For this one-paragraph survey Braudel draws on one modern work and one of the early seventeenth century, on the printed correspondence of a French ambassador, and on the archives of Ragusa, Florence, Simancas, and Naples (I, 130).

His restless piercing eye sees beyond simple geographical boundaries, even those of his own making, and where his eye goes his words follow. He considers the role of the Mediterranean islands as transmitters of material culture. Sugar, for example, passes from mainland Egypt to island Cyprus and thence to island Sicily and thence, brushing aside the Strait of Gibraltar, to Madeira, the Azores, the Cape Verde islands, the Canaries, at last to the islands of the Caribbean (I, 141). For, after all, what are islands? Land surrounded by water? But why just water? Are there not "islands that the sea does not surround"? Greece closed off by "terrestrial walls"; Naples likewise "cut off to the north by the thickness of the mountains that make its boundary with Rome"; Lombardy "a continental island between the Alps and the Apennines, between rustic Piedmont and half Byzantine Venice"; and the Maghreb and Syria, made islands by their deserts. "Scarcely exaggerating, one may speak of a whole series of peripheral islands, Portugal, Andalusia, Valencia, Catalonia, linked by Castile to the Iberian mass" (I, 146). As Braudel puts it, *forçons les termes*, make rigid words give a little, and all sorts of interesting things can happen, all sorts of new insights and possibilities can open up (II, 152). Like Humpty-Dumpty, Braudel makes words mean what he wants them to mean.

Braudel has the Rabelaisian spirit in his love not only of stray particulars but of all sorts of general notions. He seizes on any idea that comes his way—and an abundance, a plethora, comes his way—looks at it a while, applies his enormous knowledge to it, and makes something of it. The century of the Jews. The diaspora of the mountain dwellers. The perils of the plains from the mountaineers above and the malarial marshes nearby. The true human distances of the Mediterranean in the sixteenth century—the time it took men and goods to get from point to point. The impact on the Mediterranean of the Portuguese diversion of the gold of black Africa to Atlantic enterprises. The role of the Genoese as world bankers. The gross industrial output of the Mediterranean region. The decline of the Spanish bourgeoisie. The baroque as a Mediterranean incursion into the north of Europe. These are a mere handful of the colossal pile of ideas that Braudel examines in *La Méditerranée* with as much patience as his mind can muster. Then, restless, only rarely willing to push to the bottom of the matter in hand, he passes on to another idea, just as captivating for a while.

Yet Braudel's flashes of insight are not only brilliantly conceived but often beautifully documented: the frustrating snail's pace of communication in the sixteenth century, the mail that came too late, too slow, or not at all, he illustrates by letters from the empress of the Holy Roman Empire to Philip II, from Calvin to del Vico, from Antonio de Guevara to a friend, from Don Luis de Requesens at Antwerp to Philip's ambassador in Paris (I, 327). Braudel summarizes the interplay of force that made some times and distances not intervals precisely measured but a grab bag of uncertainties. "At sea a favorable wind and a spell of fine weather might make the difference between taking six months for a voyage or completing it in a week or two . . . On land . . . a war, a state of alert, roads flooded by heavy rain, or passes blocked by a snow fall" could have a like effect. "Distances were not invariable, fixed once and for all, and one could never be sure in advance before setting out or making decisions, what timetable fate would impose" (I, 328). Big features of human geography and little have their special meanings to Braudel: the big cities as consumers of wealth and creators of civilization, the many small towns along the land routes as stopovers, man's concession to the hard "arithmetic of distances," the prosperity of the small ship as an index to the general prosperity of Mediterranean trade.

All this suggests another trait of Braudel and *La Méditerranée*, another rightful inheritance from the sixteenth century. It is a trait not suggested by the formal and formidable table of contents of the book with its neatly laid out three parts, each with its sections, subsections, and sub-subsections. Braudel is a picaresque, a wanderer with the whole Mediterranean world in the age of Philip II to roam in; more, with such extension in space and time as he chooses to give to that world. The parts and the sections of the book point him in a set of rough general directions, but they do not tell him just where to go, or how long to linger at one place or another. He leaves or stays as the spirit moves him. When here or there he is attracted to something off the track, a three-star something that in his internal Michelin *vaut le voyage*, he is ingenious enough to break out of his preset itinerary.

For readers, and I hope there will be many, who turn to the English translation of *La Méditerranée* out of curiosity and for pleasure, the picaresque Braudel is the one to imitate. Do not earnestly (as I did) start at the beginning, go to the end, then stop. Rather open at random, find the beginning of a sub-section, and start there. If what you read does not interest or please you, close and open at random again. Only a most unlikely set of accidents or a most incurious mind will require you to repeat this procedure often. If the sub-subsection satisfies your curiosity, go on to another as far away or as near as you wish. If it whets your curiosity, go back to the subsection in which the sub-subsection is set and read it through.

That way, the Rabelaisian picaresque way, to think about and read *La Méditerranée* is a way that Braudel's own spirit and habits do not discourage; but it is not the only way, and it does less than full justice to the book. It fails to do justice to powerful aggregated conceptions whose force can be grasped only through reading more sustained than this chance method permits. Braudel pursues a number of such sustained inquiries: the investigation of banditry as a form of class warfare, the study of the takeover of financial operations in Europe by the Genoese, and, most interesting to me, the three case studies of *le refus*, the rejection of the civilization of their masters or conquerors by a minority or a conquered group. The instances Braudel examines are the Bulgars, the Moriscos, and the Jews. In the Balkan peninsula the Bulgars

were for centuries subject to Ottoman domination. Tillers
of the soil in the Danube plain, they fed their Moslem masters. But they never became Islamized. They clung stubbornly to the language and the religion that isolated them,
and through the centuries they remained Bulgar-speaking
and Orthodox Christian, not Turkish- or Arabic-speaking,
not Moslem. On the westmost European peninsula were the
Moriscos. The Moors had lost their last power center on the
Iberian peninsula, Granada, to the Catholic kings in 1492.
The peasants on the great estates of Andalusia, Valencia, and
Aragon were still Moslem and Arabic-speaking in the 1500s,
centuries after they had been submerged in the successive
waves of the Christian reconquest of Iberia. The policy of
the early rulers of united Spain, Ferdinand and Isabella and
the first two Hapsburgs, was forced conversion of both Moslems and Jews to Christianity. The Moors became Moriscos;
Jews, Marranos; Christians, by decree and forced baptism,
"new Christians." Their Christian rulers dispersed the Moriscos throughout Spain. In dispersion they prospered, but
they remained Arabs in custom and language and crypto-
Moslems in religion. In the end Christian Spain "solved the
problem" of Moorish Spain and its *refus*, its rejection of the
civilization of the conquerors, by deporting the Moriscos en
masse to the Maghreb. The same refusal but different out-
comes in Bulgaria and in Spain. Why? The Turks were thin
on the ground in Bulgaria. The "final solution" did not
provide a solution for them; they needed the field labor of
the conquered. It was otherwise in Spain. In the demographic upsurge of Europe in the sixteenth century the population of Christian Spain grew. There were quite enough
"old Christians" to take the place, or at any rate the land,
of the new crypto-Moslem Christians.

Finally the Jews, the eternal and ubiquitous refusers, thrust from one place, then putting down roots, not too deep, in another place. A people for whom diaspora was a way of life. A people who survived by a habit of adaptability that was never total. A people who had learned by long experience to find a resting place on the narrow shelf of a rocky precipice, and, dislodged, to seize a handhold and explore until they found another. They paid their way by quickly acquiring and providing whatever skills were in short supply in their current lodging.

It is in his studies of such phenomena as movements of men, money, and goods, banditry, the corsair enterprise, *le refus,* that Braudel at once dazzles and puts to shame historians like me. Underlying such studies are archival researches of incredible scope, a mastery of printed sources as varied as it is vast, and acquaintance with secondary works the mere setting down of which takes up most of thirty-two pages. Not only did Braudel read much; he also found in that reading the evidence for connections accessible only to a man of panoramic vision. *La Méditerranée* is a miracle of historical scholarship that shames both my narrow vision and my narrow learning.[50]

The sort of insight that went into the perception and investigation of the *refus* accounts in part, I think, for the powerful impact that the event, the publication of *La Méditerranée*, had on the structure of French historical studies. The book is a vast conglomerate of rough-hewn blocks of coherent historical substance, an implicit program, not starkly set forth as somebody's bright idea but imbedded in masses

50. The uses of Braudel's enormous store of information are also evident in the rich detail of *La Méditerranée*. He uses it to give one a sense of the expense of the rapid transmittal of news by indicating that the cost of dispatching a courier from Chartres to Toledo and back was more than the annual salary of a professor at Padua or Salamanca (I, 336-338).

of solid though incomplete historical work. In one book, although a very big one, Braudel provided French historians with both a vision of what could be done and an apparently endless vista of what was yet to do, a schedule of tasks that challenged the imagination of historians and commanded their labors. The massive list of publications sponsored by the VIᵉ section does not, of course, derive directly from *La Méditerranée*. Nevertheless, the rubrics under which the books appear—Affaires et gens d'affaires, Archéologie et civilisation, Démographie et sociétés, Les hommes et la terre, Monnaie-prix-conjoncture, Ports-routes-trafics, Civilisations et sociétés—reflect the subjects on which Braudel concentrated his attention and the attention of others in and through *La Méditerranée*. And some of the matters that he pointed to as demanding attention—the history of epidemics, the history of climate, the history of population changes—have now received that attention in part because he secured support for those who gave it. Because in *La Méditerranée* he was always ready to ask big questions about urbanism, labor mobility, population pressure, price movements, economic cycles, gross production, volume of transaction, a generation of French historians have devoted meticulous attention to studies of those matters in depth and in detail, with documentation and methods neither of which were available to Braudel in the late 1940s when *La Méditerranée* was brought to birth. In one aspect—perhaps its most important aspect— we may see in Braudel's masterpiece a seminal work in the true sense of that much-abused term. It is the seed from which, under his own laborious fostering and nurture, grew the tree, rich in fruit, which is the *Annales* school today, not only in France but wherever history as a *science humaine* flourishes.

We have now considered *La Méditerranée* from two points

of view. First as a masterpiece of picaresque Rabelaisian history, a volume to delight the reader-amateur of history in the best sense of the word, who will receive abundant rewards in wandering through its pages, following his own whim. Second, as the seminal work of the *Annalistes* in the past two decades, still a rich storehouse of inchoate ideas and shrewd insights for the most productive and lively school of historians practicing their art today. Braudel is now well aware of the powerful impact of *La Méditerranée*. As he says, "A new crop of specialized research . . . follow[ed] in the wake of my book. It began by following in my footsteps and has now completely overwhelmed me." There follows a list, which by no means exhausts his influence, of more than thirty scholars in the course of whose studies, "I have participated, often very closely" (I, 12-13). Yet to consider *La Méditerranée* only from these two angles of vision still does not do justice to the work or to its author. Indeed, although I hope not, I fear that Braudel may find my first point of view in dealing with his work frivolous. As for the second, when Braudel defended his *thèse* twenty-five years ago, the siring of a whole generation of historians can hardly have been more than a gleam in the master's eye. However well, in retrospect, our previous characterizations of *La Méditerranée* fit the work itself, they do not speak to the intentions of its author as a historian when he wrote the book.

What, then, were Braudel's intentions in writing *La Méditerranée?* We look for enlightenment to the prefaces of the two editions—and having looked we are perplexed. Not that the prefaces lack the customary statement of intention. On the contrary. The difficulty is that several intentions are stated and that they point in divergent directions. The first intention Braudel states is "to discover exactly what the historical character of the Mediterranean has been" (I, 13). A problem, then—the *histoire problème* dear to the heart of Lucien Febvre. But is it really? A problem must have manageable bounds—religious unbelief in the early sixteenth century, for example. But the historical character of a body of water and the surrounding lands that for four millennia have been sites and routes for a half-dozen or more civilizations? What *is* the problem? Indeed the problem soon undergoes mitosis and becomes "the *problems* posed by the Mediterranean," which are "of exceptional richness" (I, 15). So then which problems? A question put too late, since even before we have time to ask it Braudel turns our attention to "the grand movement of Mediterranean life" (I, 14).

Not really *histoire problème* at all, *La Méditerranée*. Rather *histoire totale*, history that aspires to embrace the whole of human activity, bringing to bear upon it all the knowledge that the sciences of man can provide—an account of the whole life of the peoples of the Mediterranean in the latter part of the sixteenth century. A task beyond the resources of any historian, even one as magnificently equipped, as learned, and as intelligent as Fernand Braudel. It is indeed a task he commits himself to but abandons quickly enough. Under the heading "Collective Destinies" we find much on certain matters pertaining to "The Economies," on precious metals, moneys and prices, commerce and transport. But on agriculture and industry there are only a few pages. Yet agriculture *was* the life of at least four-fifths of the inhabitants of the Mediterranean world. Still, 255 pages on Mediterranean economies in the second half of the sixteenth century—a generous allotment. On civilizations, only 68 pages; on societies, 46. Three durable civilizations in the Mediterranean region—Moslem, Christian, Jewish. But about Islam, Judaism, and Christianity only that their followers lived in the Mediterranean in obdurate mutual *refus*.

Of what the religions *were*, of their *mentalités*, nothing. Of course, to ask this totality of Braudel or anyone is absurd, it is too much—except that Braudel asked it of himself.

At another level Braudel sees *La Méditerranée* as an attempt to solve another problem. This one is an intelligible bounded problem. It is not, however, a problem of history, of the past, but of historiography, of writing about the past. It is "the basic problem . . . confronting every historical undertaking," how "to simultaneously convey both that conspicuous history that holds our attention by its continual and dramatic changes—and that other submerged history, almost silent and always discreet, virtually unsuspected either by its observers or its participants, a history that is little touched by the obstinate erosion of time" (I, 12). To this problem, as we have already seen, Braudel proposed the solution of a three-tiered history, or of a history that treats historical waves of varying length: *structures—longue durée, conjoncture—moyenne durée, événement—courte durée.* The concepts—structure, conjuncture, event—thus are not just guidelines for historians, notions to be kept in mind as they go about their work. At least for Braudel in *La Méditerranée*, they are the visible architectural units that pattern the entire vast edifice. Such is Braudel's plan for dealing with a problem, a question that all self-conscious historians are occasionally aware of, and that all historians who write history perforce answer even if they do not ask it. In *La Méditerranée* how well did Braudel's solution work?

Let us first listen to reviewers and others who have written about Braudel's book.

One of the richest intuitions of the author is that social change is not uniform . . . Nevertheless he translates it into the traditional divisions of historical domains (political, economic) . . .

It is hard to understand this hierarchy of rhythms . . . Because he did not make his notion of *structure* precise enough, the author too often offers a mosaic of analyses, the common direction of which escapes us.[51]

In Braudel's work the three major sections—dealing successively with geography, with society, and with "events"—never quite came together.[52]

This reviewer found the liaison of the political history with the elements of human geography somewhat unconvincing. The extent to which such elements influenced those human decisions which in turn gave direction to the events of that half-century remained obscure.[53]

Braudel's emphasis on the importance of factors of *longue durée* has made the gap between structure and event almost unbridgeable . . . As important and rich as Braudel's *La Méditerranée* . . . is . . . Braudel never fully succeeds in showing the relevance of the long-range developments for the events of the period of Philip II.[54]

There are fine pages that illuminate their subject: but they do so not because of [the] lines of demarcation so carefully laid out, but in spite of them. The parts of his "world" are all there, but they lie inert, unrelated, discrete.[55]

And finally a faithful *Annaliste* expresses his judgment in

---

51. Claude Lefort, "Histoire et sociologie dans l'oeuvre de Fernand Braudel," *Cahiers internationaux de sociologie* 13 (1952): 123-124.

52. H. Stuart Hughes, *The Obstructed Path* (New York: Harper and Row, 1968), pp. 58-59.

53. R. A. Newhall, review, *Journal of Modern History* 22 (1950): 365.

54. Felix Gilbert, "Intellectual History: Its Aims and Methods," *Daedalus* (Winter 1971): 97, n. 21.

55. Bernard Bailyn, "Braudel's Geohistory: A Reconsideration," *Journal of Economic History* 11 (1951): 279.

1971. Of *La Méditerranée*, "the greatest book produced by the *Annales* school," Jacques Le Goff writes,

> The political history is relegated to Part III, which far from being the culmination of the work is more like the bits and pieces left over . . . an atrophied appendix . . . the parson's nose.[56]

The point of quoting these fragments from appraisals of *La Méditerranée* is not that the appraisals themselves were unfavorable. Quite to the contrary, most of them were sympathetic, some enthusiastic. The point is that whatever his overall judgment of *La Méditerranée*, with varying precision each reviewer expresses similar misgivings about the success of the book in executing Braudel's explicit intentions. The plan of superimposing *durées*, one on the other, so that the whole picture of the whole Mediterranean world would become visible, does not always or often work. For whatever reason, the superposition of "transparencies" yields a final product that is in many places turbid and opaque, in others transparent enough, but for reasons having nothing to do with the overall design.

In this connection it is worth noting that the most remarkable and successful works of historians within the orbit of the *Annales* school have not been constructed in precise emulation of *La Méditerranée*. Baehrel's work on Basse-Provence, Deyon's on Amiens, Gascon's on Lyon, Goubert's on the Beauvaisis, Le Roy Ladurie's on Languedoc, Meyer's on the Breton nobility are splendid works of scholarship linked by affinity or specific inspiration to *La Méditerranée*. Each of them concerns a relatively small area, none of them engages in large-scale geographizing (which would, of course,

---

56. Jacques Le Goff, "Is Politics Still the Backbone of History?" *Daedalus* (Winter 1971): 4.

be inappropriate to their subjects). All are concerned with structures and conjunctures, but only one with a chronological account of events, and all treat structure and conjuncture as useful conceptions rather than as primary units for the organization of their material.

That a work as massive and powerful as *La Méditerranée*, a work that one way or another has served as an inspiration to two generations of French scholars, has not inspired those scholars to direct imitation seems puzzling. This fact tends to reinforce the assessments of *La Méditerranée* quoted before. The book falls short of its author's intention in one major respect. It does not solve the historiographical problem that it poses: how to deal with the perennial historiographic difficulty of linking the durable phenomena of history with those that involve rapid change.

There are several reasons for this lack of success. First, the tripartite division of *durées* may better be referred to the residual trinitarianism of a *mentalité* once Christian than to any inherent rational necessity. In the crunch Braudel himself recognizes that between the Platonic poles of total stability and instantaneous change there are *durées* of the most varied length: "ten, a hundred." Second, the three *durées* are somewhat arbitrarily attached to specific subject matters: *longue* to the geographic, social, and cultural; *moyenne* to the economic and sometimes the social; *courte*, in fact if not in theory, to the political.[57] As Claude Lefort pointed out, however, such linkages are purely arbitrary. In the Mediterranean, óne political institution, monarchy, had a *durée* of some five or six millennia; two geographic ones—

57. If these linkages do not seem consistent with every linkage that Braudel makes, it is because Braudel's own linkages are not perfectly consistent. These do justice to his practice if not to his theory.

the eruption of Mount Vesuvius, August 24, A.D. 79, and the earthquake at Lisbon, November 1, A.D. 1755—had short *durées*, indeed, a day or so, a few minutes. In fact, each of Braudel's taxonomic essences—the geographic, the cultural, and so forth—have attached to them *longues, moyennes,* and *courtes durées.* But in the Mediterranean is monarchy really political? Is it not rather social in its origin, and almost to the end religious? These questions reveal a chronic but convenient defect in our practice as historians. For our convenience we divide the domain of human experience into more or less manageable compartments—social, economic, political —and then fall into the habit of treating our classificatory devices as realities or essences, setting them against each other, even making assumptions about their relative importance. We forget that they derive their importance from the volume of particular matters we ourselves decide, often arbitrarily, to subsume under each rubric.

It cannot be justly said that as a consequence of Braudel's views on *durée,* the *événementielle* receives short shrift in *La Méditerranée.* The shrift is not all that short, 364 pages in the edition of 1949. Moreover, indirect evidence suggests that it may have worked the other way around, that the *événementielle* received its shrift before Braudel got around to writing about *structure* and *conjoncture* in the Mediterranean world. At least it is certain that Braudel had no second thoughts on the *événementielle* between 1949 and 1966 when the second edition of *La Méditerranée* was published. Although in that edition large chunks are added to and subtracted from the first two parts of the book, and modifications appear on many pages of "The Role of Environment" and "Collective Destinies and General Trends," the last section, "Events, Politics and Men," remains unaltered save for a few added footnotes that produce no corresponding change

in the text.[58] This lack of revision does not indicate that
Braudel was satisfied with the third part of *La Méditerranée*.
On the contrary, he was satiated, fed up with it. He very
much hesitated to publish it at all in 1966 (II, 223). If it
were permissible to be as bold in reconstructing the history
of the composition of twentieth-century texts as twentieth-
century scholars are in doing the like for sixteenth-century
texts, one might go further. Braudel refers to the third section as *franchement traditionelle*. Of all the parts of *La
Méditerranée* it would for that very reason have been the
most difficult to write in the German prison camp, whence
chapter after chapter of *La Méditerranée* came forth. It depends, like the rest of the book, on a colossal mass of data,
but it also depends, as the rest of the book does not, on the
exact chronological sequence of that data; such sequence is
the very nature of traditional diplomatic and military history. Doing that sort of history without reference works or
notes would be, I should think, practically impossible. Moreover, an examination of the third part shows scarcely any citations from works written between 1939 and 1949. All of
this suggests that the third part might have been written before 1939, before Braudel's imprisonment brought to a de-
cisive climax his disengagement from and discontent with
traditional history; that it may have been in the main the
traditional *thèse* he was preparing before, so fortunately for

58. This statement is not based on a page-by-page comparison of the
third sections of the two editions, for which time was lacking. However, all
the subheadings and sub-subheadings in the edition of 1949 appear in that
of 1966. The few added sub-subheadings in the latter edition are simply
interjected into sub-subsections without any further alteration of the text.
In six chance samplings (10 percent of the total text of the third part) only
two additions to the footnotes appeared, accompanied by no corresponding
alteration of the text.

the development of French historical scholarship, his own discontents and Lucien Febvre led him astray.

Be that as it may, the third part of *La Méditerranée*, though an adequate and erudite sample of "the old learning," would have caused no stir in the world of historians. Its very nature disables it from performing the function that Braudel assigns it. One cannot bring the course of political events into effective relation with the more durable and patterned phenomena of history by tacking a tired Sorbonne *thèse* (intellectual vintage of 1925) onto a lively collection of *Annales enquêtes*. The evidence does not suggest that Braudel failed to solve the historiographic problem he envisaged; it suggests that he did not really even try.

Yet that problem is not insoluble. One solution lay within Braudel's reach, and in fact time and again he reached for it and caught it. He caught it, for example, when he asked, "Why did banditry flourish in the Mediterranean toward the end of the sixteenth century?" "What accounts for the considerable flood of Christian renegades into the service of the Turk and the Barbary States?" "Why did the Spanish ultimately expel the Moriscos?" One answer to the problem of bonding event, conjuncture, and structure is provided by *histoire problème*.

As a contrast with the fruitful sprawl of *La Méditerranée*, let us consider an example of *histoire problème*, a short essay by Edmund Morgan. In the third winter of the Jamestown colony in 1610, of the 600 men who had come there since its founding three years earlier only 60 were alive. In May 1611, Sir Thomas Dale found the colonists "at their daily and usuall workes, bowling in the streets." Problem: "why did men spend their time bowling in the streets when their lives depended on work," in a situation that required that they "clear and plow and plant the crops that could have kept them alive?

Were they lunatics?" In a colony "teetering on the verge of extinction" why did even stern governors exact only four to six hours of labor? How are we to account "for this chronic unemployment or underemployment at Jamestown?" Partial answers were supplied at the time by contemporaries: too many gentlemen, unaccustomed to labor, among the settlers, too much hunger, too much disease. Another answer later: the rules of the Virginia company stifled private enterprise and individual initiative. There remains a problem un-solved: "what ideas and attitudes about work, carried from England would have led the first English settlers to expect so little of themselves in a situation that demanded so much?" Morgan has posed the problem; let us follow his quest for a solution.

First, English ideas about the New World, ideas that had been a century in the making—a *mentalité*, a *structure*, a *modèle*. The Spanish model, the Spanish experience made easily available by Richard Hakluyt, with two components—an abundant land, and a native population available to do the hard work. That was what 100 years of Spanish literature of colonization had prepared the English settlers to expect in America. That was what they did not find on the sandy spit at the mouth of the James River or in its hinterland. Willy-nilly, to live they would have to work.

What notions about work did they bring with them from England early in the seventeenth century? Those ideas were formed during a century of rising population that outstripped both food supply and opportunities for full employment. By modern standards, in Tudor England "the population . . . was idle much of the time." To prevent total idleness, the government adopted policies of "conservation of employ-ment," work "rationed so that every one could have a little," policies that "helped maintain social stability," but by the practice of spreading work thin "discouraged energetic labor and nurtured the workingman's low expectations of himself." Poorly rewarded in an England where the Price Revolution steadily widened the unfavorable gap between cost of living and wages, many an Englishman was ready to seek a better life in the New World, "but a life devoted to more and harder work than he had known at home might not have been his idea of a better life."

Settling a wilderness, too, had an English model—movement into the hill pastures of the north and the west of the island kingdom. There herdsmen supplemented their earnings with cottage industry and a cottage garden and traded for grain. The Spanish found profit that way in the West Indies. A model disastrously congenial to the settlers of Jamestown, who would not dig or plant, disastrously ill-suited to their actual situation.

Another model for the Jamestown settlement—the military expedition, like that of Cortez, but not much. Rather, a standard sixteenth-century English expedition made up of misfits, thieves, and the idle retinues of its idle gentleman-officers. "Soldiers on campaign were not expected to grow their own food. On the other hand they were expected to go hungry often and to die like flies even if they never saw an enemy." A poor model for the requirements of colonization on the Virginia coast, a fair fit for what actually happened in Jamestown in the early days.

Finally, a conception of the Virginia enterprise as a small-scale model of England, with its specialized exclusive crafts, and craftsmen who did not readily turn their hands to whatever work needed to be done. "Jamestown had an oversupply of glassmakers and not enough carpenters or blacksmiths, an oversupply of gentlemen and not enough plowmen." And no jacks-of-all-trades.

The Virginians did find a profitable crop after a while, tobacco. And they found a solution to the labor problem, indentured servants brought over from England. A poor solution, however, since the new arrivals "brought with them the same haphazard habits of work as their masters." As soon as they were out of their indentures (those who survived them), "they struck out for themselves, . . . demanding rather than supplying labor."

At last came the solution of the *longue durée*, "a cheaper, more docile, more stable supply of labor." As the seventeenth century wore on, Virginia's position in the market for black slaves improved. As against tobacco prices, the price of sugar, the competitive consumer of blacks, fell. The supply of blacks increased. Mortality declined in Virginia, reducing the risk involved in the initial outlay. And so "the Virginians at last were able to acquire substitute natives for their colony and begin, in their own English way, to Hispanize Virginia."

Such is Edmund Morgan's solution of the labor problem in Jamestown, 1607-1618,[59] and of the historiographic problem that perplexed Fernand Braudel.

What binds together the event—the bowing scarecrows of 1611; the conjunctures—the curves of population, wages, and prices in England, of sugar, tobacco, and slave prices in the Atlantic world; the structures—the established image of colonial settlement, the ingrained English patterns and habits of work and leisure, the "military mind" of the sixteenth century, the climate and human geography of Virginia? What does it? The problem precisely defined at the outset: why were the settlers of Jamestown unready for hard work? And what of the adjacent social science disciplines? Economics, sociology, social psychology come in, just as much of them

59. *American Historical Review* 76 (1971): 595-611.

as helps solve the problem and no more. Just as many events, conjunctures, and structures, and just as much about them as helps solve the problem, and no more. And all this in sixteen pages of spare lean prose without a superfluous reference or a dispensable phrase.

It is elegant. Indeed, history-as-problem proceeds under the sign of elegance. It is the point in the constellation of its forms where history comes closest to mathematics. For elegance of demonstration is a mathematical conception and criterion; the elegant solution employs the minimum number of signs and symbols and proceeds to proof in the minimum number of steps. The best practitioners of history-as-problem—Edmund Morgan is among the best—are almost as economical in their solutions as good mathematicians.

Such is the historiography of *histoire problème*. It is not the historiography of Fernand Braudel or of the *monde braudellien* of the VIe section. That world proceeds under the signs of a deluge of information, of exhaustive documentation, of a torrent of words, of abundance at the risk of surfeit. Its proudest products are Deyon's Amiens—606 pages, Goubert's Beauvaisis—653 pages, Baehrel's Basse Provence—842 pages, Gascon's Lyon—999 pages, Le Roy Ladurie's Languedoc—1,035 pages, and Braudel's Mediterranean—1,218 pages. And why not? History is a house of many mansions. Its rooms are large, and if we historians are wise we will follow the precepts of the *Annalistes* and be ready to add more rooms as the occasion suggests. If we are even wiser, we will not, as Braudel sometimes seems to suggest, tear down the rooms we already have, but preserve them as structures, however ill furnished. One never knows when a historian will come along to make something of them, a Garrett Mattingly, brilliantly to redecorate that stale old attic, diplomatic history. Indeed, in one of his more expansive moments—he has many of them—this is Braudel's view, too.

At the risk of being taxed with an impenitent liberalism, I say . . . that in order to mount the multiple thresholds of history, all the doors seem to me to be good. None of us knows all of them. At first the historian opens onto the past the door he is most familiar with. But if he wants to see as far as possible, necessarily he will knock on one door, then on another. Each time a new vista will open to him, and he is not worthy of the name historian if he does not juxtapose some of them: cultural and social vistas, cultural and political, social and economic, economic and political.[60]

Histoire problème marches under the standard of elegance; *histoire totale*, under the standard of abundance; but all history and all historians worth the name march under the standard of curiosity—and excellence. So, let Fernand Braudel, a magnificent entrepreneur of history, a great historian, the author of a marvelous book, *La Méditerranée et le monde méditerranéen à l'époque de Philippe II*, have the last word. In a thoughtful study he has been seeking to understand and help sociologists understand the relations of history to sociology. He knows, however, that his effort will be in vain unless sociologists grasp history in a way that very few of them have. "I would wish that in the years of their apprenticeship young sociologists would take the time to study even in the most modest archive the simplest of historical questions; that once at least beyond sterile manuals they might have contact with a craft that is simple but one that cannot be understood without practicing it."[61] Amen!

1972

60. *Annales E.S.C.* 14 (1959): 318-319.
61. *Traité de sociologie*, I, 97.

PART THREE

In Particular: England

4.

Lawrence Stone and the English Aristocracy

"A landmark in the historical landscape"—*The Economist*;
"A major contribution . . . an impressive achievement, which
must in future put all historians in his debt"—*The Listener*;
"A remarkable achievement . . . an outstanding study of a
very real and great value"—*History*; "A mammoth and
marvellous book"—*American Historical Review*; "Immense
value"—*English Historical Review*; "A model"—*Journal of
Economic History*; "A major historical contribution . . . a
magisterial and seminal work"—*Journal of Modern History*;
"A brilliant and original contribution"—*New York Review
of Books*; "Social history at its absolute best"—*Past and
Present*.

Such was the chorus of critical encomium that greeted the
publication of Lawrence Stone's *Crisis of the Aristocracy,
1558-1641*.[1] Despite the chorus Stone could hardly have
helped being disappointed at the actual reviews. One or two
were almost as fatuous as they were brief. Others, sensible
within their limits, were still too short. This seems to have

---

1. Lawrence Stone, *The Crisis of the Aristocracy, 1558-1641* (Oxford:
Clarendon, 1965).

been the fault of editors, so intimidated by the pejorative sense of the term "discrimination" that they refuse to discriminate between a work worth more than twenty pages and one worth less than twenty words, performing their editorial duties in the matter of book reviews with a sort of timorous and lunatic egalitarianism. Moreover, in considering Stone's work, many of the reviewers hastily plunged into what has come to be called "the gentry controversy" or "the storm over the gentry," and some became almost totally immersed in it. This tendency is unfortunate because so much of what Stone wrote stands on a base quite independent of its ultimate relation to that area of high historiographic turbulence and deserves attention simply on its own merits. Only three reviewers were given anywhere near enough space to do justice to the most important work on the period from the accession of Elizabeth I to the Great Rebellion written in the past quarter century or longer. In consequence of the ancient rancor of unappeased academic feuds and out of a certain condescension among economic historians, two of the three spent most of their time carping, sometimes justly, sometimes trivially, at Stone's inferences from a small cluster of his statistics. The exception to all these strictures—and it is a notable exception—is G. E. Aylmer's thoughtful and perceptive review in *Past and Present*.

The intent, then, in what follows is somewhat to redress a corporate injustice by historians to a great piece of history writing; and this requires a doing of justice, a rendering to Stone's book of what is clearly its due, and at the same time a making explicit of several reservations, doubts, and questions. Why then is *The Crisis of the Aristocracy* "an original contribution," "a seminal work," "a landmark," and a great monument?

If one is to find an answer to this question, the first step is to ask what substantively the book seeks to do. Mainly it seeks to cope with three questions:

1. What was the way of life of the English aristocracy between about the middle of the sixteenth and the middle of the seventeenth century? What was the "total environment of [this] *élite*" (p. 7), and in what respects and to what extent did it change between about 1558 and about 1641?

2. What was the economic condition of the English peers during this period? What ups and downs did they suffer individually and collectively—how high up, how far down, and when?

3. How did it come about that in the early seventeenth century the leadership of concerted opposition to the actions of the ruler, exercised by English peers and magnates in the Middle Ages, fell to men about one step down on the social pyramid—the parliamentary gentry and lawyers?[2]

Stone's heart is so set on finding answers to the second and third questions that he refers to the answer to the first as a secondary object. In doing so he greatly undervalues his most remarkable achievement. It is no deprecation of his very serious effort to answer all three questions to say that he is most successful in handling the first question. Some of what he says on the second and third questions may be subject to qualification, and he defines the answer to the third

2. The key words here are "concerted opposition to the actions of the ruler." This phrase is intended to eliminate localized and uncoordinated revolts of peasants and other social groups. The opposition meant is not so much the Civil War itself but the activities both in Parliament and in the country during the preceding twenty-one years, which along with the actions of James I, Charles I, and their officials and courtiers constituted the situation from which the Civil War resulted. My three-point analysis of *Crisis of the Aristocracy* diverges slightly from Stone's own two-point analysis to make possible what I believe to be a more satisfactory account of what he has done (pp. 7-8).

question in a way that in part puts that answer out of his reach. His reconstruction of the patterns of life of a social group, "the aristocracy," over a period of almost a hundred years, however, is surely not surpassed in the historical literature of any country in the world.[3]

Stone's remarkable effort "to describe in as much detail as can reasonably be tolerated the way of life" (p. 8) of the English aristocracy entailed much more than a narrow historical description of the outlook and activities of a small cluster of men; or rather, to his credit, he saw it as entailing much more than that. Those activities impinged directly on other centers of activity in England—the ruler and the central government, the business community, the schools, the law, the lesser landed classes, the tenantry, and so on. Moreover, the shifting self-image of the aristocracy and the shifting image of it entertained by others were integral elements in the social cosmologies and cosmogenies, not always wholly self-consistent, sometimes rather sharply divergent, and not entirely stable, which contemporary Englishmen saw as the legitimate regulators of the relations of the lesser communities that joint-

3. It is touched by one small bias that readers might keep in mind. In his category of "the aristocracy" Stone includes the rich gentry, some five hundred families in 1640, as well as the peerage. Much of his nonquantitative data, however, centers around the court and courtiers, and almost all of his quantitative data have to do only with the peerage. Proportionately the peerage was more heavily represented at court than the upper gentry. Thus 25 percent of the peerage held office between 1625 and 1642 as against 12 percent of the knights. G. E. Aylmer, *The King's Servants* (Cambridge: Routledge, 1961), p. 324. Since peerage is hereditary, however, a considerable number of peers were too young to be courtiers, thus increasing the disproportion. Therefore, the available evidence and Stone's book provide a less biased image of the peers' way of life than of that of the five hundred gentry families, except for the comparatively small proportion of the latter who were also courtiers.

ly composed the whole commonwealth. In *The Crisis of the Aristocracy*, responding to this complexity, Stone does not merely present a portrait of a cluster of men, their outlook, and their activities. While the figures of the men in that cluster stand at the center of his vast canvas, they are figures in a landscape, and that landscape is English society and culture from about the accession of Elizabeth I to the outbreak of the Civil War. While he paints his cluster of figures with elaborate and careful (though not always loving) detail, in doing so he often brings into brilliant relief traits of the landscape that few historians had observed before and none observed so well. So abundant and richly textured is Stone's work in this respect that no review can do it more than scant justice. Given the scope of the activities of the aristocracy, each of which Stone resolutely tracks down, investigates, and explains, merely to list those activities would produce a series impressive in its length but both tiresome and unenlightening. The details of a specific instance may more adequately illuminate and pinpoint some of the peculiar excellences of *The Crisis of the Aristocracy*.

An instance superficially most unpromising is that of the beneficial lease (pp. 313-317). A legal instrument for letting land, it is one of those technical devices of estate management which offer so little probability of interest and so high a promise of dreariness that lesser historians tend to render them bewildering and stultifying by lack of imagination or to avoid them in fear of a boring outcome. Not Stone. He resolutely plunges in and wrestles with the difficulty. In the end he achieves a model essay in the social history of law. The beneficial lease was the most common instrument for leasing land during the time span that concerns him, and during that span landlords aimed to replace copyhold with leasehold. The beneficial lease divided the tenants' liability between a lump sum payment at the outset, called the entry fine, and an annual rent fixed for the duration of the lease. The principal negotiable terms of such a lease were its duration and the apportionment of payments between entry fine and annual rent. From the point of view of both landlord and tenant, the worst duration was an uncertain one of considerable probable length. Such a lease prevented adjustments of rent to movements of prices, so that one party to the lease or the other was likely to be painfully squeezed by long-term price movements. If so the blind bet on price changes was added uncertainty as to the actual duration of the lease, the gamble would be compounded and the incentive to prudence minimized. Over a large part of England, however, the beneficial lease was made for three lives; it terminated with the death of the last of three parties named in the lease. Such an arrangement might run a very long while or a fairly short one, but in an age at once violent, harsh, and unhygienic, it was as uncertain as the uncertainties of life itself. The lease for lives thus maximized disutilities for both parties.

Similarly, the worst division of entry fine and annual rent for both parties was the heavy fine and the low rent. It encouraged improvidence on both sides, leading the landlord to gamble on a quick recurrence of the windfall of an entry fine and the tenant on its long postponement. It tempted the landlord to accept disadvantageous terms for the sake of ready money, and the heavy initial outlay deprived the tenant of the capital for improvement of his holding, improvement for which the lease for lives with its uncertain duration of tenure gave him little incentive. Yet in the period Stone studies, landlord and tenant alike preferred an increase in entry fine to an increase in rent. Thus the actual beneficial lease was a topsy-turvydom in which all parties seemed stubbornly set on doing the worst for themselves. In making this piling up of irrationalities intelligible, Stone shows himself at his best. The arrangement suited great landlords because for unforeseen contingencies—marriage portions, building costs, and so on—it enabled them to lay hands on ready cash otherwise hard or expensive to come by, because the large initial investment of the tenant gave the landlord a reasonably good security for the regular payment of the agreed rent for the duration of the lease, and because for each individual landlord the immediate tangible gain of a lump sum had strong attractions, not sufficiently offset by a gradually accruing net loss which, after all, would like as not fall on his heirs rather than on him. He was thus not strongly moved to preserve his successors from inconveniences that he himself had suffered by the like doings of his predecessors. Or as Stone puts it in one of the sparkling and shrewd asides that illuminate his book: "Like flogging in public schools, the beneficial lease was an institution in the perpetuation of which its former victims always ended by acquiring a vested interest" (p. 315). On the tenants' side, Stone's explanation of an ultimately irrational preference is even more perceptive. Obscuring any long-term economic calculations of gain or loss was the tenants' whole "vision of life on earth," into which the uncertainty in dimension and timing of the fines nicely fitted.

When man is at the mercy of disease and the weather, in health today, crippled or dead tomorrow, gorged today and starved tomorrow, with money to burn today from the sale of a bumper crop, plunged into debt tomorrow because of harvest failure, the human condition is one of perpetual flux. The beneficial lease was just one more card in a large pack of jokers, and leaseholders and the customary tenants positively preferred a few years of misery and hardship while the fine was being paid, followed by a long period at a low rent, to the regular payment of a reasonable annual sum. (P. 316)

Now this is history writing in the grand manner. It is also history writing in the old-fashioned manner. Stone makes visible a revelatory pattern between a legal instrument or device and the social and cultural context in which it flourished. He is able to make it visible because an enormously wide reading of the records of the period has rendered him aware of what that culture and society were like. His exposition manifests that rare historical tact characteristic of the work of the greatest of English historians, Frederic W. Maitland.

Stone does this sort of thing not just once but at least half a hundred times in *The Crisis of the Aristocracy*. He thus gives their intelligible places in the intricate fabric of social relations, in the pattern of culture of the period, to the passion for fancy dress, to pedigree peddling, to gambling and heiress hunting, to the arranged aristocratic marriage, to the temptations and terrors of the mortgage before Chancery created the equity of redemption, to the impact of the accurate survey on the management of large estates, to those potlatches of building, feasting, and funerals in which aristocrats blew not only income but capital assets in orgies of mutual emulation—the list could go on and on. Nor is the final effect static. Stone has succeeded in doing what anthropologists who deal in patterns of culture often fail to do: he examines a society (or a section of a society) in flux, acted on by forces external to it and reacting on them, so that the reader can observe a society not in an artificially frozen posture but in the process of dynamic adjustment (and turmoil); and he renders understandable specific changes by relating them to the social context in which they were generated. For example, having described the large number of converging circumstances that were restricting the wonted propensity of members of the aristocracy to hasty violence, he turns to describe the charms for them of that moral or at least quasi-

pacific equivalent of private war, litigation. A really pro-
tracted lawsuit

> would with its complexity and prolixity consume their time, their
> energies, and their substance for years and years on end. The very
> deficiencies in the machinery of the law, its great cost, its appall-
> ing slowness, its obsession with irrelevant technical details, made
> it an admirable instrument for the sublimation of the bellicose
> instincts of a leisured class. Sixteenth-century litigation combined
> the qualities of tedium, hardship, brutality, and injustice that
> tested character and endurance, with the element of pure chance
> that appealed to the gambler, the fear of defeat and ruin, and the
> hope of victory and the humiliation of the enemy. It had every-
> thing that war can offer save the delights of shedding blood. It
> gave shape and purpose to many otherwise empty lives. Litiga-
> tion, therefore, remained the most popular of indoor sports, de-
> spite unanimous agreement upon the folly of such behaviour and
> the rapacity of lawyers. (Pp. 241-242)

Stone's vivid sense of what the way of life and the milieu of
the aristocracy were like enables him to correct archaic stereo-
types about both the peerage and the greater gentry, and then
to go further and correct recent corrections of those stereo-
types. One of the most tired clichés about the Tudor-Stuart
peerage has been that it was "feudal" and therefore, practically by definition, inimical to the "progressive" economic innovations and activities of the (by now somewhat scaled
down) "first industrial revolution" from 1540 to 1640. Faint
intimations that this view of the matter did injustice to the
facts began to emerge some seventeen years before the publication of Stone's book.[4] Since that time awareness and documentation of the role of the aristocracy as a source, and often
the most important source, of investment capital for indus-

---

4. See the earliest version of J. H. Hexter, "Myth of the Middle Class in
Tudor England," read at the American Historical Association, Dec. 1948, and
published in *Explorations in Entrepreneurial History* 2 (1950): 128-140.

trial enterprise not only in England but throughout northern Europe have sharply increased. Stone contributed heavily to that awareness and documentation for England in a study that, revised and expanded, has become chapter 7, "Business," of *The Crisis of the Aristocracy*.[5] That chapter makes it clear that in sixteenth-century England neither bourgeois capitalists nor even the rising gentry, but the English nobility, assumed the greatest share of the risks involved in industrial innovation (pp. 338-355, esp. pp. 343, 348, 352) , with George Talbot, Earl of Shrewsbury, the richest of Elizabethan peers and one of ancient lineage, far out in front of the pack (p. 382) . In this Shrewsbury was exemplary rather than eccentric. It was the pre-Stuart peers rather than the risingest of the middle class of rising gentry, those whom James I and Charles I ennobled, who were most forthcoming with venture capital for long-term investment in industrial enterprises (pp. 378-380) . Here and elsewhere in his book Stone more than fully justifies his flat dictum, "There was nothing particularly feudal about the peers in 1641" (p. 11) . At the same time his intimate awareness of the activities, the aspirations, and the attitudes of the nobility secures him against the anachronism opposite to that of envisioning them as feudal lords: that of viewing them as businessmen. Many of them were unmistakably *in* business; businessmen they were not, although a study confined to their business activities might tend to create that illusion. The wide sweep of Stone's vision prevents him from falling into error on this score and from passing the error on to his readers (pp. 382-384) . What concerned most of the peers most constantly was the advancement of themselves and their families in pres-

5. Initially Lawrence Stone, "The Nobility in Business, 1540-1640," in *The Entrepreneur* (Cambridge: Economic History Society, 1957), pp. 14-21.

tige and wealth. In its command of their time and energy, and perhaps in its potential for yielding the advancement they sought, "business" ran a bad fourth to office at court, marriage, and estate management.

Still, while all this is new and fresh in substance, it is not particularly newfangled or new-fashioned in form or (to submit to current jabberwocky) in methodology. But Stone prides himself, and rightly, on being new-fashioned in precisely this respect. In his investigation of the way of life of the aristocracy, what in his view is new-fashioned? First, a consistent concern with statistical data; second, an openness to insights provided by the social sciences. How he usually deploys these new weapons is perhaps best seen in chapter 3, "The Inflation of Honours."

First, as to statistics. Stone provides statistical tables on the distribution of honors from the bottom rung of the ladder up —first into the ranks of the gentry through grant of arms, then to knighthood, baronetage, and the degrees of peerage. The tables show the numbers admitted to the various ranks of honor over approximately equal periods of time from about 1558 to 1641. Because grants of arms were controlled not by the ruler but by the College of Heralds, which had a financial interest in peddling them, the available statistics on admission to the gentry are ambiguous and in any case unenlightening with respect to the policy of the crown. It is the statistics on newly granted honors of knighthood, of baronetcy, and of peerage in its various grades that reveal crown policy, since such grants required royal sanction, direct or indirect.[6] Here the rough outlines of policy are easy to discern.

6. The knights created by the Earl of Essex as commander of the Cadiz expedition of 1596 and of the Irish expedition of 1599 are an exception to this rule.

Throughout her reign Elizabeth was at least as closefisted about honors as she was about money. She made so few knights that, because the honor was not heritable, their number probably fell as much as 50 percent between her accession and 1583. She even permitted the ranks of the hereditary peerage to undergo some small depletion, from fifty-seven at her accession to fifty-five at her death. From the accession of James I to the assassination of the Duke of Buckingham, the Elizabethan policy is reversed; in every category of honors directly granted by the ruler, the inflation is on. Throughout Elizabeth's reign the creation of knights averaged about twenty per year, and this included the 170 men knighted by the Earl of Essex, almost half of them on the Irish expedition in defiance of the Queen's prohibition. From the accession of James to 1630, the total creations shot up to almost three thousand, a more than fivefold increase in the rate of knightings per year. From 1630 to the summoning of the Long Parliament, creations fell back to about twenty-two per year, close to the Elizabethan rate. As to peers, Elizabeth made only eighteen, less than one every two years; eighty-four were created from 1603 to 1630, almost eight times the Elizabethan rate. Moreover, while Elizabeth maintained a fairly steady ratio of one earl to two barons in the House of Lords, by 1628 there were sixty-five earls and forty-seven barons, or about four earls for every three barons. Piled on top of the population explosion in ancient honors between 1603 and 1630 was the exploitation of new ones—threescore Irish peerages[7] and the whole baronetage, an invention of James I. From 1611 to 1630 292 men acquired the title of baronet for

7. The Irish peerages were not wholly new, but in her whole reign Elizabeth had created only three.

their families, all for a price.[8] Finally, as in the case of knighthoods, Charles sharply constricted the grants of other honors in the eleven years of personal rule. Such was the curve of creation. What of the price? In general, honors controlled by Elizabeth were literally priceless; they were not for sale. But Stone has enough scattered documentation of fact and rumor on honor prices under the early Stuarts to indicate the curve that it followed: baronetcy—£1,095 in 1611, £700 in 1619, £220 in 1622, less than £200 about 1628; barony—£10,000 in 1615, £8,000 in 1624, £6,600 in 1628 (pp. 93, 116).

The statistics are simple enough. What of their interpretation? Here Stone turns to the other social sciences, and first to economics. The exercise is not intricate. Since like modern paper money the necessary certificates of honor can be inexpensively produced at the ruler's command, once honors become venal, the temptation and pressures to flood the market with them are very strong.[9] The oversupply of titles of honor, however, reduces their exchange value. From a fiscal point of view the rate of profits on sales of honor declines with the glut of creations. Beyond this simple-minded

8. The figure 292 excludes more than one hundred Irish and Scottish baronetcies.

9. Stone refrains from considering the implications of the egregious slump in baronetcy prices and the widespread unwillingness to accept knighthood at any price or no price at all, compared with the more stable prices for peerages in the very late 1620s. The divergence at least suggests that the differential in price movement, the unevenness of the inflation, resulted from the situation on the demand rather than the supply side. It is what one might expect if, as Stone himself suggests elsewhere, legal innovations, reforms in estate management, and improved access to credit were of advantage principally to the greatest gentry landlords and were not readily accessible to the lesser. The improved economic position of the great landlords may have supported prices at the higher levels of honors-buying while an economic pinch and an excessive supply ruined the market for honors at the lower levels.

economic analysis lie questions calling for social analysis. In a society like that of Jacobean England, what are the social implications of the inflation of honors? The actual impact of the market in honors between 1603 and 1628 could scarcely have been worse than it was. For English society was status-bound, and powerfully status-conscious, built on "degree, priority and place." The observance of precedence and deference and acceptance of their legitimacy guaranteed social stability. The situation created by James and Buckingham whetted men's appetites for the gratification that any considerable upward shift in their own status would afford them. At the same time the overrapid shifts in the precedence men had hitherto enjoyed were certain to produce a revulsion, a sense that legal status coincided ill with legitimate rank. The long Elizabethan dearth had created a backlog of demand for honors that might have seemed insatiable. Nevertheless, in their readiness to supply the market for a price, James and Buckingham succeeded in depreciating the money value of honors. Worse, by their indifference to the social viability of the persons on whom they bestowed honors, they severely shook a social system of which a widely acceptable structure of honor and an acceptable dynamic of progression in status were important stabilizing elements.

Both in the use of statistics and in the use of related social sciences, Stone's chapter "The Inflation of Honours" is exemplary for the entire historical craft. With respect to statistics his decennial and quinquennial tables of grants and honors provide hard-core data for analysis. They accurately relate the "how many?" to the "when?" They thus make it possible to replace with categorical assertion the sort of waffling that historians are driven to, when in matters involving the relation of quantity to chronology they do not know "how many," either because they have been unable to find out or because they have been too dainty or lazy or remiss to count. At the same time Stone avoids that other and reverse sort of daintiness which afflicts the new puritans of economic history, the econometricians, who so fear contamination by figures less precise and refined than annual price series that their output becomes as sterile as their input, but in a different sense. Stone's quantitative data on honor price, while less tidy than one might wish, are good enough to permit a hypothesis and, *along with qualitative data*, good enough to lend that hypothesis support. Thus in the instance under consideration, the statements about the effect of the cheapening of honor made by the Commons in their impeachment of Buckingham and the rueful analyses with which in the 1650s royalists tried to account for the disasters of monarchy serve to corroborate what the quantitative data suggest (p. 120).

Stone's own explicit statements about the use of statistics occasionally are opaque and ambivalent, though not perhaps mutually contradictory.[10] A man who performs, however, is entitled to be judged on the basis of his actual performance

---

10. For example, "Statistics . . . compose the bony skeleton of this book . . . This statistical frame is as necessary to the book as the bone structure to a vertebrate; without them both would be inert lumps of amorphous flesh" (p. 3). "Statistical measurement is the only means of extracting a coherent pattern from the chaos of personal behaviour and of discovering which is a typical specimen and which a sport" (pp. 3-4). "Statistics make a dry and unpalatable diet unless washed down with the wine of human personality. They have been used, therefore, merely as controls to check the significance of the tangled jetsam of anecdote and quotation thrown up by three talkative, quarrelsome, idiosyncratic generations of noble men and women" (p. 4).

rather than on his statements of method and intent. In *The Crisis of the Aristocracy* one occasionally can turn up an ambivalent performance. It starts with a modest appraisal of the weight of the statistics that follow. Then come the statistics themselves, and finally a dictum in which, despite his earlier judicious commitment to a modest appraisal of the value of his quantitative evidence, Stone lands with a great thump and all his weight on one side of the scale, the one in accord with his general views. To anyone who has tried to sweat statistical data out of mean, niggardly, unyielding sources of supply, the psychodynamics of this process will be familiar enough. Having gone through an agonizing process to come up with any quantities at all, one finds it hard to believe that their value is actually proportional only to their relevance to the argument and not to the energy invested in producing them. Given the great masses of statistics that Stone has quarried out of meager veins in unauspicious places, the wonder is not that his control occasionally slips, but that it slips so rarely, and that his own evaluations of his quantitative data so frequently correspond to those of readers whose pleasure in criticizing them is unalloyed by any of the pains involved in digging them out. By and large in his dealing with statistics, he is a paragon of openmindedness, ready to use them for about what they are worth in particular cases, uninhibited either by the humanistic snobbishness of those who in the period of their gestation as historians appear to have absorbed a prenatal dread of numbers or by the scientific priggery that conceives a pure worship of quantities as not only an adequate but a necessary surrogate for historical understanding and imagination. He never lets himself be lured into the silly trap of opposing quantification to the other modes of advancing historical knowledge in face of the manifest fact that those modes sometimes work badly apart from quantification and often work well together with it.[11]

For historians Stone's way with the other social sciences, as illustrated in "The Inflation of Honours" and with great frequency elsewhere in *The Crisis of the Aristocracy*, is also exemplary. Again one had best look for that way in his actions rather than his affirmations and not be put off by his early pledge of allegiance to a "sociological interpretation of historical causation," whatever that may be. In practice Stone is no renegade turning his back on history to worship at the shrines of the Baalim of social science. Quite the contrary. As the old church fathers would have pointed out, he is engaged in the operation, so congenial to the Elect, of "plundering the Egyptians." As the Chosen People robbed the Pharaonic kingdom of whatever they deemed good, and as the Fathers themselves took what they found valuable from classical culture and put it to the service of the Lord, so without compunction and in a most eclectic manner, Stone takes from the economists, the sociologists, the social psychologists, or the anthropologists whatever at any particular point in his investigations seems useful and turns it to the purposes of history. On the Marxians, the Freudians, the Weberians, and the Paretans, on Veblen and Malinowski, Schumpeter and C. Wright Mills, Aron and Titmuss, he levies tribute with fine impartiality. That at the level of metasocial science the systematic structures created by those

11. Like mere mortals, historians too seem doomed to reenact the past as a result of having forgotten about it. The clash between the innumerate and the overnumerate in the trade seems to go on not from one generation to the next or sporadically but continuously and eternally.

For criticism of some of Stone's inferences from his statistics, see especially G. E. Aylmer, "Crisis of the Aristocracy, 1558-1691," *Past and Present*, no. 32 (1965): 113-125; D. C. Coleman, "The 'Gentry' Controversy and the Aristocracy in Crisis, 1558-1641," *History* 51 (1966): 165-174; anonymous review, *TLS*, April 17, 1966, pp. 285-288.

he draws on are quite incompatible and irreconcilable one with the other, that they are the occasions of fierce party wars among their adherents, does not bother Stone at all; this incompatibility does not diminish the utility of the insights imbedded in those structures for illuminating the ways of life of the early modern English aristocracy. If Stone's free and easy way of deploying conceptions from the social sciences in historical analysis induces frissons of horror among the faithful band of "pure" historians for whom social scientists are as the unclean, his free and easy way of picking up and using these concepts probably inflicts an equivalent dismay on the purer social scientists. Indeed the only thing to be said for his procedures is that usually they work and that for historians they are the only ones that most of the time do work.[12] This is what happens in the case of "The Inflation of Honours." The general economic notion of the operations of supply and demand for goods in the market is loosely applied to titles of honor, and then by examining the impact of the inflation on the status-oriented, deferential, and traditional society of seventeenth-century England, Stone moves the whole argument from the domain of economic analysis into that of social (or sociological) analysis. Whether or not social scientists would approve of such uninhibited methods, in the case under consideration historians have found the results unreservedly enlightening.[13]

What Stone achieves in connection with honors, he achieves

12. This is not to decry or deny the possible utility of an effort, by historians so inclined, to apply highly systematized structures of social science generalization to specific historical situations with a view to testing the generalizations rigorously. *Chacun à son gout.*

13. As far as I have been able to determine, "The Inflation of Honours" has gained the unanimous if occasionally grudging approval of all the reviewers who mention it.

again and again elsewhere in *The Crisis of the Aristocracy*
in dealing with aristocratic habits of consumption, with life
at court and the pursuit of office and favor, with the shifting pattern of parental authority over the marriage of heirs
and heiresses, and above all in the magnificent chapter on
power, where he traces the processes and policies by means of
which the descendants of and successors to the turbulent
magnates of the mid-fifteenth century were transformed into
the peaceful aristocrats of the seventeenth. Whenever possible, Stone follows the same sound general recipe for getting the most for his efforts, combining old-fashioned historical methods and newfangled social science notions with
an offhand disregard for any sort of orthodoxy. It does not
work every time; but it gets results so often as to defeat captious critics, and it certainly enables him to attain his first
objective—to present a study in depth of a social group, rich
in detail and abundant in insight.

Beyond and above his methods of investigation, Stone
brings to *The Crisis of the Aristocracy* qualities of mind and
character without which mere method would have yielded
little. Of those qualities only one seems to have created any
difficulties for him. He is at heart a man of intellectual-
academical-puritanical-Jacobinical temper, the temper of the
meritocrat, which is constitutionally averse to those who
owe a privileged place in society to riches, birth, fortune, and
favor rather than to personal achievement, hard work, devo-
tion to a calling, and the luck of the draw on brains. For
such a man any hereditary aristocracy, even the relatively
serious and serviceable aristocracy that Stone is concerned
with, is somewhat hard to take. With rare self-knowledge
and engaging candor he early makes explicit both his bias and
his own doubts of its soundness (pp. 6-7), but like most people convinced against their will, in less guarded moments

he remains of the same opinion still. That opinion affects the rhetoric of his statements even when it does not touch their logic. Thus the idleness of the aristocracy receives frequent emphasis in face of evidence that service, civic concern, and public activity, not wholly self-regarding, had gotten amalgamated into the value structure of the aristocrats, and into the actual pattern of life of a considerable number of them.[14]

In fact the situation in this matter is more ambivalent than the rhetoric congenial to Stone's bias permits it to appear. Occasionally the vocabulary of his bias even triumphs over some of his hard-earned statistics, nowhere more so than in the matter of the marriages of peers. Thus with respect to the quest of peers for heiresses to marry in the early seventeenth century, he ascribes the grumbling it occasioned to people's thinking back to an age "when the preservation of class distinctions took precedence over the quest for optimum financial benefits" (p. 618). In the most sensitive area —acquiring gold to brighten poverty-tarnished aristocratic blazons by noble marriages to city heiresses—he speaks of a "new trend" beginning about 1591 and ending in 1599 in which "a few bolder . . . spirits . . . began to leap across the barrier that . . . divided peers from merchants" (p. 629). Yet on the basis of the statistics Stone himself provides, none of this seems to amount to very much. The "trend" actually produced just one marriage of a peer to a city heiress; there were just two such marriages in the fifty-seven years between 1561 and 1618 as against five in the twenty-one years between 1540 and 1561, a decline of 80 percent, a sort of great leap backward. Between 1540 and 1660, 91 percent of all peers'

---

14. Thomas, third Earl of Sussex, and Henry, third Earl of Huntingdon, to name two outstanding examples of the Elizabethan period.

marriages were into the families of gentry or other peers; and in each of the four 30-year periods composing the 120-year span, the deviation from the 91 percent median was never more than 1 percent. The one possibly significant figure is an increase of marriages to heiresses from about 20 percent to 34 percent as between the first two and the last two quarters of that span. Even here some of the apparent differences may result from the superior density of information on the women that peers married from 1600 on. Still, with respect to the way of life of the aristocracy, Stone's slips into a temperamentally induced censoriousness are venial and relatively rare, usually hedged by qualifications, and almost wholly overshadowed by the rare and invaluable traits that he brings to his task.[15]

The most conspicuous of those traits is simple industry, apparently endless and indefatigable. The sheer mass of work Stone shouldered in the fourteen years his book was aborning would surely have crushed many lesser men and is massive enough to have filled the entire scholarly careers of several reasonably energetic investigators. "Extents" laid on the property of debtors in the Chancery archives, registers of recognizances of debt "in the nature of Statute Staple" in the archives of the lord chamberlain, mortgages and sales records in the Close Rolls and Feet of Fines, the *Valor Ecclesiasticus* —these are but a beginning. Published calendars of state papers and private archives; manuscript records, public and private; correspondence, published and unpublished; architectural plans for lordly palaces and the palaces themselves; estate surveys and estate accounts of all sorts; memoirs and histories by contemporary figures of every magnitude; ge-

15. Stone provides the pertinent evidence justifying my summary. See pp. 617-619, 627-632, 789.

nealogies; lists of almost everything that the peers chose to list for a century and of a good many things they did not; the plays and much of the ephemeral literature of the period; contemporary and later treatises on law; almost everything that recent historians have written on the period that has a close bearing on his subject—all these are grist for Stone's tireless and insatiable mill.[16] Beyond his industry, and indispensable to its function, is something far more impressive than mere collocations of data by a hyperthyroid scholarly pack rat—his readiness to deal with hard questions in the line of duty and his determination to pursue the answers at whatever cost to himself in time and labor. Some of the questions he wrestles with were initially raised by other scholars in the course of a long and intricate controversy in which he participated; others he framed for himself in the course of his own investigations; to all he has given laborious, patient, imaginative, and fruitful attention.[17] For example, although in a general and ill-defined way the problem of changes in the relation of the peers to the structure of political power had come up before, only Stone raised questions to which firm answers, some quantitative, some qualitative, were possible and then patiently ferreted out the answers himself. The result, the chapter entitled "Power," is the most exciting and most persuasive in *The Crisis of the Aristocracy.*

Perhaps it is characteristic of minds fruitful of hypothesis that they do not regard themselves forever bound to ideas, their own or those of others, to which they committed themselves in their youth. There is in truth no reason, besides an

16. I say *almost* everything by recent historians; the exceptions (and they are important) are political-constitutional and religious history.

17. Two important exceptions to this statement, of which Stone himself was aware, will be noted later. They are religion and the peerage in its corporate capacity as the House of Lords.

unhealthy aversion to admitting that one has ever made a mistake, why scholars should so entrap themselves. To unfreeze oneself from the posture of early (or late) infallibility is of all kinds of emancipation the most profitable for a historian. In this matter Stone is almost always a paragon. He usually displays a refreshing unwillingness to spend his life in lost battles in defense of youthful errors. No notion or hypothesis is sacrosanct; his own or anyone else's notion, rendered plausible by a respectable bit of supporting evidence, is treated as worth checking out. In all this there is nothing irresponsible. On the contrary, the irresponsible historian is the one who avoids the responsibility of coherent statement and makes it his whole career to hoard great stocks of erudition for the sole purpose of having enough at hand for occasional and sporadic sniping. The courage to be found wrong is the precondition of getting anything important right. In a profession in which all too many scholars effortlessly achieve intellectual sclerosis before they are thirty, Stone retains a lively curiosity, an ebullient youthful spirit, an openness to chances for new insights that are enviable. His industry, his energy, his imagination, his flexibility of mind constitute a combination of qualities that in historians are as excellent as they are rare. They are what make his study in depth of the way of life of the late Tudor–early Stuart aristocracy a historical feat the like of which may not be seen again for many years.

II

A book of such broad scope as *The Crisis of the Aristocracy*, written over a period of fourteen years by a writer like Stone, who learned steadily as he worked his way along, is more than a monument of history writing; it is also a monument of the history of history writing. Examined closely, it reveals the changes in habit of thought and outlook characteristic of lively-minded historians concerned during the past quarter of a century with the period of English history it covers. It also reflects broad changes among historians who during those years wrote of other times and other places. Specifically, the book bears strata marks of the phases that historical thinking about the century preceding the outbreak of the Civil War in 1642 has passed through in the last twenty-five years. Stone early identifies the underlying substratum of that thinking—the place where it all began. In the 1930s, he says, "most young historians were powerfully influenced by Marxist theory, and were in varying degrees supporters of some kind of economic determinism in human affairs, an attitude of mind which was—and is—far from being confined to those of a politically leftward inclination." (p. 6). In relation to the outbreak of 1640, that theory was vigorously though naively formulated in a little volume celebrating the three hundredth anniversary of the English Revolution.

The period 1640-60 saw the destruction of a whole social order — feudalism — and the introduction of a political structure within which capitalism could freely develop. For tactical reasons, the ruling class in 1660 *pretended* that they were merely restoring the old form of the Constitution. But they intended by that restoration to give sanctity and social stamp to a new social order.

The Civil War was a class war, in which the despotism of Charles I was defended by the reactionary forces of the established Church and feudal landlords. Parliament beat the King because it could appeal to the enthusiastic support of the trading and industrial classes in town and countryside, to the yeomen and progressive gentry.[18]

By the time Stone became engaged in long arduous study of the English aristocracy, R. H. Tawney had somewhat shifted

18. Christopher Hill, ed., *The English Revolution, 1640* (London: Lawrence and Wishart, 1940), pp. 80-81, 9.

the base of the argument. Quietly dispensing with the other groups whose effective force before 1640 was rather hard to document, he emphasized the economic rise of the gentry as "an insular species of the . . . genus" of change usually described in other lands as "the transition from a feudal to a bourgeois society."[19]

Stone's first emergence into the historical domain of which he is now indisputable master took the form of an attempt to clinch Tawney's argument by demonstrating the economic decline of the aristocracy contemporary with and in a sense concomitant to the conquest, first of wealth, then of power, by the gentry, viewed as the rural middle class. His early efforts to drive this point home by means of statistics came a cropper. In *The Crisis of the Aristocracy*, armed with fresh statistics, Stone returns to the hard-fought field of controversy over the fortunes of the aristocracy. In chapter 3, "Economic Change," he fires salvo after salvo of these statistics at his enemies of old. It is evident that in a work in which he spared himself no effort, the most herculean labor was spent on mounting this new assault on an old battleground. The opposition, however, has not been silenced. With new recruits it has counterattacked the new statistics that Stone so energetically assembled. To summarize the whole of Stone's evidence and argument and the counter-arguments it has evoked would require an inordinate amount of space and be incredibly tedious. What is attempted here (doubtless very rashly) is to use Stone's data to make a few computations he did not make and from them to derive an argument or hypothesis. If the data on which that argument is based are even

19. R. H. Tawney, "The Rise of the Gentry, 1558-1640," *Economic History Review* 11 (1941): 6.

approximately accurate, the computations fully validate it.[20]

Stone's position has two statistical foundations: (1) an attempt to estimate from a very extensive range of documents the gross rentals of all peers in 1559, 1602, and 1641; (2) an attempt to compute for several groupings of peerage families the attrition in ownership of manors between 1559 and 1602 and between 1602 and 1641. By Stone's own very candid admissions the first foundation is seriously defective, based on *"fragmentary information* from private sources about the financial positions in 1559 of only about a third of the total peerage" (p. 130; italics added), and evidence "rather greater" (how much greater?) for 1602. The attempt to eke out this information from tax returns which "it is self-evident . . . must be treated with extreme caution" (p. 131) does not seem promising enough to provide a very solid base for a broad *general* argument, although it may cautiously be put to a number of specific uses.[21]

Then what of the counting of manors? The use of manorial counts first employed by Tawney as a basis for estimating

20. For various views originating in or engendered by the statistics offered by Tawney and Stone, see Economic History Review 11 (1941): 1-38; Lawrence Stone, "The Anatomy of the Elizabethan Aristocracy," ibid. 18 (1948): 1-53; H. R. Trevor-Roper, "The Elizabethan Aristocracy: An Anatomy Anatomised," ibid., 2d ser. 3 (1951): 279-298; Lawrence Stone, "The Elizabethan Aristocracy: A Restatement," ibid., 2d ser. 4 (1952): 302-321; H. R. Trevor-Roper, *The Gentry, 1540-1640,* ibid., Supplement 1 (1953); R. H. Tawney, "The Rise of the Gentry: a Postscript," ibid., 2d ser. 7 (1954): 91-97; J. P. Cooper, "The Counting of Manors," ibid., 2d ser. 8 (1956): 377-389; Hexter, *Reappraisals,* pp. 127-162.

For the opposition's counterattacks, see *TLS,* April 17, 1966, pp. 286-288; Coleman, " 'Gentry' Controversy," pp. 165-174.

21. The information will be put to such specific uses several times in what follows, where the use itself seems to keep the likely range of error from markedly affecting the conclusion. For a summary of the results of Stone's effort, see pp. 760-761.

the current financial condition of the owners of the manors counted has run up against serious objections. The first objection is that manors were not homogeneous units of value; what a manor was worth might vary enormously from manor to manor. The force of this objection diminishes, however, if one can show that for a considerable random sample of manors at given points in time, the values of a very high percentage of them cluster closely around their mean value. If the dispersion of values is not very extensive, the margin of error in any sizable sample in which no inherent bias of selection can be discovered will be correspondingly small. Using values of manors chosen at random from the *Valor Ecclesiasticus* of 1535 and from the Close Rolls between 1597 and 1608, Stone demonstrates that at both these dates value dispersion around the mean price of manors was not very large (pp. 144-150). This makes manor counts a serviceable index of gain and loss of income on one further condition—that the sample be large enough to balance out possible egregious eccentricity in the values of one or two manors in the sample. Thus statistical dispersion tables and computations of standard deviation can say nothing useful about a sample limited to a half-dozen manors. This objection, however, can be overcome by use of large samples. Finally, even a large sample may maximize error at one or another end of the scale if the way the sample is chosen has a built-in bias. To avoid such errors, one must be extremely careful to avoid such a bias. Or one can attempt to counteract the bias by introducing a somewhat arbitrary but manifestly adequate correction.

Are any of Stone's statistics about manors almost wholly impervious to any of the objections just specified? One set seems especially impressive, although he himself makes relatively little use of it and consequently does not provide a key tabulation. The set is that of decennial purchases and sales of manors, and net losses of manors through purchase and sale from 1561 to 1641 by forty-two peerage families extant from 1559 to 1641, including only those transactions "of which the precise dates are known."[22]

TABLE 4.1
PURCHASES AND SALES OF MANORS

Date	Purchases	Sales	Net Loss
1561-1570	33	100	67
1571-1580	41	153	112
1581-1590	41	138	97
1591-1600	17	180	163
1601-1610	26	143	117
1611-1620	22	60	38
1621-1630	13	38	25
1631-1640	15	31	16
Total	208	843	635

The set is impressive for several reasons. (1) The aggregate figures are very large, more than one thousand manors. (2) Up to 1611-1620 the volume of transactions in each decennium is also considerable enough to reduce the danger of sampling error—between a minimum of 133 and a maximum of 197 exchanges per decade. (3) The sample of aristocrats is the most consistent and homogeneous possible, the one group that *as peers* underwent all the vicissitudes of the period under consideration. (4) It also is a reasonably large sample, about two-thirds of the peerage both at Elizabeth's accession and at her death and still one third in 1641. The table is of major significance, granted three assumptions. The first assumption is simply that Stone has not egregiously miscounted the purchases and sales summarized in his table. There is no reason not to make and no option but to make

22. The table is taken from app. XI, C, p. 766.

this assumption. The second assumption is that any bias in the figures of dated purchases and sales should weigh on the side of the purchases rather than the sales. A study of Stone's statistics suggests an actual overweight of about 20 percent on dated purchases as against dated sales.[23] The third assumption is that a marked and persistent overbalance of purchases by sales of major capital assets creates a presumption of overall capital losses. Surely it does so in the absence of a showing that the capital realized by the net sales is being reinvested in such a way as to produce a profit equal to that lost by disinvestment. But, as Stone notes, from 1559 to 1641 and certainly to 1603 there was no major alternative to land as a long-term investment. At any rate no one has produced any evidence that the peerage profitably transferred assets from land to alternative forms of investment at the appropriate dates, and in the absence of such evidence the burden of providing it ought to fall on those who would account for the recorded disinvestment in land in that particular way. Since during the eighty-year period there were four sales for every purchase, the overall ratio of disinvestment for the best sample of the peerage looks reasonably disastrous. But the overall figure does not tell the whole story or at least tells it badly. It is far more noteworthy that net losses were disproportionately high in the two successive decades between 1591 and 1610. In that quarter of the whole period, 44 percent of

23. This can be seen by comparing the figures in app. XI, B, col. IV, with those in app. XI, C. According to the former, thirty-three peerage families bought 141 manors between 1558 and 1602 and sold 756 manors, a ratio of only one recorded purchase for every 5.4 recorded sales. According to the latter table *at determinable dates* between 1561 and 1600, forty-two peerage families bought 133 manors and sold 571, a ratio of one dated purchase for 4.3 dated sales. Why sales should be less easy to date than purchases I do not know.

the net losses took place, a fact that seems not only to indicate an economic crisis of the aristocracy but to pinpoint it.

Inconveniently missing here, however, is a tabulation Stone
did not provide. Clearly what matters most in gauging the
dimensions of the crisis is not the ratio of sales to purchases
or of net losses at a particular time to overall net losses, but
*the relation at particular times of net losses to total manors
then owned.* But for the forty-two families under consideration, Stone does not indicate the total manors owned because
for nine families the data are inadequate. For thirty-three of
these families, however, he says that the data for 1559 do
permit a reasonably accurate estimate of total manors then
held; he puts that total at 1,670. This would make possible
the computations needed, if for those thirty-three families
(still a pretty satisfactory sample) he provided a decennial
purchase and sale table like that given above for forty-two
families. It is this key set of numbers that Stone omits. To
carry the analysis further, therefore, an arbitrary figure large
enough to exceed the probable holdings in 1559 of the nine
peers omitted from the estimate of total manors must be added to the 1,670 manors and the sum used as a basis of computation. As a guide for making such an allowance, there are
only Stone's rough estimates of relative rental income of the
peerage broken down into income categories running from
I at the top to VIII at the bottom. In 1602 the average place
of a peer on the I-to-VIII scale was 6.3. The nine peers omitted were presumably somewhat better-off, since their average
place was 5.9. Let it then be first assumed that the nine peers
held manors, at least in numbers proportional to those held
by the thirty-three for whom Stone provided the overall figure of 1,670. That would give them 456 manors to start with.
But since they were a bit richer than average, adding half
that number again, 228, to their total, gives a very generous

estimate of 684 manors for their holding in 1561. Adding this figure to Stone's count of 1,670 manors for the other thirty-three families results in an estimate of 2,354 manors in 1561 for the forty-two families to whom the disinvestment table applies. On this basis a decennial rate of disinvestment can be computed and also a rate for three unequal periods, 1561-1590, 1591-1610, 1611-1641 (table 4.2 and figures 4.1 and 4.2).[24]

TABLE 4.2
RATE OF DIVESTMENT OF MANORS

	Date	Manors	Net Loss	Loss Rate (%)
(a)	1561-1570	2354	67	2.85
	1571-1580	2287	112	4.90
	1581-1590	2175	97	4.46
	1591-1600	2078	163	7.84
	1601-1610	1915	117	6.11
	1611-1620	1798	38	2.11
	1621-1630	1760	25	1.42
	1631-1640	1735	16	0.92
(b)	1561-1590	2354	276	11.72
	1591-1610	2078	280	13.47
	1611-1640	1798	79	4.39

The computation indicates a fairly high rate of disinvestment in manors in the first three decades of Elizabeth's reign

24. A further objection may be raised to the procedure here adopted. It is that to treat 2,354 manors as of 1558 as a base from which to make a series of deductions for net loss in each decade does not take account of gains and losses of manors from other sources than purchase and sale between 1558 and 1602. It can be shown, however, that over the time span in question gains and losses from other sources did not markedly affect the relation between probable net losses and probable manorial holdings. Between 1558 and 1602, according to Stone, thirty-three families acquired 400 manors and lost 186 by means other than purchase and sale, a balance of 214 acquired. Ibid., app. XI, B, col. IV. Correcting this by a factor of 1.4, that is 2354÷1670, to allow for the estimated increase in manors ascribable

which then climbs catastrophically in the following two. A cluster of families that squanders 12 percent of its main assets in thirty years and then sheds 13 percent of what is left in the next twenty is not doing very well for itself. The indication here is the same as it was in the earlier and cruder calculation. Some of these forty-two families came to the verge of catastrophe in the decade or so around 1602. But another fact also seems to emerge from these figures: not many went over the brink. For many of these aristocrats the economic crisis ended more abruptly than it started. By 1610, after a last spell of property liquidations, it was over; and if manorial counts mean anything, they mean that seven years after James I's accession to the throne, the only group of aristocrats whose family fortunes are traceable from 1558 to 1641 were in a sheltered financial harbor where they remained for the next thirty years. For them the rate of disinvestment is certainly trivial in the three decades before 1640, and the disinvestment itself may possibly be illusory. What manor

to the addition of nine families gives an estimated net gain of 300 manors by means other than purchase and sale for forty-two families between 1558 and 1602. Against this, however, must be set what has been noted about the relation of *dated* to *actual* purchases and sales. A correction of 140 percent in the combined net recorded losses of 615 (756 — 141) manors for thirty-three families between 1558 and 1602 takes into account the addition of nine families. From the result, 861 manors, is subtracted the net dated losses for forty-two families during the same period, 438 manors. (See table 4.1) This gives a net undated loss of 423 manors due to the excess of sales over purchases. This counterbalances by more than one hundred manors the estimated net gains by means other than purchase and sale. The preceding computation of rates therefore has introduced no significant probable increase of error, and indeed it is likely that these computations minimize rather than maximize rates of disinvestment in manors by the forty-two peerage families between 1561 and 1602. Stone's own figures for the dated purchases and sales of the thirty-three families with 1,670 manors in 1558, were they available, would make unnecessary some of these conjectural corrections.

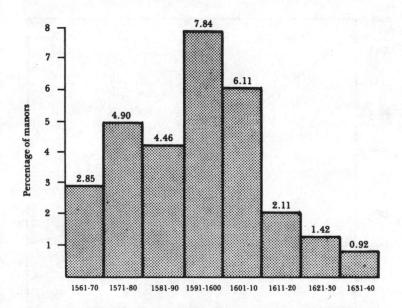

Figure 4.1. Rate of divestment of manors (1561-1640 by decade).

counts alone actually appear to reveal is "the crisis of the aristocracy, 1591-1610."

Or do they? Will not that depend on what one means by 'the crisis" and by "the aristocracy"? Since Stone's statistics on manors do yield what looks like solid evidence as to both the timing and the amplitude of the financial ups and downs of forty-two peerage families, what does this finding signify in the broader context of the history of the period, a history on so many aspects of which Stone's other findings throw new or brighter light? And first what *was* the crisis that Stone's manor count reveals and that the small statistical exercise above may have brought into slightly sharper focus? In the

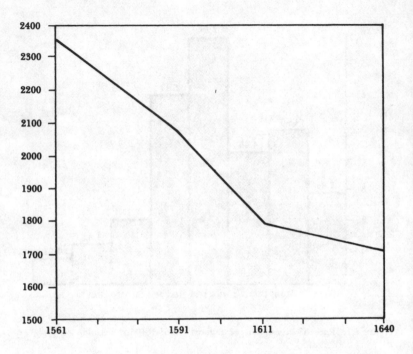

Figure 4.2. Rate of divestment of manors (number of manors divested per period).

very narrowest sense it was a crisis in the family fortunes of several families among a sample of forty-two families that already held peerages in 1559 and still held them in 1641, a crisis that may have extended to some families that acquired titles between 1558 and 1603 and to some that became extinct before 1603.[25] A very considerable number of families

25. Only ten families were ennobled between 1558 and 1603, of which eight survived beyond 1603.

entered the Elizabethan age bloated with monastic spoils, gathered quickly at bargain rates, which as courtiers and peers they were in a favored position to gobble up. A decade or so of disgorging was therefore perhaps in the cards and indeed took place. In the 1580s, however, the rate of disinvestment declined. What requires scrutiny is the resumption and the appalling rapidity of the dispersion of landed assets by this cluster of peerage families from 1590 to 1610. The new wave of disinvestment seems to have followed the conjuncture of a number of loosely related or unrelated circumstances reaching special intensity at just this time. It is a rather long list:

1. Habits of extravagance acquired earlier in very rich families continued to consume capital assets even when such consumption reached the peril point (ch. 10).

2. The success of the long Tudor campaign against aristocratic and other forms of civil violence reduced the incentive to land hoarding which existed when landlordship was a condition of manlordship, and when manlordship might be a life or death matter (ch. 5).

3. The temptation to sell grew with the rising value of land and in the absence of strict settlements to protect heirs from spendthrift fathers. It was even stronger in the case of spendthrift brothers, uncles, or cousins who did not particularly like or sometimes particularly disliked the apparent heir. To the satisfactions of running through a fortune they could add that of impoverishing someone they detested (ch. 6).

4. The primitive condition of the money market raised the price of credit so high that in the short run the sale of land looked a less costly way of laying hands on cash quickly than the alternative of loans at 10 percent interest or high-

cost mortgages without equity of redemption (ch. 9). (Retrospectively it seems clear that over the half-century between 1590 and 1640, capital gains on landholdings warranted a considerable outlay on interest charges as an alternative to sale of land. At the time, however, noble sellers did not have the advantage of hindsight, or the evidence about population increase that was a precondition for prediction, or the technique of economic analysis that, given the evidence, might have made a prediction of the price movement of land possible.)

5. The costs of war in Spain and Ireland tightened the royal purse strings, never excessively loose in Elizabeth's reign, reducing the flow of royal bounty to a trickle at a time when the queen's need and demand for costly public service from the peerage were rising rather than declining.

6. A clutch of *jeunesse dorée*, weary of the restraints put on them by Lord Burleigh, spent like sailors as a prologue to the Essex conspiracy, a disastrous resort to violence aimed at restoring their momentarily shattered fortunes (pp. 481-487).

The most impressive evidence of the combined ravages of these various circumstances is in Stone's list of heavy debtors in about 1601 (app. XXI, p. 778). It is remarkable on several grounds. In the first place, it does not include the names of several peerage families that on the basis of other evidence appear to have suffered severe losses of income from land—the Veres, Earls of Oxford, the Stanleys, Earls of Derby, the Herberts, Earls of Pembroke, and the Lords Berkeley (app. VIII, p. 760). Moreover, the seventeen peers listed seem to have been considerably better-off on the average than the whole peerage as of 1602, and to have included a much smaller proportion of very poor peers than the rest of the peerage did (app. VIII, B, p. 760) .[26] Yet in ten years this group—less than 30 percent of the peers—had sold off land worth more than 125 percent of the estimated annual gross rental of the entire peerage in 1602, and even after sales they still owed in private debts a good bit more than that rental.[27] To doubt that these people were in some sort of crisis in 1602 and to refuse to recognize that for families in such straits things might have had to get a bit worse before they got any better seem to require an excess of skepticism. And yet seen in this way, the crisis was as narrow as it was short-lived. In the first place, evidence is lacking as to whether or not it sharply touched the five hundred rich gentry families whom in his broadest definition Stone includes in the aristocracy. Moreover, as previously noted, for the solid sample of forty-two peerage families dating from before 1558, for whom Stone offers dated purchase and sale figures, the crisis, measured by disinvestment, grinds to something like a complete halt around 1610. Evidence is clear that the slide stopped by 1641, when in terms of estimated gross rentals some 40 percent of these families had improved their economic position in degrees varying from moderate to spectacular (app. VIII, C, p. 761). Under the circumstances one wonders whether the *economic* "crisis of the aristocracy" did much more than permanently devastate the fortunes of a very few families and throw enough of a scare into the rest to cause them to change their ways, put their affairs in order, and thus unawares prepare themselves

26. On Stone's I-to-VIII scale the average gross rental for the peers listed stood at 6.0 in 1602 as against 6.3 for all peers. Only 30 percent of them were in the VII-VIII range as against nearly 60 percent for the rest of the peerage.

27. For these seventeen peers, sales of £173,000+ still left debts of £150,000+ (app. XXI, p. 778). Rental for the entire lay peerage (fifty-eight persons) was £140,000 (app. VIII, B, p. 760).

to enjoy and improve on the opportunities that a happier (for them) conjuncture of circumstances provided after about 1605.

Statistics—even very good statistics—can deceive insufficiently wary historians. If they are indeed good, they provide accurate and precise information with respect to the processes or situations to which they are relevant. Both "statisticism" and some kinds of historicism, however, can be misleading when applied to people who experience life neither statistically nor historically. The implications are serious, since during much of the past (and some of the present) in many matters many men did not experience life statistically or historically, but through the misty veil in which tradition and custom appear mingled with myth. This is not to argue that quantities and the past did not matter to such people. It does mean that they may have mattered in ways different from the ones that people very conscious of quantity, statistics, and what actually happened are likely to assume. So even after one has quantified as precisely as possible and considered antecedent circumstances as fully as possible, a question remains. This question is not "Did all this matter to the people under consideration?" but "*How* did it matter?" Precise computations do not always provide a notion of the response of contemporaries to the situations they reveal. Indeed they do not provide any assurance that contemporaries were aware of the situations, or if some contemporaries were aware, which ones, and what the nature of such awareness was.

The economic anguish of a considerable number of peers around 1602 is a case in point. All peers who had to liquidate a big slice of their capital assets must have been aware of what they were doing and why they were doing it. And since beyond and above their intermingling at court, in council, and in the country, they were all members of a small select club, the House of Lords, that met frequently from 1590 to 1610, it is likely that all the peers had a pretty good notion of who were in straits and how badly. Their individual responses to their troubles varied—from those of the unreformed wastrels who tried the desperate remedy of rebellion in the Essex conspiracy to that of the remarkable reformed one, the Earl of Northumberland, who improved years of imprisonment by an almost excessive indulgence in estate management so successful that in 1641 his heir was one of the five richest peers in England. Insofar as Stone's estimates of gross rentals provide a basis for judgment, a few families by bad management or bad luck continued to slip after 1602. Almost all of the rest at least held their own and about two fifths improved their landed income, a few spectacularly.[28] Less extravagance, better luck, better management, better times, better credit facilities, and better pickings at court all contributed to the happy ending of the economic troubles of the group of peers whose fortunes have here been followed. These factors also contributed to the downfall of the view of the crisis of the aristocracy that started Stone on the pilgrim's progress which ended in his great book, the view that, as Tawney succinctly put it, in the 1640s "it was discovered . . . that as a method of foreclosure war was cheaper than litigation." Foreclosure by litigation was in fact not an option. There was almost no one to sell up. If any segment of the peerage was "feudal" in 1641, it was the one composed of families who had held their titles from before the accession of Elizabeth. Yet on the whole that group was very solvent

28. Families who continued to slip were Bourchier, Hastings, Ratcliffe, Stourton, and Talbot. Families who improved their landed income spectacularly were Percy, Vere, Manners, Seymour, Somerset, and Wharton.

indeed in the 1640s on the eve of its political liquidation, far better off than it had been four decades earlier.[29]

How, then, did others see the plight of the peers around 1602? There is not much direct evidence on which to base a positive answer to this question. One may hazard a guess, however, that people not personally involved who noticed anything like a crisis saw it as the acute embarrassment of a cluster of great families temporarily in spectacular financial difficulty. What the rest saw, if they took notice, was a local lord or two who had sold some of their land but were still able to live like lords off what they had left.[30]

On the basis of indirect evidence it is at least possible to surmise what the peers and their contemporaries did not see. Neither saw a crisis of the aristocracy in the sense of a loss of respect for and acceptance of the existing hierarchically structured society based on inherited wealth and privilege, or in the sense of the loss of prestige of the peerage itself at the apex of the social pyramid. The mass of qualitative evidence for such a twofold crisis is almost all of later date and either does not relate at all to the economic difficulties of the peers or does not relate to the economic situation of the peerage fami-

29. For the quote from Tawney, see "Rise of the Gentry," p. 12. On Stone's scale of rental income the "feudal" peers climbed from an average place of 6.3 in 1602, the lowest point reached during the whole period by any grouping of peers chronologically delimited, to 5.7 in 1641 (app. VIII, B and C, pp. 760-761).

30. Again on Stone's I-to-VIII scale of gross rental income, despite the crisis that resulted in a heavy disinvestment of manors, the median shift downward by 1602 was zero; that is, more peers had either gained or not lost in real income than had lost. Only four families had slipped more than one place in the table: the Veres, the Stanleys, the Herberts, and the Berkeleys. Ibid.

lies of 1602, since it comes at a time when those families had got their economic bearings again. The indirect evidence of the social solvency of the peerage in 1602 as against the economic straits of particular peers is provided by the early Jacobean creations. During the first decade of his reign James created twenty-four new peerages. The survivors or heirs of those creations in 1641 were by far the richest single chronological grouping of peers in the House of Lords at the time. With a very few exceptions for mere royal favor, by the standards of the time the men ennobled by James up to 1613 had earned their honors by great wealth, or long and important service to crown and commonwealth, or both. Many of them would have been peers earlier had it not been for Elizabeth's curious aversion to promoting even the most deserving to the peerage. At the level of the House of Lords there was no inflation of honors in the first ten years of the reign of James I.[31]

The conclusion is a paradox. Between 1558 and 1641 the peers were probably never worse off financially, and the prestige of peerage was probably never higher, than in 1602. In 1641, after three decades of steady financial recovery by the same peerage families, the prestige of the titled nobility was at a new low and the authority of the House of Lords was heading toward rock bottom. The conclusion seems inescapable. *The economic and the sociopolitical crises of the aristocracy were not coterminous and congruent in time; on*

31. The creations considered here are those from the accession of James I to the creation of Robert Carr, Earl of Somerset (app. V, p. 757). For some reason demographic attrition in this group was very high, about 45 percent in 28-38 years. In Stone's range table this group averaged 4.6 in 1641. No other considerable group stood so high. See the 1641 list in app. VIII, C, p. 761.

the contrary they were countercyclical and traversed each other.[32]

III

The third question that Stone addresses is how it came about that in the early seventeenth century the leadership of concerted opposition to the actions of the ruler, which had been exercised by English peers and magnates in the Middle Ages, fell to men about one step down on the social pyramid —the parliamentary gentry and lawyers. This question reveals another historiographic stratum of *The Crisis of the Aristocracy.* One can only guess when Stone's view of his task began to change. Perhaps between 1953 and 1958, for it was then that other scholars proposed views on the genesis of the English Revolution that were divergent from and irreconcilable with the ones that had started him on his long journey through the aristocracy. However that may be, one suspects that his debt to others was limited and that mainly he propelled himself into a change of opinion as his research turned up more and more data. Most likely his energy, his integrity to his evidence, and his impatience wearied him of whittling his findings down to fit the exiguous dimensions of his initial hypothesis, "that the difficulties of the sixteenth- and seventeenth-century aristocracy were at bottom financial." He ceased to believe that a financial crisis "was the sole, or even necessarily the prime, cause of their troubles" (p. 6) .

32. Stone's argument for a continuity between the financial crisis and the crisis of prestige of the peerage is not highly persuasive (pp. 163-164). The evidence he offers to connect the two is exiguous and unconvincing compared with what he provides to connect that second.crisis with circumstances on which he does not focus so effectively. I will return to this point later in the text. That the adaptive moves of individual peers to meet their temporary financial embarrassment around 1602 significantly affected the prestige and power of the whole order at the time or three decades later is not impossible, but Stone's evidence that they did so is thin.

Having arrived at this crucial point, he never looked back until he reached the conclusion of the concluding chapter in his big book: the crisis of the aristocracy was a crisis of prestige, the causes of which were

manifold . . . They include the decline in the wealth of the peers relative to that of the gentry; the shrinkage of their territorial possessions, in both absolute and relative terms; the decay of their military power in men, arms, castles, and will to resist; the granting of titles of honour for cash not merit, in too great numbers, and to too unworthy persons; the change in their attitude towards the tenantry from suppliers of manpower to suppliers of rent; the undermining of their electoral influence due to the rise of deeply felt political and religious issues; the increasing preference for extravagant living in the city instead of hospitable living in the countryside; the spread throughout the propertied classes of a bookish education, acquired at school and university, and the demand by the State for an administrative *élite* of proved competence, irrespective of the claims of rank; the pervasive influence of the rise of individualism, the Calvinist belief in a spiritual hierarchy of the Elect, and the Puritan exaltation of the private conscience, which affected attitudes toward hierarchy and obedience in secular society; and finally the growing psychological breach between Court and Country in attitudes, real or supposed, towards constitutional theory, methods and scale of taxation, forms of worship, aesthetic tastes, financial probity, and sexual morality. (Pp. 748-749)

Even beyond this he came to recognize that

Particular crises arising from particular events, personalities, and policies, the ineptitude of James, the corruption of Buckingham, the obstinacy of Strafford, Laud, and Charles; the rise of puritanism, the growth of a sense of constitutionalism, the development of improved procedural techniques by the House of Commons . . . together . . . still provide the best guide to the issues which divided men one from another when civil war broke out in 1642. (P. 10)

The movement of historical thought during a quarter of a

century in the direction of sophistication and maturity implied in these long sentences may best be gauged by repeating here the sweet simplicities of 1940. In "the English Revolution of 1640-1660 . . . an old order that was essentially feudal was destroyed by violence, a new capitalist social order created in its place."[33] As both a symptom and an exemplar of this movement, *The Crisis of the Aristocracy* is indeed a "landmark in the historical landscape," a monument to what can be achieved by historians when they break the bonds of a sterile and stifling orthodoxy and accept both the intellectual delights and the intellectual risks that such an emancipation offers to and imposes upon them.

Sharply to change direction in mid-flight to a book is a hard maneuver; the path of one's earlier trajectory almost inevitably leaves traces on one's final course; evidence gathered with one view of the past in mind does not readily accommodate itself to an altered view; and a reasonable economy with the expenditure of one's own life does not warrant a return trip through the record. In his pursuit of an understanding of the subordinate role of the peerage in the events that precipitated the upheaval of the 1640s, Stone made such a shift in mid-flight when he decided that in dragging the peers down financial difficulties were secondary to a crisis of prestige and confidence. Under the circumstances it is hardly remarkable that he did not completely succeed in reorient-

33. The quote is from Hill, *English Revolution,* p. 9. This is not to argue that it is *impossible* to reduce Stone's complexities to the early simplicities. It is to suggest that those who wish to reduce the "explanation" of the English Revolution *in this or any other way* to a simplicist pattern address themselves to those complexities and not merely prescind from them on the grounds that they are unimportant. The practice of deciding in advance on metahistorical grounds and without consideration of the record of the past what is important and what is not is itself now hopelessly passé and (one hopes) past.

ing his work; it is remarkable that he succeeded so well. Insofar as he was able to deal with that crisis under the rubrics of power, education, and the inflation of honors, he could hardly have done better. A few of the traits of the age of crisis Stone came to understand well but in some degree too late. His earlier momentum deflected him from adequately conveying their importance, an importance that his shift in direction had enabled him adequately to grasp. His way of organizing his book (and his thoughts) diffuses attention from those traits rather than directing it to them. The problem is one of focus, not, except in one particular, of omission. The three traits of the age that escape rather than capture the attention they deserve are the court-country tension and the impact of Puritanism, with which Stone deals diffusely, and the position of the lay peers as the preponderant element in the House of Lords, with which he does not deal at all. What follows is an attempt, mainly in the light of evidence that Stone himself provides, to force these matters into the center of attention.[34]

Almost casually Stone himself makes the main point: *"The peerage in 1615 still retained its full dignity and respect"* (p. 103; italics added).[35] If this is so, then with respect to the

---

34. The following observations are based on a fairly extensive, if desultory, reading in sources and secondary works on the period. In almost every detail the observations themselves require direct confirmation from a systematic study of the sources.

35. Most of the data for the following paragraphs are drawn from ch. 3; app. III, p. 755; app. VIII, C, p. 761; apps. XXIX and XXX, p. 789. Only creations from Buckingham's own accession to the peerage to the end of 1628 are counted as "Buckingham peers." The choice may be faulted on several points: (1) Buckingham's accession to favor antedates by two or three years his promotion to the peerage, leaving some peers in no-man's-land between Somerset's fall and Buckingham's creation. There are only four such peers, however (app. V, p. 757). (2) It does not include promotions

crisis in the prestige of the aristocracy and of confidence in
it, the hinge date comes sometime after 1615. But as a result
of his youthful prepossessions Stone must have oriented much
of his statistical investigation to the financial crisis of the
peers around 1602. Despite his own later reorientation he
retains that statistical benchmark in several tabulations where
the issue is not financial condition but prestige, and also
where the interplay of finance and prestige renders advisable
the intrusion of an additional tabulation from about 1618
to 1628. Although Stone's statistics never systematically single out that decade, the figures for the inflation of honors
clearly mark it for special attention. James's creation of almost a thousand knights at his accession was rather hasty, but
it would not have been catastrophic had replacement been
held to the annual rate of about fifty, to which it fell between
1606 and 1615, while the King's early errors gradually went
down the drain of mortality. The doubling of the rate of
creations from 1616 to 1625, coupled with the interjection of
the baronetage, a hereditary honor, obliterated the chance
for healthy attrition. And in the succeeding decade the new
honor of baronet, kept well in bounds until 1618, went the
way of the old one of knight, with almost two hundred new
creations swamping the initial group of about one hundred.
As for the peerage itself, between the promotion of Buckingham in 1618 and 1628, the number of peers almost doubled.

within the peerage during the Buckingham era. It may be argued, however, that while these promotions may have resulted in the embitterment
of relations within the peerage, as far as impact on the country gentry is
concerned, the major harm was done only by promotion to the peerage,
since that promotion exalted those who received it over baronets and
knights. (3) The list is extended beyond Buckingham's death to the end
of 1628 on the grounds that the duke's influence reached from beyond
the grave and that the braking process on creations does not become evident until 1629 at the earliest (app. V, p. 757).

For the mathematics of prestige and confidence, this is the cohort about which statistics would be especially welcome. In only a few of Stone's tabulations, however, can it be isolated from the whole set of creations between 1603 and 1641. With respect to marriage, for example, the group can be sorted out. It appears that in contrast to the almost complete absence of such alliances among more ancient peerage families, by 1630 fourteen of these later peers had married mercantile heiresses, either before or after their creation.

The failure to draw a line around about 1618 causes most difficulty in dealing with the economic viability of the peers, for here it is quite clear that the creations of the first decade of James's reign should be treated in the main as long overdue grants of honor to Elizabethan families of means and mark—Cecil, Sydney, Egerton, Petre, Spencer, Cavendish, Stanhope, Arundell. Statistically this appropriate shift of the dividing line would sharply increase the average and aggregate manorial holdings that Stone assigns to the "old peers" and sharply set off the narrow territorial base of the creations of the Buckingham ascendancy. A comparison of their respective rental incomes in 1641 indicates the difference in landholding between the two groups of peers. In 1641 the average income of peers whose families had entered the peerage before 1613 was 5.1 on Stone's I-to-VIII scale. The average of those who had entered in 1618-1628 was 6.2. This would mean an average gross rental of about £4000 for the peers of the Buckingham era as against £6400 for peers whose families had entered the peerage before 1613; or in relative terms, on the average the Buckingham peers had just about five-eighths of the income enjoyed by peers of earlier vintage. By 1641 the peers created during the duke's ascendancy had had between a quarter of a century and about half that time to augment their landholdings. Given the tendency of the aristocracy to transform other assets into acres, the shortness of so many Buckingham peers in landed wealth in 1641 suggests that they included a more than ordinary number of lean cattle.[36]

The value of the above statistical exercise in terms of a prestige analysis depends in the first place on the contemporary social visibility of the groups examined. In this context the usefulness of grouping peerage families as ante- or post-1602 as Stone's statistics do is doubtful, because it is doubtful whether many contemporaries saw them in that chronological framework. By way of contrast, the Buckingham peers began to attain an unenviable visibility shortly after Villiers succeeded to full favor. That visibility increased throughout the favorite's life and may not have been wholly dimmed even in the period of Charles I's personal rule, when the flood of creations abated. This visibility is what gives point to the above calculation. Average income, however, is not a trait socially visible to contemporaries, and for prestige analysis the visibility of the trait quantified is important. For

36. Stone's figures already mark a sharp distinction between the landed position of the "old" and "new" peerage in 1641: the former with an average of thirty-four manors apiece, the latter with twenty apiece; proportionally twice as many families of the former as of the latter holding forty or more manors (app. XI, p. 764). With the creations of 1603-1613 added, the average member of the first group would almost certainly have double the manorial holdings of the average peer created during Buckingham's ascendancy, and while the "old" and "new" groups would be approximately equal in size, the old would include four times as many holders of forty or more manors.

Stone's data for 1641 are based mainly on royalist compounding papers. This should minimize *relative* error among considerable samples of peers. One cannot discount the likelihood that men took a chance on understating the value of land for the release of which they had to pay a mulct proportional to its worth, but there is no reason to suppose that there was a marked differential in mendacity quotient between the peers created up to 1613 and those created from 1618 through 1628.

such analysis both the number and the proportion of peers meagerly endowed with land is of special interest; in a conspicuously landed aristocracy a meager endowment confers a negative distinction. In the group of peerage families surviving to 1641, there were more land-short peers among the creations of the ten-year Buckingham period than among all the families whose peerages antedated 1613: eighteen as against fourteen. Moreover, the land-short peers made up less than a quarter of the pre-1613 group as against more than two-fifths of the Buckingham peers. Finally, there is the question of the "fit" of the especially visible subgroups of poor Buckingham peers and poor pre-1613 peers into the structure of the community. With respect to the pre-1613 peers this could hardly have been much of a problem; all but one of the families in the group had been poor before 1602, all but five before 1558. By the second quarter of the seventeenth century, enduring impoverishment should have made them assimilated bits of the local social landscape, rather like venerable ivy-clad ruins. It was otherwise with the Buckingham peers, and if they lived in the country, they were trebly conspicuous: their promotions were new; the circumstances of their promotions were often questionable or simply scandalous; and in terms of talent, service, and wealth their claims to local precedence over the upper country gentry were exiguous or nonexistent. Yet their new titles automatically conferred such precedence on them. To that same upper gentry, which five times in the 1620s and twice again in 1640 gathered for meetings of Parliament, some of the poor Buckingham peers were unduly visible in the country; some of the poor and some of the rich ones, who did not make themselves visible locally, were only too visible in London, where they swarmed after or peddled the favors of a discredited court.

The mention of favor and court leads to one last statistical point. If Stone's figures are even approximately correct, the channels of large-scale favor open to English peers, scandalously broad after the accession of James, became even more scandalously narrow twelve years later and remained so for about another twelve. During that relatively short time the Duke of Buckingham may have been the beneficiary of offices and rewards equal to those enjoyed by the entire Elizabethan peerage throughout the whole of the queen's forty-five-year reign (app. XIX, C, p. 775). In James's last days the young lover of the doting, doddering homosexual king took all, and he continued to take all for four years more as favorite of James's son and successor. Whoever else received more than scraps of reward at court enjoyed them at the hands and the behest of the Duke of Buckingham. For the English peerage this produced a dilemma not resolvable and a disaster not retrievable at the time or in the years that followed Buckingham's assassination. It transformed the diffuse difficulties of the peers into an insoluble crisis of prestige and confidence in the aristocracy. What gave form to the crisis that precipitated itself around Buckingham was a complex interplay among Puritanism, the tension between court and country, and the political position of the House of Lords. By the time he finished his great study, Lawrence Stone knew this, but like the fox he knew many things. Like hedgehogs, observant contemporary Englishmen knew scarcely more than this one big thing and often did not precisely formulate what they knew, but nevertheless they knew it very well.

Better to understand what happened and its impact on the aristocracy, one needs to examine a process of change within the social matrix of the early modern English ruling class. A no doubt oversimplified analysis may help bring into sharp focus relations between court and country, peerage and gentry, on which Stone's study casts abundant light, but light that in consequence of his chosen structure of presentation is intermittent and diffused. The components of the matrix are court peers, country peers, country gentry, court gentry, as in figure 4.3.[37]

	Peers	Gentry
Court	court peers	court gentry
Country	country peers	country gentry

Figure 4.3. Matrix of court and country peers and gentry.

In terms of legal status throughout the period, the line of division between peers and gentry is at each moment distinct. From the moment he enters the peerage, a man is legally distinguishable from a gentleman of any lower degree. So sharp a division does not necessarily separate court and country as spheres of activity and influence. Some peers and some of the gentry can be active both at court and in the country and have influence in both places. This social matrix may be thought of not only as a matrix of honors and of activity and influence but also as a *communications network* through

37. The model suggested in figure 4.3 derives from the one that Robert Walcott found necessary in order to make some sense of English politics from the 1670s to the accession of the Hanoverian dynasty. Robert Walcott, *English Politics in the Early Eighteenth Century* (Cambridge, Mass.: Harvard University Press, 1956), pp. 155-158.

which circulate and are exchanged the views and outlook of each group. In the country gentry section, however, this communications network has one peculiarity that requires special attention. That sector differs from the others in its internal structure. It is composed of the hierarchies of *local* eminence in the separate counties of England and Wales. The politically effective country gentry are those who stand high in at least one county hierarchy. Only this group—by Stone's estimate some five hundred men at any given time between 1558 and 1641—is relevant here. With respect to this group of country gentry, questions arise not only about their communication with the other three components of the social matrix but with respect to intercommunication among the hierarchies across county boundaries.[38]

Given this general structure, what follows is an attempt somewhat schematically to describe the functioning of the system that it defines at two points in time forty years apart —the late 1580s, when Elizabeth stood at the peak of her popularity, and the late 1620s. In the 1580s the line of honor between the upper gentry and the peerage had rarely been crossed in the thirty years since the queen's accession. In that whole time by creation, restoration, and resumption there had been only fifteen accessions to the peerage in all, on the average of one every two years, and only one accession in the last fifteen years. At the center among the court group there was little correlation between peerage on the one hand and

38. I know of no effort to discover whether and in what number members of the upper country gentry stood high in more than one county hierarchy; I have only a vague and unverified impression that such men were few, and that even those who had estates in more than one county concentrated their struggle for influence and preeminence in one county only. There were exceptions, however. In 1628 Sir Edward Coke was returned as knight of the shire for both Buckinghamshire and Norfolk.

power and prestige on the other. For years advancement in power and office had not brought a title to any of the court gentry, nor did possession of a title warrant expectation of official advancement. Within the framework of a deferential system, possession of peerage honors created no presumption at all as to influence on policy. The Catholicism or incompetence or relative poverty that discouraged a considerable number of peers from seeking place at a court that often demanded inputs of expenditure in excess of its outputs of rewards consigned them to "the idiocy of rural life." On the other hand, for the upper gentry places at court commensurate in power and prestige with their local authority, dignity, and "worship" were too few to attract more than a small cluster. Seen from the other direction, however, the proportion of court peers and court gentry who actively participated in the affairs of the local county hierarchies seems to have been considerable. The high place in that hierarchy legally due to the court peers by virtue of their mere titles was also practically theirs by virtue of a continuing interest in county affairs, an interest reinforced by the appointment of some of them to the recently instituted county office of lord lieutenant. And the restrictive policy that had closed promotion to peerage to the court gentry ensured that the more eminent among them would command wealth and prestige sufficient to entitle them to a high and unchallenged position in one county hierarchy or another.

This pattern determined the directions of communication. At court it flowed freely between and within gentry and peerage. And because of the local activity of court gentry and court peers alike, there was considerable communication between the local gentry hierarchies and the court. On the other hand, the intercommunication among local hierarchies seems to have been relatively slight. The one institutionalized structure encouraging such communication was Parliament, where members of those hierarchies gathered in a general assembly. But meetings of Parliament under Elizabeth were both rare and brief, rarer and briefer than in the reigns of her sister, of her brother, or, after 1529, of her father. And for whatever reason, the upper country gentry does not seem to have developed a highly effective and extralegal network of communication among the county hierarchies.[39] The central switchboard, so to speak, of the lines linking the county hierarchies was at court. Because the court gentry and the court peers maintained ready and continuous communication between court and country, they retained their leadership in Parliament. This leadership was only occasionally and not very effectively challenged by a few members of the country gentry. The efforts of this cluster of men were indeed often, and not necessarily by design, frustrated by the readiness of some of the court peers and gentry to assume a mediatorial posture between current royal policy and country misgivings about it, misgivings which they sometimes shared in part.

This set of relations among those who ruled England was remarkably effective in maintaining internal repose. It was also capable of absorbing the impact of Puritanism in its current form and state of development. For more than a decade before 1588, the program of the Puritan ministers had aimed at the substitution of Presbyterianism for episcopal government in the church, at revision of the liturgy to eliminate "Popish" elements, at congregational power over church dis-

39. No study has been made of the role of the more or less purely country peers in local affairs. It is evident that a peer like Robert Rich, second Earl of Warwick, exercised large if not paramount power in Essex. To the south in Kent, however, affairs seem to have been in control of a gentry oligarchy, and just to the north the gentry dynasty of the Barnardistons, with Sir Nathaniel as its head, dominated Suffolk.

cipline, and at an extension and improvement of preaching of the Word. Unsuccessful maneuvers to achieve the first three goals had absorbed a large part of the energy and talent of the Puritan ministry. Those goals had elicited some support from peers and gentry both at court and in the country. But in face of the queen's intransigent opposition, they had not evoked enough enthusiasm from a large enough group anywhere to polarize the governing classes along the lines set by religious issues.

While the Puritan ministry was frustrated in its ecclesiological, liturgical, and disciplinary designs, Puritan gentry and peers were not cut off from positions of honor and power either in the country or at court. On the contrary, the queen's long-time favorite, the Earl of Leicester, her principal secretary of state, Sir Francis Walsingham, and a very considerable number of court peers and gentry acted as protectors and advocates for the Puritans. Indeed in Parliament itself, where Puritan country gentry found an occasional opportunity to press for one item or another of the program of the Puritan ministry, they often received open support from highly placed peers and gentlemen of the court. This open court-country alliance of Puritans did not budge the queen's effective resistance to Puritan demands; on the other hand, it did not reduce the zeal of the court Puritans for the royal service or result in the withdrawal of royal favor from them or in any concerted action against them by the queen and the supporters of her ecclesiastical policy. The result was that Puritanism had a diffusive rather than a polarizing impact on the English governing class and did not jeopardize its relatively smooth functioning. Under the circumstances of the 1580s religious divergence did not exacerbate the tendency of court and country to polarize into two cultures incompatible and at loggerheads with each other, unable either to communicate effectively across the gulf between them or to unite their energies in a joint enterprise. The viability of the peculiar social pattern just examined was fully vindicated by effective coordination of the ruling class in court and country at the time of the Armada crisis.[40]

The passage of forty years witnessed noteworthy changes in the patterns of relations within the social matrix of the ruling class. Increase in the number of peers, and especially increased readiness to reward service in high court office with peerages, automatically enhanced the power of the court peers. This dual process correlatively and inevitably diminished the importance and power at court of the court gentry. The diminution of their power at court weakened their position within the county hierarchies. With neither the wealth nor the prestige that four decades earlier their eminence at court had afforded them in the country, they tended to withdraw from activities in which they no longer could hope to receive the respect and "worship" that their predecessors had enjoyed. This decline in status and power became markedly evident in the incapacity of the court gentry to lead that assembly of the upper country gentry, the House of Commons. In the county hierarchies the influence of the court peers did not expand proportionally to the shrinkage of the influence of the court gentry there; if anything, to the contrary. The inflation of peerage honors created a fatal dichotomy between legal right of precedence on the one hand and respect, worship, and effective power in the actual workings of the county hierarchies on the other. The latter increasingly went to those who actually did the work—the more assiduous deputy-

40. The contrast between the situation of France and England in this respect emerges in dramatic vividness from the pages of Garrett Mattingly, *The Armada* (Boston: Houghton Mifflin, 1959).

lieutenants and justices of the peace, painstaking in their attendance at musters, quarter sessions, and petty sessions. Neither court peers nor country peers exercised much control over these rulers of the countryside, whose power and influence depended on local estimates of merit and worth that increasingly diverged from the canon for advancement at court.

By 1628 communication between the country gentry and the court, which forty years earlier had proceeded smoothly, was hopelessly snarled. No analysis of the sort favored by Stone can quite do justice to the circumstances that raised the misunderstanding and cross-purposes between the court on one side and the country gentry on the other to the crisis level, where what one regarded as communication the other deemed irrelevant and intolerable noise. Month by month, year by year, for a quarter of a century, while alienation from the country and contempt for the tastes and modes of both perception and valuation current there increased at court, misgiving, doubt, distrust, and detestation of almost everything that began in and emanated from the court rose among the country gentry. The accentuation of mutual distrust started with the accession of James or perhaps a little before.[41] It was more intense in 1615 than it had been in 1603. With the accession of Buckingham, aside from one brief, adventitious respite of good will that followed the breakdown of negotiations for the Spanish match in 1624, the force of the flood of anger grew. At the dissolution of Parliament in 1629, it culminated in a sort of collective rage of mutual frus-

---

41. Some of the debates in the later Elizabethan parliaments over issues not specifically related to religion suggest the earlier date. So does the extraordinary and rapid response of the House of Commons, beginning on the very first day of James's first parliament, evoked by the case *Goodwin vs. Fortescue.*

tration and bitterness. Such a process can best be presented not in analytical but in narrative form. The story itself becomes the explanation of the series of events it recounts. Only when one follows those events in chronological sequence does one acquire a sense of the cumulative fury that was creating the situation of the later 1620s when the court and country hierarchies no longer adequately understood what the other was saying, because in matters of the utmost importance to both they had practically ceased to speak the same language.

The breakdown of understanding between the court and the local gentry hierarchies coincided with and was in fact the occasion for a most significant development of intercommunication among the local hierarchies of country gentry. By 1628 that communication had markedly increased in quantity and improved in quality. The improvement in quality was assisted by the improvement and intensification of the education of the upper gentry. In the universities and at the Inns of Court, more of them received a training that was both longer and better suited to their needs than it had been. The improvement in communication was also a function of an improved information network. Pitifully meager no doubt by present-day standards, the growing volume of newsletters flowing from London to the country provided the county hierarchies of the 1620s with a larger body of shared information (and misinformation) about current events in the great world than their predecessors of the 1580s had received. The increase in volume of intercommunication among the county hierarchies was itself a consequence of their better education and better information; men communicate more when they know more to communicate about. Above all, however, the impulse to create means of intercommunication among the country gentry across county lines derived from the common sense of a need for it. The need was the result of the divergence of outlook, opinion, and judgment between the court and the upper country gentry on an ever broader range of issues. Obligingly, though under some duress, the court itself nurtured in the leaders of the counties an awareness of how fully they shared common views on major matters and provided them with opportunities for communication unparalleled in Elizabeth's reign. In the five Parliaments that James and Charles summoned between 1621 and 1628, the greater country gentry from all over England met and worked together, day in and day out, in the House of Commons. There they unconsciously constructed a collective representation of a common enemy, the court, which temporarily obliterated all the latent divergencies in their own views.

These circumstances did not make the country gentry Puritan; about 1628 some were Puritans, some were not. To identify some country gentry who clearly were Puritan at the time is not hard; to identify many who clearly were not is more difficult unless they enthusiastically took part in or supported Archbishop Laud's measures of ecclesiastical policy; and such men were few. The transformation in Puritanism itself is what makes it hard to define the boundary zone between Puritan and mere (anti-Laudian) Protestant in the late 1620s.

Like its antecedent in this matter, Christian humanism, Puritanism slowly reeducated the English landed classes and reoriented and inflated their expectations both of themselves and of others. This reorientation touched many aspects of human existence. It especially touched public life. Puritanism did not create the idea of such a life; some such notion had begun to reemerge in the Middle Ages and had received further specification during the Renaissance. But for many people Puritanism gave a new and special poignancy to the purpose of public life. It set the goal of that life very high, no less than the *regnum Christi,* the kingdom of God on earth, where His will should be done. With so exalted an end, Puritanism made very severe demands on those who took part in ruling the English commonweal, the Elect Nation of God, the cynosure of the faithful everywhere, "as a City on a Hill." In that nation office should be precatory rather than predatory, for prayer not for prey, a dedication rather than an exploitation.

The spread of this sense of the nature of public life was slow and sporadic.[42] The propagation of the Puritan view of the right quality of life, even the effective and detailed formulation of that view, were the consequences of a paradox. They owed much to Elizabeth and James I, who opposed, frustrated, and defeated the Puritans in the arena of ecclesiastical politics. From the 1570s to the first decade of the seventeenth century, the Puritans tried to impose their ecclesiological and liturgical views on the English Church by exerting pressure at court indirectly through Parliament and directly through friends in the queen's council and near her person. Their successive defeats gradually diverted the energies of many Puritans from the divisive issues of the one right government and form of worship for the church. Deprived of access to the responsibilities and ambiguities of power, from the late sixteenth century on they turned their main effort toward the ministry and the molding of conscience. In this range of activity the central authorities failed effectively to restrain the spiritual brotherhood from propagating a ver-

42. Its earliest embryonic expression in England was perhaps pre-Reformation. There are elements of it, at least, in Thomas More's *Utopia,* with the appropriate Christian overtones, but, of course, without the emotional charge generated by the conflict with Popery, and without the special rhetoric that that conflict engendered.

sion of the gospel that was increasingly in conflict with the ethical outlook of the court.

With declining hope of access to power through the court and an increasingly well defined opposition to the way of life, the ethic, the ordering of values characteristic of the court, the Puritan ministers zealously sought a welcome for their message among leaders of the county hierarchies, who dominated life in the country. By that time the spiritual brotherhood of godly ministers in England was no longer so overtly or intensely committed as it had been to a program that required a remodeling of the whole ecclesiastical structure and therefore the support of the authority of the crown. In 1641 that ministry again turned its attention directly to the divisive problems of church government. In the interval between the successful repression of the Presbyterian movement by Elizabeth and Archbishop Whitgift and its re-emergence in the early days of the Long Parliament, the principal concerns of the godly clergy had become the effective ministry of the Word, the cultivation and sensitizing of Christian consciences, and propaganda against the Popish resurgence at home and abroad, preoccupations that the Puritans shared with a very large segment of the country gentry. These shared preoccupations make it hard for us at three centuries' distance to identify lay Puritans and may have made it hard at the time for some of the gentry to be clear in their own minds whether they were Puritan or not. The new direction of thrust of Puritan thought and action after political defeat by Elizabeth thus encouraged the symbiosis between Puritanism and the country gentry and afforded to the Puritan laity opportunities for leadership in the country that they had lost at court.

The favorable circumstances, partly accidental, partly the fruit of policy, that in the 1580s had enabled the court to en-

joy the benefits of the Puritans' energy and intelligence without having to suffer their domination, ceased to exist. By the
mid-1620s the Puritans for practical purposes were out of
court in fact and in hope. They had no place to turn but to
the country, and primarily to the country gentry. Beyond all
other issues uniting the country gentry and dividing them
from the court in the 1620s was the one that had bound court
and country together in the 1580s—the posture of the Elect
Nation in its relation to a beleaguered international Protestantism on the Continent and in the face of a victoriously re-
surgent Popery. In the present context, discussion of the
shortcomings of the views on such complex matters current
among the country gentry, of the inadequacy of their understanding, of the irrationality of their response is irrelevant.
Whether under the circumstances any policy the government
attempted to follow could have succeeded, whether the county gentry had the faintest notion of alternatives to the succession of cul-de-sacs into which James and Charles plunged,
does not matter. What does matter is that everything the
Stuarts tried failed and that, as the decade passed, responsibility for failure rested ever more clearly on the Duke of
Buckingham. And all this concurred in time with the suspicion that he was responsible for most of the doings at court
that annoyed, alarmed, and shocked the country gentry, and
with his evident responsibility for many of them. The diffuse but fervent international Protestantism of the larger and
richer part of the country gentry had at its hard core the zeal
of the Puritan gentry. The anguished cry "Avenge, O Lord,
Thy slaughtered Saints!" was wrung from a Puritan heart at
a later time, but some of the emotion it reflects—pity for the
continental Protestant victims and hatred for their Popish
tormentors—was common to the Puritan clergy, the Puritan
gentry, and the mere Protestant gentry of the country in the

1620s. And in the 1620s that emotion was powerfully magnified by impotent rage at the paralysis of English policy and by hysterical dread of the inroads of Popery at home, especially at court. Men who a couple of decades earlier would not have much troubled themselves to act in behalf of the ministers ejected for resistance to the canons of 1604 had little patience with attacks on preachers whose offense was zeal in denouncing doings that they themselves deplored, doings that in appearance and often in fact were generated and consummated at court.

How much of the Puritan ethic forced its way into the hearts of the country gentry by the way of a widely shared concern for the perils of Protestantism is hard to know and hard to find out; but it is scarcely an accident that Richard Baxter, who was well enough aware that he was a dissenter after 1660, did not know that he was a Puritan before the 1640s. It is at least likely that involvement in the care and feeding of zealous preachers of the Word absorbed into the Puritan lay fellowship a part of the gentry that had hitherto stood outside it. It also provided new means and new motives for intercommunication among the gentry hierarchies. Favorite preachers established lines of communication among the gentry of different counties; so too did the need to protect these preachers from harassment directed from the court. Finally, bonds of friendship, reinforced by a shared religious outlook originating in the several Puritan-dominated colleges at Oxford and Cambridge, carried over among the Puritan gentry after college days. The seeds for the dense growth of interrelations among the Puritans in the country, so easy to discern in the 1630s, were sown some decades earlier and matured very fast in the favorable climate of the 1620s. Puritanism, then, advanced the consolidation of the country gentry, broadened the "credibility gap" that isolated the court from the country, and intensified the nationwide crisis of the 1620s.

Supposing the foregoing description of the transformation of the political scene in about four decades to be reasonably accurate, to document it adequately would require years of work in published sources, national and local archives, and private muniments. An early study of mine detailed the intricate links of cousinship that, regardless of county lines, bound several Puritan "families" of cousins and clients into a sort of Mafia of saints.[43] A letter from a devout dowager to Sir Simonds D'Ewes about her step-grandson, Sir Nathaniel Barnardiston, the leading gentleman and leading Puritan in Suffolk, further illustrates the transvaluation of values that took place in the days of the early Stuarts:

Let me desire you further this bearer Mr. Burrell, the late and to my sence the yet minister of Wratting, if Sir Nathan:B:bee as I hope he is earnest to have him restored as well to liuing as libertye. You may out of your interest in him and respect towards him in direct tearmes let him know that he will suffer much in the opinion of his country neighbors here in these parts, many looke upon the success of this business, and surely as this man specd Sir Nath wilbe censured if it be not fully evidenced to them that he desired and indevoured to have him restored to both. The name of Barnardiston is and ever shalbe precious to me; and if any of that name, especially the Luster of the house, should undergoe justly any tart censure or incurre an harde conceit amongst his neighbors, and those of the best ranke according to Gods account, it would even much devert me, in these my declining dayes. Therefore at my intreatie be verie earnest about this desire of myne, and of this I am confident: that the work will be acceptable to

43. J. H. Hexter, *The Reign of King Pym* (Cambridge, Mass.: Harvard University Press, 1942), pp. 84-88.

god, and bring much comfort to your own conscience, which that it may doe shalbe the earnest desire.[44]

What survives of older days and older ways in Lady Anne's letter is the intense concern for "the name of Barnardiston" and "the Luster of the house." This luster depends on the place of the head of the house, Sir Nathaniel, in the county hierarchy. That place ultimately depends on "the opinion on his country neighbors." That opinion itself, however, is no longer to be won by any of the marks of favor that the court can lavish on a country man. On the contrary, it is to be won by an act of quiet but manifest subversion, in which Sir Nathaniel restores to his living a Puritan minister displaced by the clerical faction favored at court. And finally beyond court favor, the older complex measure of earthly status in the country—an amalgam based on broad acres, a loyal tenantry, riches, and ancient lineage—is made yet more intricate by dependence on the approval of a rather special reference group, a new kind of hierarchy, *"those of best ranke according to Gods account,"* an account not wholly accessible short of Judgment Day.

The crisis of aristocracy was in part a correlate of this broader crisis, which caught the peerage in a cross fire from which they could not escape. In the first place, the polarization between the court and the country gentry destroyed the capacity of the peers corporately and individually to play the mediatorial role in which they were cast by Elizabethan policy. They could not possibly harmonize the signals of discontent and disaffection that came up to them from the country

44. Anne Barnardiston to Sir Simonds D'Ewes, Jan. 1641, BM, Harl. MSS, 384, fol. 27. I thank Professor Kenneth Shipps of Trinity College, Deerfield, Ill., for calling my attention to this letter and providing me with a transcript of it.

with the demands for unquestioning trust and compliance that came down to them from the court. What was true of their activity was equally true of their mode of life. It had been hard enough to maintain a pattern of behavior appropriate to both court and country in the sixteenth century, before the demands of the two so completely diverged. In the 1620s it was almost impossible. No peer who maintained the style of life at court under Charles I that the Earl of Leicester had under Elizabeth could have gained and retained leadership of the Puritan-country "coalition." The Puritan-country ideal of zeal, sobriety, austerity, and indifference to earthly rewards was not congenial to the court; even less so were its practice of sanctimony and plain speaking and its distaste for ceremony. The courtier's ideal of grace, urbanity, and cultivated hedonism was not congenial to the Puritan-infested county hierarchies; even less so were its practice of and, worse, its tolerance of idleness, display, flattery, gambling, fornication, adultery, and sodomy. These ancient sports were surely not unknown in the country, but there they carried penalties in terms of power or at least exacted that hypocrisy which is vice's tribute to virtue. At the very time when court and country demands on the aristocracy so sharply diverged, the inflation of the peerage from 1618 to 1628 injected into that body a large increment of members without much inclination to the country ideal or practice. Their aptitudes, such as they were, seemed to lie in the direction of the court ideal and especially of court practice.

What has been said helps to provide an answer to the third problem posed early in this study: why did members of the upper gentry rather than of the peerage assume the positions of leadership in "the general crisis of the seventeenth century, 1618-1641" in England? There were, of course, perforce or by choice a considerable number of country peers.

Some, however, were disqualified for leadership by religion; they were overt or crypto-Catholics, whose religious attachment opposed them to the partly Puritan and wholly anti-Catholic leadership of the upper gentry. Many of the rest were too insignificant to cut much of a local figure. But worst of all, it may be suspected, most of them were too stupid. Inheritance of title is not a very satisfactory predictor of political talent, certainly not to be compared to ability, energy, and dedication to duty and to acquisition of power. These latter traits, not merely wealth and legal status inherited or granted by court favor, were required of those who worked their way up or held on to their places in the highly competitive, quasi-meritocracies of the counties. Not only were the peers pulled apart by the divergence of expectations between court and country; they were also trapped by the rising demand for competence on the country side, as the need for experience, knowledge, ability, and aptitude for countermaneuver against court policy increased. In this crisis situation, in comparison with the upper country gentry, the peers who cast in with them were deficient in talent, training, experience, and number. In this situation they found their place beside rather than above, as collaborators with rather than leaders of, the disaffected gentry.

So much emerges by refining and slightly altering the focus on data, almost all of which can be found in *The Crisis of the Aristocracy*. But at the very outset of his book, by declining to consider the peers as a corporate body, members of the House of Lords, Stone separates the crisis from the political collapse of the Lords. On purely historical grounds the procedure is hard to justify; it is like putting asunder whom, if not God, at least English public law had long since joined.[45] It was a joining that surely affected the positions of the peers individually as well as collectively between 1559 and 1641, for after all an important element in the prestige and the power of every individual peer was the prestige and power of the corporate body of which he was a member. And in the general crisis that took shape from 1618 on, that corporate body had a lot going against it. Specifically, it ran athwart the statistics and mathematics of the peerage in Parliament. The details of those statistics would require close, almost daily, examination as the crisis moved from one issue to another in Parliament, which after all was where much of the action was or at least where it ended up being. However, a simple and rough computation at an arbitrary date about 1641 makes the gross outlines evident enough. It goes like this:

	150	total peers ca. 1641
	76	majority of peers
minus {	26	bishops } safe for the king
	20	Catholic peers
leaving	30	non-Catholic lay peers required for court majority
i.e.	24%	of total lay peers (124) required for court majority $(30 \div 124 = 24\%)$

It is possible, of course, that the country gentry who led the House of Commons never made so crude a computation. But in parliamentary matters they were anything but stupid men; if they did not make it, it is because of its crudity, not because of their excessive moral sensibility or of defective political awareness and intelligence. Some such calculation clearly preceded the bill in 1641 to exclude bishops from the

45. Stone could well justify it on other grounds: that enough—or fourteen years' work—is enough. I would heartily agree.

upper house. It would be a little surprising if the leading members of the House of Commons did not explicitly or intuitively strike a series of trial balances rather like the one above on issue after issue in the parliaments from 1621 on. For them the House of Lords, like a lady of easy virtue, was often in demand, usually available, but never wholly to be trusted.[46]

A theory that treated the peers in Parliament as an aristocracy holding the balance of the constitution between monarchy (the king) and democracy (the House of Commons) had been propounded in Elizabeth's day.[47] It vanished under the early Stuarts. James I and Charles I were disinclined to regard their own powers in a light so unflatteringly secular and potentially restrictive. And although the Puritan-country political calculators had no theory of their own that would break the deadlock between them and the court, they had no inclination to a theory that awarded to the peers, who sat in Parliament solely by virtue of birth, royal caprice, or flat cash payment, a voice as authoritative as the one the Commons claimed as representatives of the communities of England and held as a result of the superior intelligence of their

46. That politically passive busybody, John Chamberlain, was already counting the votes of the bishops in the Addled Parliament of 1614. There are subsequent intimations of awareness in the House of Commons of the influence of the court "bloc" in the House of Lords, and in crucial matters it was clear that the bishops provided the court with the controlling votes in the upper house in the Short Parliament. C. H. Firth, *The House of Lords during the Civil War* (London: Longmans, Greene, 1910), pp. 36, 48, 66.

47. As late as 1607, with surprising docility, the House of Commons swallowed without protest the Earl of Northampton's view that only the upper house was institutionally qualified to deal with "matters of state" such as foreign affairs. As representatives of purely local interests, he alleged, the House of Commons was institutionally disqualified, regardless of any accidental qualifications of some of its members in such matters. Ibid., pp. 34-35.

leaders. In effect, from the 1620s to 1642 the peerage ran into a kind of situation that recurred in 1827-1832 and 1906-1911; in their corporate capacity they did not appear as a body that did nothing in particular and did it very well, but as a body peculiarly constituted in existing circumstances to do something in particular and do it badly. The addition of this political element to the others that Stone deals with increases the intelligibility of the crisis of the aristocracy.

It also calls attention to one of the most annoying perplexities of the period—the ultimate revival of the prestige of the aristocracy. At the Restoration the peerage regained political effectiveness after a decline and fall lasting four decades or more. The gradual absorption into the pattern of political orthodoxy of the theory of mixed government by King, Lords, and Commons, to which both court and country were inhospitable under the early Stuarts, was a symptom of this revival. This first perplexity is simply a part of a still broader perplexity that has afflicted many historians of the period, a certain uneasiness about the English Revolution when viewed as one of the series of great revolutions in the Western world—the Reformation and the English, American, French, and Russian revolutions. On analysis this uneasiness seems to have two components, one historiographic or mythographic, the other more strictly historical. The historiographic grounds for uneasiness are so well documented as to be scarcely arguable. In the patterns in which whole peoples think of their pasts, 1517, 1776, 1789, and 1917 appear to have an uneradicable place in the collective memory. However historians nowadays or hereafter may evaluate their actual consequences, men very soon afterwards thought of the events of those years as inaugurating a new era, a *novus ordo saeclorum*, and have continued so to think of them to this day. No such thing happened in the English case. For historians today to settle on a common date—1628? 1640? 1649? 1688?—inaugurating the new era in English history would be as hard as to dislodge those other dates—1517, 1776, 1789, 1917—from their time-hallowed places. In at least one clear sense in which the Reformation, the American Revolution, the French Revolution, and the Russian Revolution may be said to have made it, the English Revolution did not make it at all.

The failure of the English people as a whole to enshrine in their hearts the English Revolution of the mid-seventeenth century drove historians who believed it really was a revolution anyhow to an anxious search for plausible grounds for their conviction. Most of the search was conducted during a time span ill-starred in two respects. First, there was little consensus among historians on what to count as a revolution; yet they suffered from the illusion, at once uncomfortable and unwarranted, that the term was useless unless they could discover or define what a revolution "really" was. Since to discern a common essence in the Neolithic Revolution, the Industrial Revolution, the Scientific Revolution, the French Revolution of 1789, and the Revolution of 1830 in the Netherlands requires hallucinatory gifts not granted most historians, the search was on the whole unsuccessful. Second, the search coincided with a growing conviction that to count as a "real" revolution, any lapse of a relatively stable human community into long internecine war involving the disruption, displacement, or alteration of the prime center of accepted authority had to be a social revolution.

Instead of clarifying, this somewhat gratuitous stipulation confused. It committed historians to the view that all major or big or real revolutions were brought about by and in the interest of particular social classes. By means and as a consequence of each such revolution, the victorious revolutionary class wholly or in part achieved its conscious (or semi-conscious) social ends.[48] Its ends always encompassed the increase of its own political and economic power in the community and, as a condition of that increase, the overthrow, subjection, exploitation, and expropriation of other classes. Unfortunately this model makes something less than a perfect fit on any of the revolutions it is supposedly designed for, and on none worse than the English Revolution, on which it hangs in disarray like an ill-designed, ill-cut sack. Historians who have tried to cope with this unhappy situation have not had much luck. The more they work at the problem, the more it appears that the notion that the English Revolution, 1640-1660, was not in the foregoing sense a social revolution has something going for it, and that historians who want it the other way have a good bit going against them.

Nothing else is going as badly against them as the actual outcome of the English Revolution vis-à-vis the aristocracy. From pretty far back that class seemed destined to be overthrown, expropriated, and suppressed—both the immediate and the ultimate victim of the upheaval. Even before the revolution its prestige and social status had grown shaky. The imperatives that governed the decisions and actions of much of the aristocracy had become irrelevant and even repugnant to other social classes, particularly to those a step or two down the social pyramid.[49] Because so many aristocrats ended as

48. Consequences inverse to the intention of the revolutionaries should not count, for example, bureaucratization in Soviet Russia, Bonapartism in nineteenth-century France, or the increased secularization of politics in England after 1660. These may have been in part consequences of what the revolutionaries did; they were not at all what the revolutionaries wanted.

49. For the notion of the fabric of imperatives, see J. H. Hexter, *The Vision of Politics on the Eve of the Reformation: More, Machiavelli, and Seyssel* (London: Allen Lane, 1973), ch. 4.

allies and supporters of the Crown, once the revolution broke out, their property was sequestrated, decimated, and in some instances confiscated outright. The large packet of political authority and power once theirs as members of the House of Lords got whittled down in practice until 1649, when it too was wholly confiscated. Finally, all these changes took place over a relatively short time span at the behest of the leaders of the revolution or with their consent and in pursuit of what they deemed their proper purposes. For historians the trouble with the English Revolution is that none of these changes lasts or leaves an indelible impress on the social order.

What makes the English Revolution suspect as a social revolution is the restoration of the peerage economically, politically, socially, and ideologically after 1660. For this is what happened, and what Stone says happened, for which he will earn less than golden opinions from those whose presuppositions require them to believe otherwise. Since, by the criteria of social revolution proposed above, the peers seemed to be marked out to be the losers, the main thrust of history writing from the 1920s to the 1950s was to force them to play the role in which historians cast them. As it actually happened, the peers, who should have been the victims, were the victors. Some peerage families loyal, but not too loyal, to King Charles indeed suffered both during the Interregnum and after from the cost they incurred in compounding for the return of their estates to their possession before 1660. Other changes—more flexible mortgage arrangements, improvements in the terms of credit, stricter estate settlements— however, improved their situation. Economically the peerage still comprised England's greatest landlords. In a society in which land remained the surest route to political consequence, the peers' collective share of landed income appears to have been greater in 1688 than in 1601.[50] After the Restoration individual peers learned better how to use their wealth for political purposes. The day of connectional and interest politics was dawning, when the management of family parliamentary interests combined with access to a share of crown patronage was the key to power, a key that peers inclined to politics were long to manipulate with great success. The high noon of "the Whig oligarchy" was not far off. The political viability of the peers as individuals was complemented by that of the peerage in its constitutional embodiment in the House of Lords. The reinstitution of that house after its abolition during the Interregnum was complete and integral. It was accompanied by the gradual but almost universal acceptance of the theory of mixed government which conferred on the House of Lords the function of "balancing" the constitution, of preventing it from drifting too far in the direction of "mere monarchy" embodied in the king or "mere democracy" embodied in the House of Commons. Finally, the old social hierarchy of deference and place reestablished itself. Alexander Pope's celebration of the Great Chain of Being in the age of Newton was perhaps less grand than Shakespeare's in the age of Gloriana; nevertheless, it fitted the temper of that later age better. So did the formulation of the peers' claim to their place at the top of the social hierarchy, which was put in civil rather than theological terms. And so in the outcome of the English Revolution, the lordly victims were victors.

At least one victor in the revolution became its victim. The habits of thought associated with it no doubt continued to form the characters of many Englishmen, but at the Re-

50. The worst that can be said for the estimates of Thomas Wilson (1601) and Gregory King (1688) is that they provide no ground for believing otherwise. The estimates are given in app. XII, p. 767.

storation Puritanism had lost its power to define the expectations of the politically effective classes. After 1660 not many Englishmen in positions to exert strong political pressure brought it to bear in the service of the aspirations once evoked by conceptions like the Elect Nation, the Holy Commonwealth, the Rule of the Saints, and the New Jerusalem. The moral climate of politics had undergone an abrupt change, becoming in the process considerably less rigorous. In twenty years of power the Saints had failed and failed and failed again to construct viable foundations for the government of England, and as a major political force Puritanism itself was buried in the rubble of their failures. They had proved unable to rise to the level of their own demands, and so in the interest of a workable civil order, the expectations of their rulers that the Puritans had entertained and taught others to entertain had to be scaled down.[51] One effect of this reduction of expectations was to relieve the peers of some of the impossible demands for austerity of political conduct and dedication to selfless ends that they had failed to meet before 1640. Such an austerity and dedication, unrelated or potentially adverse to their individual and corporate interests, are extremely rare in the members of any group and are scarcely to be dreamed of in a group created by the principles of selection governing the English peerage.

After 1660 the peers were also relieved of the second impossible demand that faced them from the 1620s to the 1640s, a demand for levels and kinds of competence quite beyond their reach, though well within the reach of the combined talents of the upper gentry and great lawyers, the group from

51. The trajectory of expectations could probably be traced with reasonable accuracy by a study of the successive terms of political settlements proposed or deemed acceptable by the various Puritan groups, excepting only small clusters of apocalyptic chiliasts.

which the bulk of the House of Commons was chosen. By the quite intelligible deficiency and default of the peerage, this group had been left to meet and had met the central crisis of the age, the crisis of the constitution. This crisis abated somewhat at the Restoration and yet more at the Revolution of 1688, and with it abated the almost continuous demand for high skill as well as for Puritanical fervor that it had evoked before 1640. Once the upheavals subsided, the House of Lords could get along quite comfortably "with no pretence of intellectual eminence or scholarship sublime." In addition to the powers of adaptation that the peerage displayed, to which Stone does full justice, it was this double lowering of expectation and demand that brought the English aristocracy out of the turbulence of the early seventeenth century and the catastrophes of its middle decades into the quieter waters beyond. The accommodation was after all mutual—an adaptation of the aristocracy to a changing society, but also an adaptation of the demands of that society to what the aristocracy had a capacity to supply.

To say that the English Revolution was not in the sense previously specified a social revolution is not to say that it was trivial. An eruption that kept England in turmoil for twenty years cannot be thus casually written off. Beyond that, it did settle, perhaps more effectively than its surviving leaders thought when the Restoration came, several important political issues that were in doubt as late as 1640. How completely it settled them was not altogether evident until the foolish younger son of the revolution's most eminent victim stumbled into an attempt to alter the terms of settlement. To his loss James II learned how firmly fixed were the boundaries to the authority and power of the king of England.

With respect to the problems that the term "revolution" poses for historical discourse, a contemplation of the result of the crisis of the English aristocracy in the seventeenth century is most instructive. It suggests that the term sometimes may be sensibly applied to upheavals that did not permanently alter the distribution of wealth, the control of the means of production, or the structure of society, and that only modified but did not subvert the prior organization and distribution of political power. In the general upheaval in England between 1640 and 1660, one can discern a religious revolution that first succeeded and then collapsed, the Puritan revolution; a political revolution that succeeded and then collapsed, the republican revolution; and a potential sociopolitical revolution that flared up briefly but did not succeed, the Leveller movement. To deny that those twenty years were an era of revolution would seem to entail an excessive austerity in the use of the term, or to impose gratuitously the rather unreasonable restrictive covenant that only revolutions that were ultimately successful shall count as revolutions, which leaves one with no term to apply to the many revolutions that have not succeeded. It is even more arbitrarily restrictive to apply the term only to those upheavals the consequences of which were permanent drastic alterations in the structure and the functioning of society. And it is an act of desperation to bend and twist the evidence in order tightly to bind such upheavals to major long-run social changes to which at best they were linked casually and tangentially. In the case of the English Revolution, some scholars have engaged in such distortions in order to force that revolution to fit a simplicist model of the overall development of western or world civilization. The motive is intelligible, but the result is rarely commendable.

Equally intelligible but even less commendable is the peculiar psychological quirk that causes some historians to identify their own achievement with the magnitude or success or "importance" in the past of the events and affairs that engage their attention. There is after all no evidence whatever that merely by choosing a "big subject," a historian adds a cubit to his stature. Nor is there evidence that for the understanding of the past the investigation of failure is less rewarding than the exploration of success. The measure of a historian is not the importance in the past of what he chooses to write about, but the importance of what he writes about it, which is a very different thing. Of this the book here so closely scrutinized is the best proof. It may be hard or impossible to evaluate the overall importance in the past of two crises, both of relatively brief duration, in the affairs of some of the 382 men who constituted the English peerage from 1558 to 1641. That a history written about those men seen in the framework of those crises can be important indeed, Lawrence Stone has demonstrated beyond reasonable doubt. He has done so in the most convincing way possible —by writing about them one of the most important historical works of the past quarter century—"a milestone," "a landmark," a monument.

1968

5.

The Historical Method of Christopher Hill

Christopher Hill has published another book, *Change and Continuity in Seventeenth-Century England.* It is a collection of essays that he wrote and addresses that he delivered between 1961 and 1973. During that time Hill also published *The Century of Revolution* (1961), *Society and Puritanism in Pre-Revolutionary England* (1964), *Intellectual Origins of the English Revolution* (1965), *Reformation to Industrial Revolution* (1967), *God's Englishman: Oliver Cromwell and the English Revolution* (1970), *Antichrist in Seventeenth-Century England* (1971), and *The World Turned Upside Down* (1972). Spanning the time in which those other works were written, the essays in *Change and Continuity* naturally reflect Hill's central scholarly interests during that period. They deal with the ethical, political, and social traits of Puritanism, the quality of intellectual life at the English universities under the early Stuarts, the nature of and the changes in science during the seventeenth century in relation to society; the character and sources of radical movements and of radical ideas about politics, economy, society and religion during the Interregnum, the connections among science, religion, and social class.[1]

Therefore, without being a summary of Hill's recent work, *Change and Continuity* does provide us with a representative sample of his primary concerns and of his ways of pursuing them for more than a decade, a sort of microcosm in which one may discern the principal traits of the macrocosm. Before we go chasing that notion any further, however, we had better pay a little closer attention to what we have already said. In summary, what we have said is that in the eleven years between 1961 and 1972 Hill published seven books; that in that span close to 2,500 pages of his work found their way between hard covers. For a scholar it is a simply astounding achievement, an output at the dimensions of which the ordinary historian can only shake his head in awe and wonder.

Hill is not merely prolific; he is also enormously erudite. Taken separately, his productivity and his erudition are monumental; taken together, they are incredible, truly Pelion piled upon Ossa. With respect to his erudition, consider a few examples from his work. Documenting the chapter entitled " 'Reason' and 'Reasonableness,' " a mere twenty-one pages in *Change and Continuity*, are references to forty-seven modern historical works, thirty seventeenth-century pamphlets, twenty-four modern collections of seventeenth-century sources, forty-two seventeenth-century treatises, and twelve miscellaneous items—over one hundred and fifty different

1. Christopher Hill, *Change and Continuity in Seventeenth-Century England* (London: Weidenfels and Nicolson, 1974). Page numbers given in parentheses in the text or the notes refer to this work.

The original publication of this essay in the *TLS* (Oct. 24, 1975) was followed by Hill's reply (Nov. 7, 1975), Hexter's comment on that reply (Nov. 28, 1975), and several letters to the editor from other scholars (Nov. 14, 1975; Dec. 12, 1975; Dec. 19, 1975; Jan. 9, 1976).

works cited, counting only once works cited several times. In " 'Reason' and 'Reasonableness' " the deluge of erudition is a trifle heavier than elsewhere in *Change and Continuity*, seven and one-half works cited for each page of text; but not all that much heavier. In the forty-five-page essay "Puritans and 'The Dark Places of the Land' " the rate drops to a mere six works cited per page of text, drops in effect from a deluge to a downpour. By Hill's own impossible standards these are but mediocre displays of learning. To watch him blasting down the highway of scholarship with pedal pushed to the floor one must turn from *Change and Continuity* to the second section of the first chapter of *Antichrist in Seventeenth-Century England*. There in ten pages of text we encounter no less than 142 different people who between 1529 and 1640 identified the Pope and Popery with the Antichrist. And in six pages of footnotes we find references to the 170 different published works by means of which Hill identified the 142 different people who identified the Pope and Popery with the Antichrist, a world-class record of seventeen different works cited per page. Since *Antichrist in Seventeenth-Century England* is among his most recent works, it appears that time has not withered nor custom staled the infinite variety of his learned curiosity.

Confronted by avalanche upon avalanche of information, citations to literally thousands of different sources, what is one who seeks to evaluate Christopher Hill's historical work to do? He cannot hope to know as many things, have as many bits of information, as Hill has about any major subject to which Hill has given close attention. I doubt that a single scholar who has passed judgment on any considerable work of Hill's has ever read as extensively as he in the subject of their common concern. To get at the "essential Hill" in *Change and Continuity* through the dense cover of his erudition, then, we will have to try sampling, and take a close look at the texture of that erudition when it is set out to display one of his major themes. We need, that is, to pass over some of his excursions down byways, where he is especially susceptible to enthusiastic lapses.[2] We would do well not to base our judgment of a learned and eminent historian on lapses of this sort, short of evidence that his method or his biases or both predisposed him to them.

In the essay "Protestantism and the Rise of Capitalism" that kind of lapse is rare.[3] The essay is relevant to one of Hill's central themes, one of his *idées maîtresses*: the close interlinkages between religious commitment on the one hand and the forms and changes in the economy and society on the other. The specific topic, the link (if any) that binds

2. For example, in the essay "Radical Critics of Cambridge and Oxford in the 1650's" he tries to link Puritanism, described by some of its devotees as "experimental" religion, with modern science, an "experimental" approach to nature (p. 135). Now it is true that some Puritans used the term "experimental" in referring to their approach to the holy, just as in *Opticks* Newton referred to some of his tests as "experiments." But in this context to link Puritanism to modern science through the term "experiment" by means of a coincidence not of sense but of sound is to establish a connection on the treacherous sands of a pun. It treats "experimental" meaning "related to experiment" as synonymous with "experimental" meaning (archaically) "related to experience." A pun, however, cannot establish commonality between "practical experience of the influence of religion on the powers and operations of the soul" (experimental religion) and the series of procedures that Sir Isaac Newton went through to provide empirical foundations for the reasoned theorems of *Opticks* (scientific experiment).

3. The most conspicuous one is the illustration Hill offers of the Roman church's demand for obedience. "If she [the church] shall have defined anything to be black which to our eyes appears to be white . . . we ought in like manner to pronounce it black" (p. 85). But as a precept in St. Ignatius Loyola's *Spiritual Exercises* this total submission was required only of Jesuits during the Counter-Reformation, not of all Catholics at all times, or, indeed, at any time.

capitalism and Protestantism, is at once venerable and lively. It came to the fore long ago as the result of a gross and fairly accurate observation made in the nineteenth century: in the countries that were industrially and, before that, commercially most advanced the Calvinist variant of Protestantism had had a dominant religious role. In the early twentieth century the problem of the relation, if any, between Calvinism and economic precocity evoked two classic studies, Max Weber's *The Protestant Ethic and the Spirit of Capitalism* and R. H. Tawney's *Religion and the Rise of Capitalism*. To these brilliant works serious objections have emerged over the years. The principal ones are (1) that "capitalist" Calvinism attracted Dutch boors and Scottish cotters, Transylvanian and Languedocian petty nobles, and English gentry as well as the mercantile and industrial agents of capitalist development, and (2) that "Protestant teachings on usury, treatment of the poor and so forth" (p. 82), alleged to link the Reformed church to the unlimited rational pursuit of gain, were actually too peripheral in Reformation doctrine to have had the effect ascribed to them.

Hill confronts the latter difficulty head on. He abandons the later views that would require of ordinary sturdy lay Puritans a febrile sensitivity to the nuances of theological discourse. To replace these views he offers a sophisticated revision of the naive pre-Weberian view that found in the Reformation the seeds of freedom and therefore of free enterprise. In Hill's version, the emancipating element in the new theology did not lie on the fringes of Protestant belief; rather it was the central doctrine of that theology: justification by faith alone. The emphasis of that teaching was on the ultimate authority of the heart, and therefore of individual conscience, as against the law-structured constraints externally imposed on Christians by the Roman church. According to Hill, to appeal to the individual conscience is in actual effect to appeal to the source whence its ingredients are drawn. The individual conscience is certain to have its source in its social environment. The social environment provides the individual with the content of his consciousness and the institutional structure within which that consciousness is formed. And a man's conscience is simply the derivative of his consciousness, its superstructural elaboration. The consciences of Calvinist merchants took form in the marketplace, which sanctioned the unremitting pursuit of gain by being the institutional environment structurally embodying that pursuit.

By a happy concatenation Protestant merchants, sure in their faith, were the beneficiaries of an extraordinary Providence, getting richer and richer with God on their side—or so they believed. Or at least so Hill believes they believed. In such circumstances the more Protestant a merchant was the more intense was his trust in individual conscience and the greater his freedom to strive to accumulate. So the Puritan capitalist had the strongest incentives of all to exert himself to the utmost in pursuit of gain, and the clearest conscience in doing so. "It was in fact," says Hill, "the labour of generations of God-fearing Puritans that made England the leading industrial nation in the world—God, as His manner is, helping those who help themselves" (p. 96).

Having thus asserted the intimate connection of Puritanism with the emergence of industrial capitalism, Hill continues:

Through this emphasis on the inner conviction which inspired actions, bourgeois lay society could impose its own standards. "God's children look to the spiritual use of those things which the worldlings use carnally," said Greenham. The actions of the Scribes and Pharisees "were good in themselves, and for others," said Sibbes, "but the end of them was naught, and therefore both they and their works are condemned." "Man may with good con-science," Perkins thought, "desire and seek for goods necessary, whether for nature or for his person, according to the former rules: but he may not desire and seek for goods more than necessary, for if he doth, he sinneth." (The "former rules" include the con-venient provision that "those goods without which a man's estate, condition and dignity . . . cannot be preserved" are necessary.) The preachers attempted to spiritualize what men were doing anyway, by telling them to do it for the right reasons. One may suspect that their congregations paid more attention to the gen-eral permission than to the careful qualifications with which it was hedged around. "They are very hot for the Gospel," said Thomas Adams of such laymen; "they love the Gospel: who but they? Not because they believe it, but because they feel it: the wealth, peace, liberty that ariseth by it." (P. 96)

It seems fair to ask what this paragraph with its combina-tion of general statements and evidential quotations intends. Fair to ask but not easy to answer. It appears to say that by emphasizing conscience in commercial matters Puritan preachers opened the floodgates of individual judgment, and that in a bourgeois society this could only mean that men of commerce and industry would do what would maximize their gains, regardless of any limits that the ministers advo-cated. If we have Hill's intention right, we may reasonably expect of the evidence offered (1) that the preachers cited be Puritans; (2) that they be preaching to "bourgeois lay" congregations; (3) that they be attempting to "spiritualize" the ongoing conduct of their bourgeois auditors, relying on the consciences of the laity as the ultimate controller of their actions; and (4) that for Puritan preachers the appeal to con-science be the preferred alternative to other means of bring-ing Christian teaching to bear on the conduct of their flock in commercial matters as elsewhere. Does the evidence Hill offers meet this minimal standard?

That Richard Greenham, William Perkins and Richard Sibbes were Puritan ministers scarcely allows of doubt. Born twenty years apart in the mid-sixteenth century, they represent three generations of that brotherhood of preachers, physicians of the soul frustrated by Queen Elizabeth's denial of disciplinary power to the congregations, who, forbidden to rule the flesh of Englishmen, bit by bit became directors of the spirit of a large elite among them.

Are the congregations that these preachers addressed bourgeois, so that their words could put merchants and industrialists in good heart for the pursuit of riches, as Hill seems to suggest, by denouncing avarice? Well, it is hard to be certain to what class the words of the ministers were directed. This is so partly because we simply do not know for sure who the audiences for the particular words Hill quotes were. Partly because there is some lack of agreement among English historians as to who was bourgeois and who was not in Elizabethan and early Stuart England. We do know, however, that the actual words Hill cited from Greenham and Perkins are not drawn from sermons at all. We do know that Greenham spent almost his whole life ministering to the wretchedly poor rural parish of Dry Drayton, five miles outside Cambridge. We do know that Perkins preached in Cambridge itself, in the main, one would assume, to the sons of the gentry and the aspirants to holy orders who attended the university. We do know that although Sibbes's pulpit was in London, he did not have a parish. He was preacher at Gray's Inn, and his regular congregation came from that preserve of the gentry, the largest of the Inns of Court. So *if* Greenham and Perkins preached as they wrote, a thing that Professor Haller's discussion of the rhetoric of the spirit might lead us to doubt, and *if* the sons of the gentry at Gray's Inn, and the sons of the gentry and the fledgling clergy at Cambridge, and the farmers of

Dry Drayton were bourgeois, then Greenham, Perkins, and Sibbes were preaching to a bourgeois auditory. And to the extent that they were not, one might make bold to say—not. So much for the second point above.[4]

As to the third, do these Puritan ministers "attempt to spiritualize what men were doing anyway," thus avoiding any painful dislocation of bourgeois consciences? To the contrary. In the work from which Hill quotes, Greenham writes of the benefit of poverty as against the devil's temptation to want more, of the evil of usury among Christians—"an abomination," of "the devil's alchemistry to turn silver into gold," and of "outward things" that "are as a veil to hide God's face from us." In the sermon that Hill quotes, Sibbes points out that a man who walks with God will walk warily in prosperity because he knows its accompanying sins, "pride, insolency, security, hardness of heart." And following the bit of Perkins's treatise that Hill quotes, Perkins goes on to say that "seeking of abundance is a fruit of diffidence [that is, dis-

4. The quotation from Perkins comes from his treatise on cases of conscience, and Greenham's apparently comes from a similar sort of work. For the rhetoric of the spirit, see William Haller, *The Rise of Puritanism* (New York: Columbia University Press, 1938), pp. 128-172.

In his reply to this study Hill argues that in this passage the term "bourgeois lay society" refers not to townsmen but to "gentlemen, impropriators [sic: i.e. "gentlemen-impropriators"?] and yeoman farmers." He remarks that with respect to who was bourgeois and who was not at the relevant time I hold a "very extreme position." Whether my position is extreme or not, it does raise some problems that inhere in ad hoc extensions of the term "bourgeois." That position has been dimly visible since 1948, when it was set forth at a session of the American Historical Association, and clearly visible since 1961, when it was published in *Reappraisals in History*. Whatever its weaknesses, it cut down temporarily on the perplexing eruptions of that historical monster, the "bourgeois of convenience," into historical discourse.

trust] in the providence of God . . . ; seeking abundance is *a hazard to the salvation of the soul.*"[5]

These further quotations from the very works that Hill quotes suggest that his choice of words, both the words of the Puritan ministers and his own, do not quite do justice to the point the ministers were making. They were not trying, as Hill alleges, "to spiritualize what men were doing anyway." On the contrary, they were sharply warning their readers and auditors that a multitude of economic transactions and aspirations entailed spiritual perils. Each time they succumbed to such doings and wantings, men endangered their immortal souls. Indeed how could Greenham, Perkins, and Sibbes have preached otherwise? These expositors and preachers were not far from the pure sources of Calvinist Christianity. They knew that God put men here below to see his will as revealed in scripture done on earth. And they knew that the human instruments of that will, sinful men and their lazy consciences, were weak reeds indeed to support God's work. So they did not "spiritualize what men were doing anyway"; they denounced what men were doing —oppressing and denying charity to the impotent poor, coveting, and striving to accumulate riches without limit. Their aim was neither to trust nor to soothe the conscience of the rich but to inform and purify it.[6]

---

5. *The workes of the Reverend . . . M. Richard Greenham.* Revised . . . by H. H., 5th ed. (1612), pp. 26, 41, 27. William Perkins, *Workes* (1616-1617), II, 125. My italics.

6. In his reply I believe Hill missed my point here. He says he did intend only that "a *by-product* of Puritan preaching was a confidence in one's own conscience which in an increasingly capitalist environment could lead men to break with traditional norms of conduct," and that he "set about proving this by citing as many representative Protestant and Puritan thinkers as [he] could find." He thinks I dismiss the men he cites in the quoted paragraph

Finally, by emphasizing the insufficiency of Puritan teaching and preaching to inhibit the bourgeois pursuit of riches, Hill raises a question: why did the Puritans rely on mere preaching, a weak instrument against the power of the flesh, to instruct men's consciences? To this the answer, I think, is simply and evidently "faute de mieux." At those moments when Puritan ministers glimpsed a chance to impose serious sanctions through presbyterial or congregational discipline on sinners, they grabbed for it, Greenham and Perkins among others late in the sixteenth century, Sibbes's old associates—he died in 1635—in the 1640s, as members of the Westminster Assembly of Divines. At heart they were all new presbyters, the "old priests write large" who were the targets of John Milton's angry invective.

But what of Thomas Adams, whom Hill also quotes? The trouble with Adams is the lack of any persuasive evidence that he was a Puritan at all and the existence of some evidence to suggest that he was not. He had an un-Puritan way of turning to the existing church courts, the "bawdy courts" of Hill's *Society and Puritanism*, as a refuge for the clergy from the plundering of the laity. He was anything but an exemplar of the Puritan style of "plain preaching": into a single sermon he slid no fewer than sixty Latin quotations, maxims, and phrases. Finally, he mainly dedicated his sermons to high royal officers. He presented his complete works to two privy councillors, the Earls of Manchester and Pembroke, shortly after the Puritan-related fracas in the parliament of 1629. That was not, one would think, the moment of utmost ripeness for a Puritan to be dedicating his sermons to

---

"because only one of them preached in London." Actually, as indicated in the text, I dismiss the three because their preaching is specifically antipathetic to a free spirit of capitalist accumulation, and any auditor who believed otherwise was suffering from chronic spiritual deafness.

a couple of eminent courtiers. On examining "Lycanthropy: or the Wolfe Worrying the Lamb," the Adams sermon that Hill quotes, it turns out that just as the lambs are the clergy, the wolves are the laymen. They are only bourgeois laymen, however, if we extend that term to much of the English aristocracy from the king down. For preeminent among the wolves in human form, according to Adams, are the lay holders of impropriated church livings; and in seventeenth-century England holding lay impropriations was a particularly genteel diversion.[7]

So we complete our close scrutiny of one paragraph of "Protestantism and the Rise of Capitalism." It puts in evidence but four quotations from sixteenth- and seventeenth-century sources out of about one hundred citations to such sources in the essay. What it reveals is curious: none of the quotations is quite to the point. What defines capitalism for Hill is "industry, frugality, and accumulation as good in themselves" (p. 311, n. 3). Rather than licensing them, Greenham, Perkins, and Sibbes would have denied goodness to any of those "virtues," unless put to the service of God. They specifically condemned the crucial capitalist virtue, unlimited "accumulation as good in itself." Their unfortunate addiction to Holy Writ prevented Greenham, Perkins, and Sibbes from perceiving that sort of accumulation as anything but covetousness. And what Adams is talking about, lay impropriations, is quite beside the point. And so, perhaps, is Adams himself.

7. Thomas Adams, "Lycanthropy: or the Wolfe Worrying the Lambs," in *The Workes of Thomas Adams* . . . (London: 1629), pp. 379-392. A rather hasty look at the more obvious sources of information on Adams thickens the mystery about his religious position. He appears not to have been linked with the clusters of connected Puritan preachers studied by Haller. His *Workes* were published in 1629, and four years later he fell silent for twenty years. Then, in 1653, apparently without any church living, dependent on charity, he published two last sermons.

That quotations in text should be pertinent and bear exactly on the point about which they purport to be evidence is one of the first things a fledgling historian learns by example, precept, or the infliction of condign punishment by his preceptor. That one of the most eminent historians of our day, a mature scholar, a colossus of erudition, should miss four evidential shots in a row is astonishing. It may be an accident; it is unthinkable that it should be a mere accident. Error on such a scale is not random, it is systematic. To seek and find the defect in method or concept or both that induced such systematic error in this paragraph will be of more use toward understanding the characteristics and limitations of Hill's work than summaries of the dozen essays collected in *Change and Continuity* would be.

Before we embark on the search, however, we need one more bit of evidence ourselves. In the page following the paragraph we have just put under the lens, Hill proceeds in much the same way as he had in that paragraph. Greenham is slightly misconstrued again. Gouge's fierce diatribe against covetousness undergoes some curious moderation. Adams, perhaps a non-Puritan, is presumably caught soothing the consciences of a City congregation; and Joseph Hall, certainly a non-Puritan, is certainly caught applying balm to the consciences of the City fathers. But Hall is scarcely to the point. If he had a fault, it was his irresistible inclination to think and speak well of and, especially, *to* anybody—king, bishops, peers, aldermen—who at any future time might do him good, a habit that in a polarized society was bound to bring him trouble in the end.[8]

From our previous minute sifting we have learned to ex-

8. Hall was a bishop during Lauds's tenure of Canterbury and wrote a defense of the divine right of episcopacy. Hill does not make this point.

pect if not to accept in Hill this degree of deviation from the precise deployment of evidence. Nothing, however, has prepared us for the quotation that follows the one from Joseph Hall: "The Presbyterian preachers, Hobbes noted two generations later, 'did never inveigh against the lucrative vices of men of trade or handicraft'" (p. 97). The quotation dates from 1662, in the peak years of reaction when only the boldest man and one most favorable to the Puritans would have had a good word to say publicly for the Puritan ministers who by then were ejected from their pulpits. It referred to the Puritans of a period from the accession of Elizabeth to 1640, a span some of which Thomas Hobbes, born in 1588, could not have remembered at all and concerning the rest of which all men's memories might have somewhat faded by 1662. Finally and most important, it was applied by Thomas Hobbes. Thomas Hobbes detested Puritan preachers with an unplumbable, implacable execration. He saw them as the fomenters of the Great Rebellion, which he regarded as an utter cataclysm. Any allegation whatever that Thomas Hobbes makes about Puritans has evidential value only for the purpose of documenting his own phobia. Why in the world, then, does Hill quote this tawdry, sneering bit of nonevidence? Why, especially, since even if it were evidence, it would do nothing whatever to support the sensible argument he is making? The argument does not in the least depend on the absurd view that the Puritan ministry winked at lucrative vices. That indeed is one of its greatest merits. It depends on the view that the Protestant, and especially the Puritan, emphasis on conscience liberated English merchants from the external constraints inherent in medieval Catholic canon law and casuistry and in what Hill believes to have been the medieval attitude toward work and mercantile accumulation. Why then . . . ?

What we seek is a common explanation for two phenomena in Hill's historical writing: the somewhat ill-fitting quotations from sources illustrated by the cases of Greenham, Perkins, Sibbes, and Adams; and a wildly irrelevant quotation from a source in the case of Thomas Hobbes. Two traits of Hill's work, I believe, explain these manifestations of a deep historiographic malaise. One is procedural: source-mining; the other is a practice engendered by a set of mind: lumping. Hill is a ruthless source-miner and a compulsive lumper.

What are these two traits? Source-mining is the examination of a corpus of writing solely with a view to discovering what it says on a particular matter narrowly defined—going through the indexes and leafing through the pages of the appropriate works of the sixteenth century, for example, to find what they had to say about the cultivation of asparagus or about spiritual pride. Source-mining is not an unqualified historical vice. Under some circumstances all historians are source-miners, and should be. The investigator of the history of asparagus cultivation and use who looks at and for nothing else but references to asparagus in sixteenth-century volumes is doing the job of swotting up a chapter sensibly enough. For obvious reasons mining out of the sources all explicit references to spiritual pride would be neither a sufficient nor a necessary preparation for composing a study of views on spiritual pride in the sixteenth century. All evidence on the subject would not appear under the rubric, and all evidence that appeared under the rubric would not be as consequential as some that did not. A historian would have to engage in the delicate work of picking and choosing on the basis of some judgment as to the methods and conditions of proof.

My colleague Donald Kagan believes that the most significant line of division among historians is not the one that separates quantifiers from nonquantifiers, comparativists from national historians, Marxists from non-Marxists from anti-Marxists; it is, he says, the one that separates the lumpers from the splitters. Historians who are splitters like to point out divergences, to perceive differences, to draw distinctions. They shrink away from systems of history and from general rules, and carry around in their heads lists of exceptions to almost any rule they are likely to encounter. They do not mind untidiness and accident in the past; they rather like them.

Lumpers do not like accidents; they would prefer to have them vanish. They tend to ascribe apparent accidents not to the untidiness of the past itself but to the untidiness of the record of the past or to the untidiness of mind of splitting historians who are willing to leave the temple of Clio a shambles. Instead of noting differences, lumpers note likenesses; instead of separateness, connection. The lumping historian wants to put the past into boxes, all of it, and not too many boxes at that, and then to tie all the boxes together into one nice shapely bundle. The latter operation turns out to be quite easy, since any practiced lumper will have so selected his boxes in the first place that they will fit together in a seemly way. Hegel, Marx, Spengler, and Toynbee have at least this much in common: each of their systems possesses a large measure of internal coherence. It is the initial step—the packaging of the clutter of evidence about men and their sayings and doings in the past into an appropriately small number of boxes—that causes the trouble.

His treatment of intractible men and angular and resistant events separates the compulsive lumper from the more moderate variety. The latter do what they can to make the data of history behave reasonably one way or another, but they do not do unreasonable things to the data to make it *all* behave that way. The compulsive lumper, on the other hand, somehow gets rid of anything or anyone that will not fit into the foreordained boxes. There are various devices for consigning inconvenient entities to the limbo of nonhistory; but for the present inquiry the relevant device is the depersonalization of people. People, individual persons from Moses to Lenin, are the historical entities most resistant to lumping; but if they cannot be eradicated from the history that is the past, they can at least be shrunk to convenient and, so to speak, fitting size in the history that is about the past.

Christopher Hill's supreme contribution to historical method has been to put source-mining at the service of lumping in such a way as to insure that mere people will never get in the way. Here is his description of his primary methodological postulate: "[Since] I was advancing a thesis . . . I . . . picked out evidence which seemed to support my case."[9] How simple! And what clarity of statement! Even an ordinary historian might be able to arrive at some conclusion that he aimed at by following Hill's method; but Hill can be sure of arriving at any conclusion he aims at. Most historians know some of the published sources and scholarly works on a period or topic; Hill knows all of them for the century of English history between 1560 and 1660 and a good bit of what lies on either side of those time limits. Given his erudition and his predisposition to lumping he is bound to find evidence that *seems* to support his case; after all, he is working

9. Christopher Hill, *Intellectual Origins of the English Revolution* (Oxford: Clarendon Press, 1965), p. vii. Although Hill does not repeat this apologia for his method, it clearly applies to any work of his in which he is "advancing a thesis." My recent methodical explorations of the complete works turned up no considerable writing of his that did not vigorously advance one or more theses.

the biggest mine in the business and not examining the ore too closely.

This same process is precisely what was happening in the source-mining operation we scrutinized so closely a while back. It might be described as a transformation of contexts. The "natural" contexts of the words of Greenham, Perkins, Sibbes, and Adams are the treatises they wrote or the sermons they preached in which those words appeared. By picking them as evidence that seemed to support his case, Hill mined them out of those contexts and lumped them into quite a different one—the emancipation of capitalist acquisitiveness by the evangelical approach to conscience and the heart. The context, that is, not of Greenham, or Perkins, or Sibbes, or Adams; the context, rather, of Christopher Hill. This, of course, would be all right if the two contexts were congruent. Unfortunately, as we have seen, they are not.

Having boldly struck the great blow for methodological freedom inherent in prescribing to himself the selection of only evidence that seems to support his case, Hill appears timidly to regress into a defensive posture. "I hope," he says, "I have suppressed no facts which make against me." But, really, not to worry. He is not in the slightest danger of suppressing facts that make against him. To suppress them he would have to see them and recognize them. One as truly intent as Hill always is on picking out evidence to advance a thesis by source-mining and compulsive lumping never sees problems or difficulties, facts that might make against him. Thesis-advancing imposes on "the facts" a gestalt that prevents Hill from perceiving them as anything but supportive.[10]

10. It is here in his reply to my essay that Hill seems to have most seriously mistaken its point. He believes that I accuse him of "inaccuracy and dishonesty," that I "bring against" him "charges of distortion and cheating." In the present context cheating would involve *conscious* fiddling with the

Consider a few examples. Hill has had dealings with Thomas Adams off and on now for more than two decades. Only a little attention to Adams is enough to make one aware of his oddness. Two or three hours of investigation in the more obvious places confirm the impression that he is a peculiar fellow indeed. But in the years that Hill has had to do with Thomas Adams there is no sign that he has taken note of Adams's peculiarities. Hill does not encounter him as a person but as a sentence here and a sentence there, selected for seeming to support this or that thesis that Hill happens to be advancing. Indeed, given the methodological postulate there is no reason why Hill should have encountered Adams at all. That precept in effect liquidates him, transforms him into a series of discrete quotations, that is, into a nonperson, who naturally cannot speak coherently.[11]

In the quotation from Hobbes examined earlier, Hill illustrates the outreach of his methodological postulate at its

evidence to make it fit one's argument. I do not know of any instance in which Hill appears to have done any such thing, and I greatly doubt that a search would reveal an instance. When I say that given his way of going about dealing with evidence he has no need to cheat, I do not mean that if he did need to cheat he would; I only mean that in the circumstances the question does not and will not arise.

11. Adams appears in Hill's *Economic Problems of the Church* (Oxford: Clarendon Press, 1956) as well as in *A World Turned Upside Down* (New York: Viking Press, 1972). In his reply Hill says that in the paragraph I have quoted from him he cited Adams not as a Puritan minister but as "a contemporary critic who ascribes views to lay Puritans." He further points out that in several works he has indeed attended to people, notably in *Puritanism and Revolution* (London: Mercury Books, 1962), *The World Turned Upside Down*, and *God's Englishman* (New York: Dial Press, 1970), a book about Oliver Cromwell. The point is well made. If there is still something in my point (and I think there is), it requires accounting for this apparently contrary evidence, not merely overlooking it. I shall not attempt that operation here, but simply leave the paragraph as it is as a reminder to others and to me that even the most resolute splitter sometimes lumps.

maximum. What he does with that quotation seems to suggest that any statement whatever on a subject, a statement irrelevant to or even contradictory of the thesis being advanced, can be seen as "evidence which seems to support my case." The advantage of enlisting such a powerful research principle in the work of advancing a thesis is surely apparent. It reduces the tiresome business of classifying one's notes and of reflecting on and ordering one's evidence into a mere matter of reaching into one of the several lumping bags that contain the yield of one's source-mining and of setting down the bits that come out in whatever order they happen to come. The time saved by adopting this accidental style of historical composition can then be invested in further source-mining.

Despite the varied attractions of Hill's historical method, a reviewer whose prepossessions in such matters are conservative, perhaps reactionary, may interpose a doubt. It rises from the effect of amassing evidence that "seems to support a case" on the economy of historical investigation. Such investigation can often be abbreviated by giving some thought in advance to the conditions of proof of a thesis or, perhaps better, a hypothesis. A little reflection, for example, would suggest a fairly rigorous and quick way to test the hypothesis of "Protestantism and the Rise of Capitalism." The hypothesis is that a sense of their own purity of heart, induced by the Protestant emancipation of conscience, liberated the English bourgeoisie to pursue gain without scruple and without limit, since that was the way gain was pursued in the marketplace, which formed their consciences. Such a hypothesis surely suggests that one seek out the writings and utterances of men of the market to find if directly or indirectly they reveal the imputed connection between acquisitiveness and a clear Protestant conscience. Now out of ninety-nine citations in Hill's essay, four are to laymen. Of the four, Fulke Greville was a courtier; Sir Walter Raleigh was not only a courtier but, as a result of royal favor, the holder of a patent of monopoly, that antithesis of gain through industry and frugality; Thomas Hobbes was the client of one Earl of Devonshire and the tutor of his son and grandson, his successors in the earldom; and Oliver Cromwell was—well, Oliver Cromwell (pp. 88, 93, 97, 90).[12] One does not wish to raise doubts about the applicability of the passages Hill quotes to the illumination of the Protestant view of conscience. One may, however, entertain some reservations about Hill's selection of those four men *alone* to represent the views of Protestant "bourgeois lay society." On the face of the evidence the linkage of these four men to the middle class or the "industrious sort of people," the bourgeoisie, seems a bit tenuous, if not wholly illusory. Given the subject of "Protestantism and the Rise of Capitalism," would it not have been well to reinforce what a captious critic might regard as the somewhat flimsy evidential base those four provide with the views of a few merchants, tradesmen, and artisans, at the point where those views bear on the relation of conscience to buying, selling, riches, and work? If the views were appropriate they might give us an even more intimate grasp of the connection between Protestantism and capitalism than Hill affords us by quoting Raleigh's last words before his execution.

It is possible, of course, that in the abundant outpouring of the press between 1530 and 1660, and in the mass of manuscript from that period since printed, not a single English

12. John Milton also appears (p. 88). After some reflection on his background and his career before the 1640s, I decided to put Milton in a footnote rather than in the text where a consideration of the perplexities and ambiguities involved in classifying him socially as a bourgeois, ecclesiastically as a layman, even religiously as a Puritan might engender such bafflement as to hamper the reader in his pursuit of my argument.

Protestant or Puritan merchant, tradesman, or artisan uttered a word from which we could properly infer his views on capitalist economics and activity. But, if this is true, we would like to know it, and if it is not, we would like to know what they did utter. We cannot find out, however, from reading "Protestantism and the Rise of Capitalism," or, so far as I know, from reading any other work by Christopher Hill. Nor can we find out whether Hill found out, or even whether he tried to find out. Of only one thing can we be reasonably sure: within the feeble constraints set by his own methodological postulates Hill could go on forever writing about the relationship between capitalism and Protestantism in England from 1530 to 1660 without for a moment feeling impelled to inquire whether any Protestant capitalist of the time expressed any views relevant to the matter.

And so in "Protestantism and the Rise of Capitalism" things end rather much as they began. They began with Hill's attractive hypothesis to account for the putative link between Protestantism and capitalism. Following his methodological rule, since he was advancing a thesis, Hill picked out evidence that seemed to him to support his case. As a consequence of his compulsive lumping, his source-mining, and his relaxed views on relevance, in the end we still have an attractive hypothesis treading water, as it were, waiting for the solid ground of proof to be shoved under it. And that is not good enough.

Lest the coincidence of Hill's statement on method, his actual method, and its fatal outcome in "Protestantism and the Rise of Capitalism" be assumed to be a wildly freakish and unique accident winkled out by the reviewer with sinister intent, let us briefly examine another essay in *Change and Continuity*, " 'Reason' and 'Reasonableness' " (pp. 103-123). At the outset Hill indicates that the aim of this exercise is to assess changes in thought in seventeenth-century England as reflected in the uses of the terms "reason" and "reasonableness" in those hundred years. Given the lush outpouring of the press in seventeenth-century England and the general modishness of the terms reason and reasonableness, Christopher Hill here found himself a source mine of oceanic dimension. And out of this marvelous miscellaneous treasure trove, he had only to pick out fifteen pages of evidence that seemed to support his case—that the senses in which men in the seventeenth century used the terms reason and reasonableness was significantly related to their position in the socioeconomic structure. It is the professional gambler's dream, the no-lose wager, like being able to place your bet after the results of the race are in. For given Hill's method there was no way that in his source mine he could miss finding fifteen pages of fragments that seemed to support his case, indeed to support almost any case he chose. He stood at that joyous pinnacle of power shared with rulers of totalitarian states and Humpty-Dumpty: words—at least the words reason and reasonableness—meant anything he wanted them to mean. Enjoying the unlimited potency of his method to the full in this essay, Hill cheerfully disregarded his stated intention to focus on the terms reason and reasonableness. The fifteen pages in which he sets out what purports to be the evidence contain ninety-four footnotes. Just about two-fifths of these actually refer to the use of "reason" and "reasonableness" in the seventeenth century; fifty-five concern themselves with other matters that in the nature of his thesis cannot be germane. Perhaps because of this idiosyncrasy in exposition, the reviewer found himself somewhat less powerfully persuaded by " 'Reason' and 'Reasonableness' " than he had been by "Protestantism and the Rise of Capitalism."

Several years ago a social scientist of singularly opaque

and wooden mind chided me condescendingly about the "impressionistic evidence that you historians use." Aside from noting that his intimacy with numeric data might be either the cause or the consequence of an inadequate mastery of his mother tongue, I gave the statement little further thought. If it meant anything, it was an ill-put cliché rooted in ignorance and illusion. Now after a long and almost total immersion in Christopher Hill's historical writing, utter disregard of what the social scientist said seems to me to be less appropriate. That poor strangled soul might have been laboring to say that he was suspicious of the way historians constructed proofs of their hypotheses out of nonquantitative data. One can imagine him reading in Christopher Hill's work and, with his natural eloquence at full voltage, sputtering, "See? That's what I mean. Impressionistic!" Of course that is a very poor way to describe the trouble.

The trouble nevertheless is there. It has nothing to do with the kind of evidence: "impressionistic" or qualitative against "objective" or quantitative, a sadly incompetent taxonomy in any case. It has rather to do with the nature and conditions of historical proof, and with the obligations of historians with respect to the uses of evidence for the purposes of proof. Proof is a very sensitive region historiographically. In matters concerning proof historians probably deploy and need to rely on a larger share of what Michael Polanyi calls "personal knowledge" than do those who work in any other human science. If this is so—and there are good reasons why it should be—then any general or comprehensive historiographic statements about the conditions of proof, about "scientific method," are likely to be even more nearly vacuous than those made in sister disciplines.

Since deficiencies in the provision of proof by a historian often can only be brought home by a critic through a time-consuming process very like that replication of experiment which scientists rarely undertake, each historian lives under an especially heavy obligation to police himself. Far from just looking for evidence that may support his thesis, he needs to look for vulnerabilities in that thesis and to contrive means of testing them. Then, depending on what he finds, he can support the thesis, strengthen its weak points, or modify it to eliminate its weaknesses. He should in effect always be engaged in an inner dialectic, compensating for history's limitations with respect to codified, externalized conditions of proof by being a hard master to his own mind. A historian of great erudition and vivid imagination who fails to do this fails his colleagues, places on them a burden that should have been his. Christopher Hill so fails his colleagues. It is too bad.[13]

1975

13. Readers should be warned that an able and thoughtful historian, Quentin Skinner, has described my essay on Hill as vituperative, intemperate, and unfair (*New York Review of Books*, March 23, 1978, p. 6). The "intemperate" does fit with a friend's characterization of the essay as marred by overkill. As to "vituperative," it does not seem to me the *mot juste*. Harsh, perhaps? Not kind, certainly. What perplexes me is the "unfair," particularly considering the source, Skinner's review of Hill's book on John Milton. My perplexity rises from Skinner's magisterial marshaling of evidence that in the three major points Hill makes about Milton, he concentrates on the proof-texts that might support his position. He is, according to Skinner, correspondingly blind to far more powerful and persuasive evidence, part of which Skinner addresses, that Milton arrived at the positions he took by routes quite other than those Hill alleges he followed. In short, the deficiency that Skinner notes in Hill's way with evidence in the book he reviews is identical with, an exemplary instance of, the deficiency I regard as characteristic of Hill's work, a deficiency that renders it unreliable. This leaves me wondering in what major way I have been unfair to Hill.

PART FOUR

Panoramic Vision

6.

Republic, Virtue, Liberty, and the Political Universe of J.G.A. Pocock

J. G. A. Pocock has written a book called *The Machiavellian Moment*. One would be ill-advised to try to hold one's breath until that moment passes. The book is about 550 pages of text—big, big pages. From one particular angle of Pocock's multiangled vision the Machiavellian moment stretches in an enormous panoramic sweep for twenty-two centuries from Plato to the foothills of European Marxism and American "manifest destiny." In that perspective the book is an account, variable in diversity and detail, of the ways men in the Western tradition have perceived the passing of earthly time and the succession of earthly events—that is, history—and of how they have related it to their lives, fears, and aspirations.

From another point of view, one that seeks to take into consideration the variabilities in density and detail of *The Machiavellian Moment*, Pocock offers in chronological order (1) a sketch of master ideas about politics up to the end of the fifteenth century; (2) a full account of the reorganization of thinking about politics between 1494 and 1530 in Florence, a reorganization that thrusts to the center of at-

tention the problem of the republic of *virtù* and its relation
to other than living political and cosmic notions; (3) a history of the transplantation of Florentine, civic-humanist republicanism with all its unresolved tensions and dilemmas
from cinquecento Italy to England in its mid-seventeenth-
century upheaval; and (4) a description of the transformations of this republican thought in the Anglophone world
from James Harrington in later seventeenth-century England
and the neo-Harringtonians in early eighteenth-century England to Adams, Jefferson, Madison, and their associates in
the remarkable galaxy of talent that assisted in the birth of
the American republic. (By its inordinate length, its multitude of explicit and implicit qualifications, and its conscious
straining to convince the reader at once of the actuality and
of the convolution and complexity of the interrelations that
are its concern, the preceding sentence bears witness to the
force of the Pocockian impress and rhetoric on the mind of
this reviewer, a mind ordinarily tilted toward simplicity, clarity, and triviality rather than complexity, impenetrability,
and depth.)

More generally, *The Machiavellian Moment* is an investigation of the invention, alteration, rejection, restructuring,
and renovation of the paradigms of the Western world in the
realm of its thinking about time, history, and politics. In his
adoption of the notion of paradigms, Pocock draws from the
apparently inexhaustible reservoir of inspiration and stimu-
lation with which, in *The Structure of Scientific Revolutions*,
Thomas Kuhn endowed two decades of American scholars.
Pocock traces the alterations engendered in Florentine political thinking when into the midst of medieval paradigms, all
tending to focus the ultimate human values in eternity and
its apocalyptic prologue, the Florentine humanists thrust the
conception of the *vivere civile* and of the republic of Florence

itself, a particular and temporal society, in which some men believed it possible to realize universal and ultimate human values. At a later stage and in another land, England, Pocock examines a sort of paradigm explosion beginning in 1642 with the "King's Answer to the Nineteen Propositions" and continuing in a Fourth of July paradigm display right up to the Declaration of Independence and on to the Constitution. The centerpiece of this display, says Pocock, was a considerably modified version of the republican Machiavellian moment that had happened in Florence over two centuries before.

Finally, on the strictest construction, the Machiavellian moment happened mainly in the minds of three Florentines —Niccolò Machiavelli, Francesco Guicciardini, and Dino Giannotti—as they turned their experience and learning to a consideration of the mysteries of politics as reflected in the death throes of their native republic. To the Machiavellian moment in this sense Pocock gives his closest attention and longest scrutiny.

These are some of the main ways to catch hold of the Machiavellian moment over the long arc of its passage through history and through Pocock's book. There may be several other ways that I failed to perceive. As one intricate and shrewd argument after another appeared on the pages of Pocock's book, I was so busy trying to figure where each one fit within those dimensions of his political perception which at the moment I believed I had grasped that I had little inclination and less time to look for other dimensions to rack my mind on.

Some scholars have voiced complaints about *The Machiavellian Moment*. Because of their sources the complaints cannot be dismissed out of hand. The reviewer has heard them from half a dozen historians whose areas of scholarly interest are scattered through the time-and-space span of the "Machiavellian moment." Severally, their primary interests were Renaissance Italy, Stuart and Augustan England, and colonial and federal America. In the cluster of complainants are two historians who are among the very best in their respective fields during the past half-century.

One does not have to look hard to discern in *The Machiavellian Moment* traits that a critic, even one not wholly given over to captiousness, might incline to fault. Occasionally one feels that some of Pocock's astounding feats of intellectual prestidigitation are touched with hocus-pocus. Consider, for example, how he treats the argument of Augustine that the affairs of *civitas terrena* had nothing to do with the city of God, man's final abode and first concern. Pocock concludes that Augustine's devaluation of life on earth was insufficient and unsuccessful, that even in Christian commonwealths under grace earthly life seemed to those involved to be more significant than the spinning of Fortune's wheel. Therefore, he adds, "The revival of the Aristotelian doctrine that political association was natural to man logically entailed the reunion of political history with eschatology" (p. 43). By the end of that sentence I have a sense of being had. Did the revival of the Aristotelian doctrine logically entail any such thing? Wasn't the Church itself in its own eyes a *corpus mysticum*, a mystical body politic, one whose history was not secular but sacred, and therefore especially endowed for the management of the *eschaton*, the last days and last things? And was not this one of the reasons why the Church could and did comfortably swallow not only most of Aristotle's metaphysics but also most of his politics? And anyhow, what is the sense of talking about what is "logically entailed"?

After all, *The Machiavellian Moment* is about history, and what happens in history is notoriously not coincident with logical entailment.

A few pages later (p. 49), summarizing what has gone before, Pocock firmly distinguishes between the organization of politics in medieval customary communities, nonparticipatory in character, and its organization in citizens' republics. In doing so he says nothing about the functions of counsel and councillors in pre-Renaissance European monarchies, although the right and duty of the king to seek and get advice in "the arduous affairs of his realm" was an institutionalized political cliché in the Middle Ages. The silence is peculiar because a good bit later in the book we hear that "English humanism developed its civic awareness by projecting the image of the humanist as counselor to his prince" (p. 338). Civic consciousness through counsel to the crown—so what else is new? Newer, that is, than Simon de Montfort? Again the critic may wonder what Pocock is trying to get away with.

Still, he had better not wonder too hard. What the critic knows—and can hardly miss on any page of *The Machiavellian Moment*— is that Pocock is juggling a large number of complicated ideas, ideas of the people he is writing about and ideas of his own. At the same time he is trying to describe the shape of the ideas, and his own method of coping with them, in a way that will give readers a sense of the intricate transformations that have taken place over time in the internal dispositions and relations to each other of the idea clusters that he is juggling. He is so busy keeping the big show going that he scarcely notices if a bit of one idea cluster or another breaks loose and clunks to the ground. Such accidents or oversights are minor and detract only trivially from the great big glorious show that Pocock puts on in *The Machiavellian Moment*. The gaffes quoted (and there are others) are not disingenuous; they are the slips of a most hard-working mind that occasionally overworks itself.

Pocock has a passion for explication that tempts him to draw out ideas connected only tenuously, if at all, to any of his several Machiavellian moments. Consider, for example, his dense, three-page discussion of the divergences and convergences of Plato and Aristotle (pp. 19-22). As ever, the exercise is intelligent—in this instance, particularly clever; but does it have anything at all to do with the next 530 pages? Nothing that I can make out. Again, Pocock speaks of "politics and the *vita activa*" as against "faith and the *vita contemplativa*," and then goes on, "though it has to be kept in mind that contemplation is an activity, and the activity most appropriate to life in the *civitas Dei*" (p. 40). But by whom does it have to be kept in mind? Not by Pocock, evidently. Contemplation of God as an *activity* never comes up again in *The Machiavellian Moment*. Like the excursus on Plato and Aristotle, contemplation as action is a nonstarter. There are others scattered through *The Machiavellian Moment*. Their presence has nothing to do with the sense or substance of Pocock's book; they add nothing to it and detract little from it.[1]

More serious is Pocock's frequent choice of lumbering, crookbacked, mammoth sentences to carry the burden of his argument. For example, to convey the drastic "epistemological and . . . philosophical consequences" of the humanist exaltation of grammar and philology over logic, he writes:

---

1. One of my favorites is on p. 86: "civic *virtus* or *virtù* (the choice between Latin and Volgare could itself be significant) might . . . rise triumphantly above the insecurities of fortune." How it could be significant Pocock does not testify.

The more it was stressed that an author long dead was speaking to us in the present, and the less we made of any structure of timeless universals through which his voice was mediated, the more conscious we must be of communication across time and of the time-space separating him from us; and the more carefully we facilitated this communication by studying the text and the context in which he had spoken or written, the more conscious we must become of the temporal, social, and historical circumstances in which he had expressed his thought and which, in shaping the language and the content of it, had shaped the thought itself. (p. 61)

That sentence pretty well describes the impact on the sense of the past that humanists produced when they investigated what Greeks and Romans had meant to say in ancient times. To try to grasp what the words of the ancients meant when they used them and to those to whom they used them is, as Pocock shows, to perceive that language itself has a historical dimension. But while one could do the job of showing it a lot worse, one could hardly do it more perplexingly than Pocock does in that blockbuster of a sentence. A reader with a quick eye and only a moderate appetite for beating his own brains out on 112-word sentences might skip a bit and look further along for slightly less demanding Pocockian syntax. Since he would not find much of it, he might skip out of *The Machiavellian Moment* altogether. And that would be too bad, because *The Machiavellian Moment* is a magnificent historical work, which more than repays the effort it exacts.

Though some of that effort may appear to be inflicted gratuitously, most of it is indispensable. The set of ideas, the situations in which men had them, and the shadings of the meanings of the words men used to express them provide the structure of *The Machiavellian Moment*. As Pocock frequently says, the facts, situations, and shadings are themselves complex and stand in complex interrelation with each other.

And he is not an author who shirks the unpacking of any complexity or the exploration of any interrelation, however intricately tangled.

Rather, he is a scholar with an extraordinarily informed, agile, and fertile mind. He displays his agility of mind by remarkable feats of linking the pieces of information he controls. He displays his fertility of mind by providing firmly articulated intellectual structures into which the linked materials fit; in the terms I have used elsewhere (chapter 5) he is a lumper. Moreover, he displays both the fertility and the agility of his mind by keeping the movement of structured information through his system orderly by a pattern of considered and refined distinctions. Those distinctions prevent his elaborate structuring of the relations of ideas from becoming a maze enveloped in a fog; if one pays close attention to the distinctions one can move through Pocock's exposition not quickly but at least sure-footedly. Indeed, unless one is ready to consider the book as it considers its subject, painstakingly and systematically, one will not even be able to spot most of its brilliance or to have more than a misty perception of the rest.

This need for painstaking reading brings us back to the main complaint that scholars have made about Pocock's book. Most often and most emphatically they complain that *The Machiavellian Moment* is an extremely difficult book. And they are right; it is an extremely difficult book. Yet though true, the complaint may not be justified. It is justified only if the difficulty of the book is largely gratuitous. As we have seen, once in a while Pocock does treat his readers to an allusion that is probably intelligible only to the rather small class of academic sons of antipodean professors of classics. And once in a while he plunges into a thicket of distinctions, and the reader who follows him and sees where he has gotten for his pains may incline to ask, "Was this trip necessary?" Such allusions and excursions, however, do not account for the mass of complaint; what accounts for it is that most pages of *The Machiavellian Moment* lay out several layers of intricate argument internally, while externally they carry references back to elaborate lines of reasoning strenuously pursued since the early pages of the book and forward to theses that may not fully emerge for the next hundred pages. Yet there is no way one can stick one's thumbs into such a confection and pull out a plum or two and still get the good of the whole pie. It is not only for the length of *The Machiavellian Moment* that—as Pocock says—"the complexity of its theme stands as a justification"; that complexity also justifies the density of thought on every page of the book. At a certain risk one can skip considerable sections of *The Machiavellian Moment*. It is risky because one cannot be quite sure whether a section is going to be central to a subsequent argument. Several pages of exposition on Aristotle that I had skipped turned out to be essential; and the initial skipping ended by costing me rather than saving me time. Actually, one can skip the sections on Calvalcanti and Contarini at the small expense of not grasping two subsequent back-references, but the saving is only 15 pages, a 3-percent drop in a 550-page bucket.

Although with considerable risk one can skip a few pages of *The Machiavellian Moment*, one cannot skim a single page. The Pocockian prose style with its metaphorical twists, its syntactical turns, its sometimes perplexing allusions, its involutions, convolutions, and intricacies is the ultimate disincentive to skimming. I do think that Pocock's peculiar rhetoric serves a purpose—whether it serves his conscious purpose or not is hard to say. There is no way to understand the interlaced structures and processes of argument that constitute *The Machiavellian Moment* except by giving them one's whole attention. You do not gently glide from full stop to full stop; you swink and sweat and pull yourself along. By the time you have struggled through a Pocockian sentence, you know what it says, what it has to do with what Pocock has said recently, and—sort of—how it fits with what he said a couple of hundred pages back. In short, the difficulties a reader encounters in *The Machiavellian Moment* are not usually the consequence of obscurity, much less of obscurantism, on the author's part. They are not in the author's mind but mainly out there in the past. Pocock tells a most complex story about complex phenomena in all their complexity. It is hard to follow, though not all that hard, if one keeps one's mind on it; but it is impossible to follow if one lets one's mind stray. It is not a book for the reader who seeks to pick up a few names and ideas for purposes of academic chit-chat or to earn intellectual brownie points. *The Machiavellian Moment* more than adequately rewards all the effort of mind that it demands; it demands a major effort and gives a major reward.

The difficulty of reading and the feasibility of grasping *The Machiavellian Moment* are both increased by the conceptual apparatus Pocock uses to provide markers of continuity and of change in men's perceptions of politics and time as his story moves through three main historical epochs: fifteenth- and early sixteenth-century Florence, England from the mid-seventeenth to the mid-eighteenth century, and the continental colonies of Britain that became the United States in the late eighteenth and early nineteenth centuries, with a prelude on the Classical-Christian era before the fifteenth century. As a device for coming to grips with this apparatus let us turn to the excellent index that Mrs. Pocock made for

The Machiavellian Moment. The first thing one notices as one glances through it is the predominance of entries under general subjects—apocalypse, experience, fortune, tradition, and so on.[2] As one attends more closely to the lengthier index entries, suggestive patterns emerge. For example, (1) although some of those entries occur frequently in present-day structured discussions of politics—democracy, republic, equality, experience, society, (2) still, a good many surely do not —apocalypse, aristocracy, custom, God, grace, millennium, monarch, virtue; (3) but scarcely a single political term frequently indexed (only "personality," perhaps) is of recent coinage or recently introduced into the common language of political discourse;[3] and (4) with the overwhelming bulk of the recurrent terms men writing about politics between the sixteenth and eighteenth centuries would have been quite at home.

These patterns reflect a significant trait of Pocock's discourse and of the method it expresses. By and large, in leading his readers into the minds of the past, he does not try to translate the political terminologies men once used into the

2. In "quantifying" the language of *The Machiavellian Moment*, my unit of counting is the line of index entry. I preferred it to the occurrence of the individual terms in text (because every occurrence is not indexed) and to the page entry in the index. Since some of the page entries for a given term mark brief references to it, others small essays on it, merely counting such entries would obscure the actuality of imprecision with the appearance of precision. I chose an imprecise unit of counting that at least corresponds to the imprecision of what the count represents. This does not mean that the results of this line-counting are insignificant. The forty lines that the index devotes to "corruption" and the forty-six to "republic" as against the three lines of entries on "hierarchy" and the zero on "oppression," "rebellion," and "obedience" tell us a good deal about the foci of concern of the book.

3. According to the OED, "personality" in the sense in which Pocock uses it appears in the late eighteenth century.

ones with which his late twentieth-century readers are familiar. Quite the other way about. He starts by setting out what for his purposes are the key conceptions in political thought before the sixteenth century, and then he relates each new or modified conception that appears subsequently to those earlier terms. For example, Pocock does not translate the "manifest destiny" of early nineteenth-century America into the "imperialism" of the twentieth century but, rather, relates it to the "millennium" and "apocalypse" of the sixteenth and seventeenth. So in a sense Pocock's first and perhaps heaviest demand on his readers is that they master a new vocabulary made up of a small but highly mutable set of terms. Readers can test their mastery of this vocabulary only by trying to make sense of *The Machiavellian Moment* with it. With Pocock's way in the patterning of vocabulary made explicit from the evidence of the index to *The Machiavellian Moment,* we can sort out his preoccupation with four matters—language, models, paradigms, and time.[4]

1. *Language.* The intellectual genealogy of Pocock's longstanding preoccupation with what he calls language would be interesting to trace. Since historians have come to share that preoccupation,[5] though for different reasons, we can

4. "Models" and "paradigms" might seem to be exceptions to the third pattern described above. Pocock certainly uses them in a sense they have borne for less than thirty years. They are not political terms, however, but generic terms of intellectual discourse. Nor do these terms appear at all in the index to *The Machiavellian Moment,* perhaps an indication that Pocock shares my view of their functions.

5. The reviewer, for example, shares Pocock's historical preoccupation with language even to the point of a special concern with its place in the investigation of political ideas, and, all unaware of the fact, shared it as early as the early 1950s. See J. G. A. Pocock, *The Ancient Constitution and Feudal Law* (Cambridge: Cambridge University Press, 1957); and "Languages and Their Implications," in J. G. A. Pocock, *Politics, Language and*

here skip to a matter of substance: what does Pocock mean by "language" in *The Machiavellian Moment?* One might say that in the sense in which Pocock uses the term, "language" was born when the relatively static words "terminology" and "vocabulary" caught up with the dynamism implicit in the arrangement of the *Oxford English Dictionary.* Words and clusters of words change in meaning over time, and the character of the change becomes visible only upon a close examination of the contexts in which particular words occur. "Democracy" and "aristocracy," for example, have drastically different resonances in the seventeenth century than in the twentieth, and even point to substantially divergent actualities. In a historical sense the "language of politics" is the language (vocabulary and syntax) that at a given "moment" (a moment can last from two to two thousand years) men use to voice their perception of political life. In one of its dimensions, Pocock remarked some years ago, the study of political thought involves "the systematic exploration of political texts in quest of answers to such questions as 'what was he saying?', 'what language was he saying it with?', and 'what was he talking about?'" Directly the second question, inferentially the other two, can be answered only if one has grasped not merely the orthographic surface of the key political words used during a given time span, but also, and in their full range of nuances, all the meanings, overtones, un-

---

Time (New York: Atheneum, 1971), pp. 3-41; J. H. Hexter, *"Il Principe* and *lo Stato,"* (written in 1953-1954) *Studies in the Renaissance* 4 (1957): 113-138, now included in J. H. Hexter, *The Vision of Politics on the Eve of the Reformation* (New York: Basic Books, 1972), and "Retrospect and Historical Prospect," in J. H. Hexter, *Reappraisals in History* (London: Longmans, 1961), esp. pp. 202-210. I know of no evidence that Pocock and I came under any shared influence in the 1950s other than a common sense, accessible to everybody in the craft, of the impropriety of anachronism.

dertones, and moral resonances those words had in the contexts in which they were used for the men who used them.[6]

This is what it is to know the language of politics during a particular "moment." And this accounts for the fact that the words Pocock recurs to most often are words that men who wrote about politics in early modern times would have been familiar with and that many of them would have used often. That they did use them is evident on a glance at the index. It reveals the scatter of the vocabulary of the language of politics that Pocock is describing. That vocabulary recurs throughout the book and throughout the writings of the men that the book tells about from Machiavelli to John Adams. It is this recurrent use of the same words in similar though modified senses that entitles Pocock to a Machiavellian moment enduring for about 375 pages and 275 years.[7] To know the political language during a time span, then, is to know what men in that span perceived particular political utterances to mean. In one of its dimensions *The Machiavellian Moment* seeks to familiarize its readers sufficiently with the republican language of Machiavelli, Guicciardini, Giannotti, Harrington, "Cato," Bolingbroke, Thomas Jefferson, and John Adams that they can understand what each was saying and in what respects it was like, in what respects different from what the others had said before.

2. *Models.* Pocock starts his book with a section called "Particularity and Time," the first two subsections of which schematically present a model of the structures of political thought that Florentine civic humanist writers of the quat-

---

6. Pocock, "Languages and Their Implications," pp. 37-38.
7. Through Parts II and III of *The Machiavellian Moment* and from the collapse of the Florentine republic in 1512 to the American Constitutional Convention in 1787.

trocento took off from. The model consists of "a system of hypotheses which serves to explain the significant relationships among the concepts"—those key concepts, *experience, custom, usage, prudence, providence, fortune, virtue,* by means of which men in the later Middle Ages evaded confrontation with the succession of events in time that we call history and therefore avoided the need to make sense of it.[8] The shifts in the language of politics that Pocock concerns himself with make their mark on the mass of index entries under the seven terms listed above, the terms that were, so to speak, lying in wait for the Machiavellian moment. Some of those terms and others that were the common material of medieval political discourse tend to fade out in the era of Italian civic humanism; some resound in the Florentine political vocabulary in the early 1500s and dimly in England a century and a half later. One of them—*virtus-virtù-virtue*—swells through *The Machiavellian Moment* from beginning to end. It is the political word that occurs most often throughout, and its modulations in meaning make it the most sensitive indicator of the character and direction of the shifts in the language of politics that Pocock investigates. Under the impact of the multiple modifications in meaning of such key terms, the medieval model itself was transformed.

3. *Paradigms.* When words such as experience, custom, usage, and prudence are linked together in particular ways and linked as well to other words about politics, so that they form a structure of more or less coherent, compatible, and widely accepted propositions, they constitute what Pocock

8. The definition of a model set in quotation marks in the text is a modification and conflation of the definitions given in the *Dictionary of Behavioral Science,* ed. B. B. Wolman (New York: Van Nostrand, 1973), s.v. "model (4)" and "model, schematic." It seems fairly to describe what Pocock means when he writes about "models."

calls paradigms.[9] A political paradigm, says Pocock, is "a conceptual constellation performing a diversity of authoritative functions in the political speech of a society." The notion of a paradigm as a cluster of related ideas and assumptions shared by the members of a community of knowledge and learning over a determinable time span had its origins in Thomas Kuhn's *The Structure of Scientific Revolutions*. An account that will explain and render intelligible the *succès fou* that the notion of paradigm so rapidly attained in recent decades—a conception around which workers in one field of intellectual endeavor after another found they could organize apparently disparate aspects of their inquiry—will someday make a major chapter in the history of American thought. Kuhn himself may entertain some doubts as to the relevance to his initial conception of some perceptions of the meaning of "paradigm" and of some uses of the term, including Pocock's. Be that as it may, Pocock appears to have a pretty good notion of what he has in mind when he uses the term. He uses it pretty consistently to point to language structures that perform a like function in the politics of different societies: the function of summarizing a commonly held view about politics and expressing it in such a way as to license some forms of political behavior and belief and to inhibit others, to encourage reflection and even action on political matters to flow in one set of directions rather than in others.

9. Unfortunately, the otherwise excellent index to *The Machiavellian Moment* has no entry for "paradigm" or "model," so only a reviewer who had the time to index those two terms himself (or the foresight to have done so from the outset) would be able to say precisely in what sense or senses Pocock uses them. I can only hope that I have an adequate grasp of the meaning patterns that "paradigm" and "model" acquire in Pocock's use of them, and of the weight he puts on them in his argument.

Pocock illustrates the impact of paradigmatic structure in politics on what societies will consider and accept, what they will avoid or reject, and what they will not see at all, through the paradigm sets by means of which, he says, medieval man dealt with time and the passage of time. The central paradigm set in medieval thought focused on the ultimate value of the eternal and the universal. It directly devalued the temporal, the stream of events in time on earth. As medieval minds perceived it, that stream tumbles from a meaningless past through a meaningless present toward a meaningless future, mere sound and fury signifying nothing. Into this muddle of time, God's redeeming grace intervenes from eternity. Grace intervenes both sporadically in special providences and ordinarily in the eternal institutions God gave to man —the Church and the Empire. But on earth things have meaning, make sense, only by virtue of their relation to the eternal and universal, not by virtue of their temporal and spatial relationships, that is, their contingent historical relationships to each other. Given the perspective provided by the medieval paradigm, History, the daughter of Time, is as idiotic, as senseless as her father.

Since, however, areas of discernible order do exist in human affairs, a second set or subset of medieval paradigms developed to take account of such order here below. The subset divided events into those that repeated past events or were readily assimilable to them and those that did not and were not. In dealing with the former, the proper rules were provided by experience, especially as recorded in those treasuries of experience, the customs of the land, and guarded by the judges learned in the law, which was itself the crystallization of custom. In this orderly region of politics, the ruler, whether one or many, did not know or decide anything but merely administered the judgments of those who by long experience did know. He enforced what the judges declared to be the law. At the other extreme lay events—civil turmoil, foreign war—for which precedent was so slight, dim, and ambiguous, and chance was so clearly in the saddle, that there were no rules to go by. In these matters rulers actually ruled, but paradoxically and perforce they did so without rules. Of law, which was immemorial if not eternal, there was a science, a mode of knowing; of warring there was only a craft, a mystery, at once temporal and irrational, left by God's ordinance in the hands of those whom He ordained should have it. So law and policy, two major ingredients of politics, were recognized in this paradigm but denied a true historical existence, that is, an intelligible role in the intelligible flow of events. Law as custom has no true history because it is immemorial and essentially changeless; policy can have no history, because history requires the presence of some sort of discernible and intelligible order in its object, but in the paradigm policy appears as random, ruleless, orderless.

Christianity also provided medieval men with a political paradigm that implied a devaluation of time and history. By conquering Rome, Christianity conquered a society in which civic values and a sense of civic obligation, however attenuated, survived. Christianized Romans still recognized that good service in earthly office was a kind of virtue. They also recognized, however, that such service, though virtuous, distracted them from the higher virtue—contemplation of the heavenly city—and subjected them to Fortuna, the goddess of the random chance of events in time. Bound to fortune's wheel, men moved up to worldly greatness and down from it under circumstances wholly beyond their control. Yet that is not the whole story. In truly Christian perspective, what men without faith see as fortune, the random-chanciness of the here-below, is actually Providence, the will of God working in an instant yet eternal now, the *nunc stans*. That will appears to men as senseless fortune only because to men trapped in the illusions of this life, the way of God is inscrutable, an ultimate reality with which they can come to terms not by reason or experience but only through faith.

The procession of events in time has no goal in time, and therefore earthly time and history have no meaning or end of their own. Still, that procession does have a goal on earth, the second coming of Christ and the end of days; and prophets may still scan the procession, as prophets did of old, for signs and intimations of millennium and apocalypse, signs the correct reading of which is at once the proof and the seal of their prophetic mission. Yet though the signs are *in* the earthly city they are not *about* it, not about secular history, but only signals of the coming ultimate event in sacred history, the Day of Judgment, which will mark the destruction of the earthly city and with it the destruction of time and the end of history.

Thus, with Pocock's help, we can begin to grasp the profound ahistoricity of the medieval mind by spelling out the paradigms that were the ground and foundations out of which medieval thought grew. We have just seen by means of a simplified presentation or model that, given the political language medieval men used, they saw politics within a framework of political paradigms or acceptances and assumptions that directed their attention away from earthly time and history by denying those concepts meaning. Our minds are also now open to understanding how complicated it would be for a political paradigm that made much of time and history to find a place for itself within the bounds of the medieval paradigm system. We can see, too, how, in the course of developing a language of politics to explore the possibilities of such a history-and-time-centered paradigm, a society—unconsciously or consciously—might jostle, alter, or destroy the medieval paradigms that were partly or wholly incompatible with a consciousness attuned to history. The emergence of a time-and-history-centered paradigm might then be envisioned as a first but major step in a complex and elaborate process of paradigm transformation. And the process itself, which actually happened, may be described, with a more precise meaning than historians are wont to indulge in in such matters, as a transit from medieval to modern.

To tracing precisely such a transformation Pocock devotes the last 500 pages of his 550-page book. In different parts of the European world between the middle of the fifteenth and the late eighteenth century, Western men's vision of politics shifted from one in which the values of stability or immobility, monarchy, authority, eternity, hierarchy, and universality stood as the core of politics to one in which all these values had become peripheral or adversary. At the end of the period they had been replaced at the core by republicanism, secularism, progress, patriotism, equality, liberty, and utopia. By that time, of the language of medieval politics only a few words—reason and virtue and experience, for example—had survived. Some of the surviving words had lost connection with each other. And they survived in a political language that one way or another took time and history not trivially but seriously.

The firm orientation of Western thought toward the fixed and the eternal was shaken in the fifteenth century in Italy in the city of Florence. Early in that century despotic rulers of other Italian states subjected the liberty of Florence to severe external threats. Florentine humanists of the early quattrocento were steeped in Roman history of the republican era as against the age of the imperial Caesars. The threats from outside made them patriotically conscious of their city's institutions, of the parallel republicanism of Florence and Rome. In declamatory pieces that frequently took the form of praise of the active above the contemplative life, these humanists declared that above all things on earth free service to one's city ennobled human life—indeed, that the highest mode of existence for man here below was not ascetic withdrawal but citizenship, not future citizenship in Augustine's eternal City of God but present citizenship in quattrocento Florence.

The succeeding generations accepted and had to learn to deal with their predecessors' commitment to the values of political life. To those Florentines who grew up around the turn of the sixteenth century the susceptibility of their own republic to the winds of chance, accident, and fortune, to time and the tides of history, was a part of their personal experience, interspersed with the daily round of their lives. Their native city, their *patria*, had stumbled from crisis to crisis. By the 1520s, they had seen the overthrow of the Medicis in 1494, the brief but stirring years of apocalyptic republicanism under the influence of Savonarola, the beginning of barbarian—first French, then Spanish—domination in Italy; the collapse both of the Savonarolan regime and, in 1512, of the republican order that succeeded it; the restoration of Medici domination with foreign aid; and finally, the control of the republic not by Medici near at hand but from Rome, by members of the family, Leo X and Clement VII, who occupied the papal throne between 1513 and 1534.[10] How at the same time to actualize the potentiality of civic life in Florence and to organize the republic to survive amid the chaotic rush of dangers, chances, and accidents that were its

10. There was an interregnum, so to speak, between Leo's death in 1521 and Clement's accession in 1523.

political milieu in the early sixteenth century became a central preoccupation of several extremely bright Florentines whose political perceptions were formed during those decades—Francesco Guicciardini, Dino Giannotti, and above all, Niccolò Machiavelli. To the republican thought of these three men Pocock devotes the longest part of *The Machiavellian Moment.*

To the penetrating political inquiries that they pursued, these men brought certain common equipment. In the first place they brought a knowledge, common to all educated men of Renaissance Florence, of the literature and history of ancient Rome. They also brought an assumption common among humanists, though not always explicit, that an active life, a life spent in coping with the contingencies and uncertainties with which events confronted men in political societies, was superior to a contemplative life spent in reflection on the eternal verities. That mind-leap beyond the medieval paradigms gave the Florentine thinkers a fresh line of access to the enormous and worldly riches of Aristotle's *Politics.* They explored a vein of the ore-laden Aristotelian mass that medieval men had not discovered because, according to Pocock, their gestalt, their political paradigms, could make no sense of it. What the intense preoccupation of the Florentine humanists with the affairs of their city enabled them to come to grips with in Aristotle was his assertion that man was a *zöon politikon,* a political animal in that his *telos,* his end, the purpose and fulfillment of his being, could be realized only within the *polis,* the political society, the republic. The only complete human being was the citizen. The republic was universal in that within it and only within it all human values were potentially present and realizable. The republic, however, was also and all too evidently temporal, bound to time, coming into being in time, continuing subject to the accidents of time, and under the impact of chance ceasing to be in time. It was enmeshed in history.

Guicciardini, Giannotti, and Machiavelli found in Aristotle a system for classifying political systems by their number of rulers—the One, the Few, or the Many—and a criterion for judging actual governors—good if they ruled for the good of all, evil if they ruled only for themselves. Finally, they found in his *Politics* the idea that in the best government power would be divided among the One, the Few, and the Many. All would participate in ruling and being ruled, all giving to the polity the good they were capable of offering and receiving the good they were capable of using. In a good or virtuous republic, according to Aristotle, the good or virtue of all was maximized for each and for all.

Before the minds' eyes of the Florentines—besides the theories of a Greek philosopher who had been dead almost two millennia and the image of Roman civilization that had vanished more than fifteen hundred years earlier—was the actuality of Venice, or at least a myth about the actual Venice. The actuality was that Venice was a republic with little faction and no army of its own, and that it had flourished for centuries on its lagoons, free of serious internal disruption and secure against the designs of enemies. The myths of Venice were two in number. One was that its political order had existed unchanged from time immemorial, so that it was the oldest, the most stable, and the most durable of all republics —as it officially called itself and was called, *La Serenissima*. The other myth was that the evident stability of Venice, its effective resistance to change, chance, and fortune, was the result of its mixed and balanced constitution. It appeared to some Florentine observers that the Venetian Doge, Senate, and Consiglio Maggiore achieved just that initial balancing of the One, the Few, and the Many that Aristotle and Polybius had perceived as the precondition of a good political order and therefore of a good or virtuous life for man. In any case, no Florentine in the sixteenth century could write about republics without cocking an eye at Venice.

The emergence of Florentine civic consciousness and the catastrophic political experiences of their city after the expulsion of the Medici in 1494 confronted Guicciardini, Giannotti, and Machiavelli with the identical primary questions: on what conditions, if any, can the Florentine republic be saved? More generally, what are the conditions under which a republican regime—or any regime—can survive, given the novel situations and contingencies, usually adverse, that time and history impose? How can a republic save itself from would-be despots within and from enemies without?

According to Pocock, the principal building blocks that the three Florentine thinkers had at hand for constructing answers to such questions were the items we have already mentioned—the paradigms of medieval thought, knowledge of Rome and its republican glory, the Aristotelian corpus of political ideas, and the actuality and myth of Venice. As Pocock's account indicates, Guicciardini, Giannotti, and Machiavelli shaped these elements in different ways to provide divergent answers to the acute questions that Florence's political crisis raised. Yet the general similarities underlying their answers are as consequential as the specific differences among them. All three gave their answers on two Aristotelian assumptions: (1) that the only political order worth saving is one in which a body of citizens participates in ruling— a republic; (2) that the character of the society depends on how office and authority—in effect public power—are distributed and how the social orders—the One, the Few, and the Many, or the Prince, the Elite, and the People—are politically rewarded. Moreover, all three considered that the maximizing of virtue in the citizen body is the ultimate test of a republican order. Conversely, the perpetuation of a free republic demands virtue of its citizens; civic virtue is indispensable for its survival, so virtue is at once the material and final cause of the republic. And last, although the three writers differed in the details of their characterization of republican virtue, they all imparted to it a strong ascetic quality. In the end, republican virtue, like Christian virtue, insists that the way to self-fulfillment lies through self-denial, that self-indulgence of any kind is incompatible with civic virtue, and that self-restraint is a first ingredient of such virtue. With their common equipment—the medieval paradigms, the Florentine experience, the humanist's education in Roman antiquity, and the Aristotelian politics of participatory republicanism—all three writers had to face the fragility of the republic. It was the only order in which man, the zöon politikon, could fulfill his potentiality, but its survival was always threatened by fortune, the flux of things in time. History was the enemy of human fulfillment in a civic order.

That, at least, was the way that Guicciardini and Giannotti saw things. The former an advocate of the elite state, the latter of the popular, both aimed to provide Florence with a republican constitution that would achieve Aristotelian ends: a static republic, maintained by a balance among the One, the Few, and the Many, a republic not living and moving with history but escaping it, a changeless bulwark of order and a refuge of excellence in a sea of change, chance, and fortune. For them, the republic of civic virtue was in history but not of it. Machiavelli alone, Pocock believes, burst out of the Aristotelian shell. He did it by turning to history instead of away from it, by building the new into his structure of ideas rather than building his ideas as a wall against innovation.

The new—that is, the dynamic and historical as against the static—says Pocock, stands at the very center of Machiavelli's most famous or notorious work, *Il Principe*. For that book is precisely about new princes, men who have shaken the order of things and for good or ill changed their world, innovated, made history by getting hold of a state that they did not inherit. Such men have truly cracked the cake of custom; their power is outside the law, illegitimate; and their problem is how to hold what they have one way or another— but not legally or legitimately—acquired. That Machiavelli believed that there was *anything* to say on this subject was one of the most startling originalities of that startlingly original man. It was original because it suggested that for some men history need not be the domain of sheer contingency, that virtue lay not in bearing the tricks of time but in mastering and doing them, that sometimes fortune itself might be conquered and controlled. From one angle of vision, *Il Principe* is a book that tells the political innovator, the destroyer of order, how to get away with it, how to establish a new political structure for his own benefit. In the *Discorsi*, Machiavelli turns from innovators, new princes, to republics. He asks the very same questions about them: How can they win a place in the world? How can they hold it? Instead of following Guicciardini's course of arguing that the way to save a republic is to barricade and strengthen it against the onslaught of history, Machiavelli proposes that the republic enter the stream of history and dominate it by dominating the republic's enemies. Its dynamic goal prescribes its internal arrangements; a conquering republic must have the means of conquest, and the means of conquest are disciplined, fierce, hard soldiers. Such soldiers ready in great enough number to fight and die for the republic can only be drawn from a large body of fierce, disciplined, hard citizens with a stake in the country. A state that breeds such citizens is a popular republic, but it cannot be a peaceful one. Machiavelli, like Guicciardini and Giannotti, starts with an Aristotelian model, a participatory republic with office and authority divided among the One, the Few, and the Many. He manipulates the model, however, with a view to showing how to establish not a tranquil, inactive commonwealth but a dynamic, active one. His ideal state is not the most serene republic, modern Venice, but the most brawling, bellicose one, ancient Rome.

Rome, Pocock points out, is the "new prince" among republics, ready when it can to attack and destroy all other states, republican or not. And the virtue of Rome is the virtue of the new prince: it is military valor, audacity, youthful readiness to seize fortune as soon as the main chance, the historical chance, comes, and to squeeze out of her by will and strength whatever it can. The danger to the republic is the decline of military ardor, and that decline comes from corruption. Corruption is the seeking of private good or class good rather than the public good. It can come, as it came in Rome, from the self-seeking and power-seeking of the consuls (Rome's corporate One) or of the senatorial class (the Few). It can also come when the Many, the citizen soldiers, go soft, preferring their own ease and pleasure to austerity and battle. And so, says the hard-eyed Machiavelli, it is the fate in the end of a conquering republic like Rome to destroy other republics by defeat and itself by corruption.

Such, very briefly, is Pocock's account of the shorter Machiavellian moment when several Florentines worked their way through to a conception of the conditions for republican life in the face of history seen as fortune. It is thoughtful, perceptive, and sound. In its treatment of Florentine thought as a reach of the great stream of Western reflection on politics it has no equal. Pocock renders clear and intelligible the way the Florentine thinkers found themselves at home with the Aristotelian paradigms, and marks out precisely the places where one Florentine or another diverged from or went beyond the Aristotelian vision of the *zöon politikon*. He also explicates those elements of political thought revived or created by the Florentines that were to carry over into the next great chapter of republican theory in early modern England. Finally, he catches the Florentines in the act of confronting history rather than turning from it, and thereby making the first hesitant steps on the path that the West would follow in becoming the most history-minded of civilizations.

Yet for all its qualities, the central section of *The Machiavellian Moment* is disappointing. It is flawed by one major error, an error, it appears to me, not of commission or omission but of addition and proportion. It is not hard to describe what has happened. The first hundred-odd pages of *The Machiavellian Moment* are dense with ideas, moving fast to achieve an exposition of the medieval political thought-structures that will impinge on the Florentines. And the last 220 pages are an exciting trip through the extraordinary complexities of Anglophone thinking about participatory politics and their relation to liberty from the sixteenth to the eighteenth centuries, a brilliant description of the assimilation of the Machiavellian moment into a world such as Machiavelli never could have imagined. In it Pocock makes contact with and makes some sense of the relations among the advocates of a stunning array of political ideologies—fundamental-law constitutionalism, divine-right monarchy or royal absolutism, "populist" democracy, millenarian elitism, classical republicanism, and Harringtonian republicanism. And that takes care only of the seventeenth century, with other sets of ideologies ready to crowd forward in the eighteenth. As Pocock skillfully makes his way amid these intricate idea-sets, he locates himself and his reader in relation to such highly visible intellects as Edward Coke, John Selden, John Milton, Thomas Hobbes, James Harrington, John Locke, David Hume, Adam Smith, Edmund Burke, John Adams, Alexander Hamilton, and Thomas Jefferson. To make a circle of such giants the visible perimeter of one's thought is to force oneself to add a cubit to one's stature.

In the 250 pages of *The Machiavellian Moment* devoted to the formation of republican thought in Florence, one encounters only two intellectual giants, Aristotle and Machiavelli, although they are indeed supergiants. Besides them there are a few figures of considerable intellectual stature—Guicciardini and Giannotti, and perhaps Bruni and Savonarola; and then there is a cluster—Vettori, Alemanni, Contarini, and so on—of pretty small potatoes. Moreover, what was going on in Florence in the domain of political ideas in the relevant time span may have been as important as what went on later in England, but not as much was going on in Florence. As we have seen, what was happening was the emergence of a republican ideology that diverged from Aristotle's in its preoccupation with history, innovation, and the organization and uses of military force. That emergence is indeed significant, but it is not particularly complex or difficult to grasp. Yet Pocock gives considerably more pages to the Florentine episode than to the Anglophone one, despite the comparative intellectual meagerness of the former.[11] Now it may

11. Florence gets 247 pages to England's 220, about one-eighth more.

be said that no examination of political thinking that has Machiavelli at its center can suffer from even relative intellectual meagerness. There is something to that argument, but it thrusts an odd pair of questions to the fore. Is Machiavelli at the center of thought about politics in sixteenth-century Florence? No one would or ever did doubt it. Is he at the center of the Florentine episode of *The Machiavellian Moment?* Well . . . the discussion devoted to the three figures central in the Florentine section of the book takes up 191 pages, and of that discussion almost exactly a third goes to Machiavelli. Fair shares, one might say, but that would suggest that in his mature years Pocock had fallen victim to a lunatic obsession with equality that has never afflicted him before. Guicciardini and Giannotti—good, thoughtful men, no doubt; but equal in excellence to Machiavelli in the Machiavellian moment? No way. And anyhow, they do not get equal treatment. Giannotti comes short, but in *The Machiavellian Moment* Pocock tells us a third again as much about what Francesco Guicciardini said on politics as about what Niccolò Machiavelli said.

Even more curious oddities appear in the proportioning of attention among the writings of the three Italians. Most historians of ideas would say that the key Italian work in the revival of republican thought was Machiavelli's *Discorsi sopra . . . Tito Livio.* To it Pocock devotes twenty-eight brilliant and closely argued pages. To Giannotti's somewhat less widely admired *Trattato della Repubblica Fiorentina—* a little more than half as long as the *Discorsi—*Pocock gives twenty-one pages. His treatment of Guicciardini's most celebrated political discourse, the *Dialogo del Reggimento di Firenze,* is even more generous. The work is just about half the length of the *Discorsi.* The explication of it, however, takes up almost double the space given to the *Discorsi* in *The Machiavellian Moment*.[12]

One can hastily contrive a hypothesis to account for the disproportions in the attention given the three writers. Perhaps despite the title of Pocock's book, Guicciardini and Giannotti exercise an influence nearly equivalent to Machiavelli's in the formation of the republican tradition whose history he is pursuing? But no, at least not according to Pocock. For after he transfers his attention from Florence to England, only seven references to Guicciardini occur, and only seven to Giannotti. The same span of *The Machiavellian Moment* contains more than seven times as many references to Machiavelli, fifty-one in all. Indeed, even if Pocock had made frequent references to Guicciardini and Giannotti in his treatment of the extension of the Machiavellian moment to England, a difficulty would remain. Although Giannotti's *Li-*

12. The words per page in the Palmarocchi edition of Francesco Guicciardini, *Dialogo e discorsi del regimento di Firenze* (Bari: Laterza, 1932) come out on a rough count pretty close to the number in the Bonfantini edition of Niccolò Machiavelli, *Opere* (Milan: Ricciardi, n.d.) that Pocock used. The pages in Donato Giannotti, *Opere*, 2 vols. (Florence, 1850) carry about four-fifths as many words as the other two. For whatever it is worth, I have tabulated the essential information about the length of the works discussed and the length of Pocock's discussion of them in *The Machiavellian Moment*. I give the numbers of pages as they occur in the editions cited in this note. The reader will keep in mind that the Machiavelli and Guicciardini editions used are roughly equivalent in words per page, the Giannotti edition, about one-fifth less:

work	pages	pages in Pocock
Machiavelli	416	61
Guicciardini	225	82
Giannotti	446	48
Machiavelli, *Discorsi*	333	28
Guicciardini, *Dialogo*	170	52
Giannotti, *Trattato*	230	26

bro della Repubblica de'Vineziani was published in 1540, the *Trattato* on Florence did not appear in print until 1721, too late to have much impact in England. Indeed, whatever impact Giannotti had there, if any, does not appear in *The Machiavellian Moment*, where Pocock's infrequent references to him in the post-Florentine section suggest that few seventeenth- or eighteenth-century Englishmen or Americans cared or even knew anything about him. And they certainly cared and knew nothing about any of Guicciardini's numerous essays on politics and government in Florence, unpublished until the nineteenth century.

Pocock perhaps has a reason that he does not make explicit for lavishing undue attention on Giannotti and Guicciardini and especially on the *Trattato* and the *Dialogo*. Before *The Machiavellian Moment* there existed in English no full account of Guicciardini's political ideas and no account of Giannotti's.[13] In working his way through the writers of Florence's time of troubles, Pocock evidently made careful précis of the works of both men. Then in writing the solid, detailed summaries of the political works of Giannotti and Guicciardini that take up almost all of chapters 5, 8, and 9 of *The Machiavellian Moment* he appears to have overfaithfully followed those précis with only slight changes. Intrinsically, these summaries are thoughtful, conscientious, and reliable; and they reach out to interlink the writing of Giannotti and Guicciardini with those of Aristotle and Machiavelli and with each other. As such they will be useful to scholars who wish to get a clear and ample view of the spectrum of Floren-

---

13. Felix Gilbert's fine treatment of Guicciardini in *Machiavelli and Guicciardini: Politics and History in Sixteenth-Century Florence* (Princeton: Princeton University Press, 1965), though more than adequate for the author's purpose, does not offer a comprehensive and inclusive guide to Guicciardini's political thought.

tine republican thought in the sixteenth century. Placed in *The Machiavellian Moment* they are too large and too leisurely. They slow to a snail's pace a work that begins with a powerful intellectual surge in the first four chapters. Pocock regains that pace in the two splendid chapters on Machiavelli himself, and comes on with a stunning burst of ideas through all the last six chapters—like a miraculous marathoner sprinting the last ten miles of the race. In the chapters on Guicciardini and Giannotti it is as if Bugs Bunny had been transformed into Tubby the Tuba.

The most remarkable section of *The Machiavellian Moment* is the last, "Value and History in the Prerevolutionary Atlantic." It investigates the history of republican thought in England and America from the middle of the seventeenth to the end of the eighteenth century. In that span of time and place, the world underwent transformations in polity, economy, society, and culture that were intricate and interpenetrating. Pocock's chapters on English and American republicanism are densely packed. The changes in English and American republican thought were frequent and kaleidoscopic in the face of rapid changes in the circumstances of the English-speaking community. Used by many people with divergent and shifting goals, the language of Machiavellian republicanism underwent many modifications and metamorphoses. Under such circumstances, even an expert might find it hard to give an account, both intelligible and brief, of what was going on either in the period or in Pocock's book. And on these matters the current reviewer is not expert.

In the matter of the introductory chapter of that final section, "The Problem of English Machiavellianism: Modes of Civic Consciousness before the Civil War," the reviewer feels more at home. Before Pocock deals with the unfolding of republican thought in England, he has to confront a critical question of formidable difficulty: how the devil did republican thought, of all things, get a footing in England, of all places, in the first place? In the early part of the chapter entitled "The Problem of English Machiavellianism," Pocock devotes himself to the forbidding task of rendering it intelligible that classical republicanism took root in a land that above all others in Europe carried its hierarchical medieval political structures, central and local, intact and functioning into the early modern age. In contrast, Florentine republican thought, as we have seen, had as its foci two interrelated conceptions: (1) that the only secure foundation for republican liberty was the military *virtù* of the arms-bearing citizen-soldier and (2) that men achieved their full humanity only as active participants in the political process. How could these indispensable republican conceptions find lodgment in a land "dominated by monarchical, legal and theological concepts apparently in no way disposed to require the definition of England as a polis or the Englishman as a citizen" (p. 334) ? In short, how did Englishmen make the transit from thinking of themselves as subjects to thinking of themselves as citizens? Easy enough, of course, for Florentines, long since actual participants in the government of a medieval commune; but the English . . . ?

The fifteen pages in which Pocock solves this problem are the most remarkable, the most intellectually exciting, in *The Machiavellian Moment*. They show the author at his very best—intensely economical, extremely demanding of and rewarding to his readers, bold in generalization but sharp-eyed in recognizing and making explicit the bounds that limit each generalization he offers. In this short span he makes his way through the unique, dense tangle that is English political thinking in the period. He does more, for in those few pages he also comes to grip with many of the most evocative recent efforts to find a way through the tangle to an orderly understanding of the English mind in a period of intellectual as well as political and constitutional upheaval. He considers and brings into a manageable synthesis the central themes of Michael Walzer's *Revolution of the Saints,* Christopher Hill's *Society and Puritanism in Pre-Revolutionary England,* Donald Hanson's *From Kingdom to Commonwealth,* Arthur Ferguson's *The Articulate Citizen of the English Renaissance,* William Lamont's *Godly Rule,* and William Haller's *Foxe's Book of Martyrs and the Elect Nation.*

Pocock's quest for the grounds of republicanism in England, for the bases of "the revival [there] of the ancient notions of political *virtus,*" starts with a characterization of the English thought patterns that were rooted in medieval paradigms. That characterization will serve as well as any other passage in a long book full of stunningly bright passages to illustrate Pocock's capacity for compressing a mass of intricate ideas into a small space, and thus producing exposition of unusual density, the penetration of which exacts the closest attention from the reader. In a "territorial and jurisdictional monarchy," such as England, he says,

the individual took on positive being primarily as the possessor of rights — rights to land, and to justice affecting his tenure of land — and a structure of "ascending authority" existed mainly as a structure of customs, jurisdictions, and liberties, in which such rights were embodied and preserved and which rose to meet the descending structure of authority that existed to command its continuance and enforcement. In the world of *jurisdictio* and *gubernaculum* the individual possessed rights and property — *proprietas,* that which rightfully pertained to him — and was subject to authority which, since it descended from God, was never the mere reflection of his rights; and the central debate was, and has remained, how far the two conceptual schemes — ascending and

descending powers, *jurisdictio* and *gubernaculum,* rights and duties — were integrated with one another. (P. 335)

Having clearly identified the basic elements in sixteenth-century English habits of political thinking, Pocock further identifies what cut that thought off from Florentine civic-humanist republicanism: "It can be strongly affirmed, however, that
to define the individual in terms of his rights and his duties,
his property and his obligations, is still not enough to make
him an active citizen or a political animal" (p. 335).

On an irregular schedule between 1560 and 1650, Pocock
points out, Englishmen explored the series of new or modified thought structures that came to dominate their minds
during the upheavals of the mid-century. Many of them believed England was the Elect Nation, a new Israel chosen by
God to do His will on earth. Even Englishmen of humanist
background might subscribe to the conception of the Elect
Nation, but they also saw in the giving of counsel the way in
which educated men served their princely commonwealth.
Some of them also held that the place above all where such
counsel should be offered was Parliament, where the whole
political nation was personally or representatively present.
Others saw the meaning of Parliament in a different light.
To them it was an element of the ancient constitution, that
body of customs and rights imbedded in the common law,
which it was the duty of Englishmen to preserve as their heri-
tage from the past and legacy to the future. Finally, the mil-
lennial chiliasm that emerged toward the end of the period
drew not only on the sacred-secular idea of the Elect Nation
but also on the secular-sacred idea of a law which had its roots
in the historical English nation over a vast time span and
which incorporated the part of the law of God that was also
the law of nature and of reason.

All these thought structures were species of genera that were long antecedent to them. Some, indeed—the idea of the Elect Nation, for example—had emerged long before the dawn of the Christian era. But in England each of these structures had traits that marked it off from its genus; and those traits were peculiarly local in time and space, peculiar to England between the 1560s and the 1650s. Moreover, each structure shared a common trait with the others. For its attainment or perfection each required the participation in the work of ruling of the particular Elect or elected that it singled out, whether it was the Chosen Community of Saints or the chosen members of the House of Commons and the commissions of the peace. Clearly, then, not one of these structures had built into it the indispensable blocks of Machiavellian republicanism. But clearly, too, each of them had in it elements that were compatible with Machiavellian republicanism. Thus Pocock renders the otherwise mysterious success of Florentine theory in mid-seventeenth-century England intelligible. As the structures to which they adhered collapsed into failure or were gutted in the course of civil strife, men of a most varied set of intellectual origins found refuge in the republican political conception of a "mixed monarchy." That conception, born freakishly in Charles I's "Answer to the Nineteen Propositions" in 1642, was nurtured into a sociological theory of republican liberty by the English Machiavellian, James Harrington, during the Commonwealth.

A first-rate historical study is often distinguishable from the ruck not only by the problems it solves and the questions it raises but also by the questions whose clear formulation it makes possible. Pocock's account of the rebirth of republican thought in Florence and its transit to and development in the Anglophone world bears all three marks of excellence. With respect to the third, it led me to formulate two such questions, one minor, and one, I think, major, using *The Machiavellian Moment* as a firmly established reference point.

First, given the history of the secular, republican Aristotelian language of politics as set forth in *The Machiavellian Moment*, how are we to deal with the actual occurrences of the term "republic" and its equivalents in those sixteenth-century writings on politics which do not readily assimilate to the republican model mediated to England via Florence? After all, the major sixteenth-century work on politics by a Frenchman was *De la République* by Jean Bodin. Bodin, the formulator of the doctrine of monarchical sovereignty, was anything but an addict of Aristotelian participatory politics and a balanced constitution. An Englishman, Sir Thomas Smith, a contemporary of Bodin's and a secretary of state to Elizabeth, wrote *De republica Anglorum*, and somewhat earlier, another Englishman composed *A Discourse on the Commonweal of England*. Claude Seyssel, a Savoyard in the service of Louis XII, knew northern Italy well in his youth, and Florence later. He also knew Aristotle's *Politics* surely and Polybius possibly. His treatise *La Monarchie de France* (1515) refers to royal France as a *chose publique*, a *bien commun*. And Seyssel favorably compares the monarchic *chose publique*, literally the *res publica*, of France with the aristocratic republic of Venice and the democratic republic of Rome. Indeed, "republic" and "commonwealth" did not become bad names in monarchic Europe until a republic that proclaimed itself a commonwealth took off the head of a king of England in 1649. Up to then the language of European politics had both those terms in an extended sense as part of its vocabulary, free of invidious connotation. Indeed, Seyssel and Smith gave them a faintly Aristotelian aroma, despite the strongly monarchist inclinations of their thought. Conversely, there is some ambivalence in Machiavelli about the rule of the One. In the vestments of Caesar and his successors it is a horror, but when the One is Romulus, and his successors are Numa and Tullus, they found a *regno* that is not a republic, but may possibly be a *vivere civile*, and certainly is *bene ordinato*, as France perhaps is in Machiavelli's eyes. These fragments of data intimate a considerable complexity in the relations between the civic republicanism of the Florentines and the political language of monarchists of the northern kingdoms who had a place in their vocabulary for royal republics and commonwealths. It will now be possible to explore that complexity from the secure base provided by *The Machiavellian Moment*.

The other question Pocock's study makes it easy to formulate clearly is this: what is the relation between the language of liberty worked out by the great Florentines and maintained and modified by political writers in Anglophone lands from 1660 to 1800 and the other tradition of political liberty that Europe, and especially England, lived with from "time immemorial" to the nineteenth century? There may have been two languages of politics that had "republic" as part of their vocabularies in the 1500s, as is suggested above; there were certainly at least two that had "liberty" as the key word in their vocabulary throughout the time span of the Machiavellian moment, c. 1500-c 1800.

As Pocock makes clear, the Machiavellian moment was triggered by a dual threat to Florentine liberty—the threat of subjection to a foreign conqueror without, the threat of domination by a Medici principate within. As he also points out, this double peril moved Florentines to deep and earnest reflections on the conditions for the survival of liberty, thus generating a sociology of liberty. The Florentines' views on liberty share a common core. That core derives from Aristotle and is the mark of the common profound debt of the Florentines to him. The fundamental condition of liberty, they agree, is participation in political life. To be barred from participation, to be excluded from the common activity in which the decisions are made and the deeds done that affect the lives of all, is a kind of servitude. Participation is also the fundamental and indispensable condition of virtue. Without it the highest virtue, civic virtue, never comes to life. The citizen manifests his civic virtue by acting to his fullest capacity in the political life of the commonwealth for the common good, not for his own good. Citizenship, liberty, and virtue are thus inseparably intermingled. They are positive, active, and as Pocock says, dynamic. Adapting Isaiah Berlin's distinction, they imply "freedom to" rather than "freedom against."

There is, of course, in the political tradition of the West a long, complex history of a conception and language of liberty as "freedom against." That other language of liberty does not focus on participation. The liberty that is its object can be enjoyed without political activity, and indeed without virtue. As Pocock traversed three hundred years of talk about politics in pursuit of the Aristotelian-Machiavellian language of republican liberty, he was bound to encounter that other language of liberty, which men, especially Englishmen, spoke with even greater fluency and perhaps with more powerful conviction than they spoke the first. When he does encounter it, his sharp, recording mind grasps the substance of the other idea of liberty firmly and describes its prime features with elegance and precision. Thus he sketches the outlook of "God's Englishman," that member of a strange generation or two who accepted the idea that they were born in an "Elect Nation": he was "an inheritor at common law, receiving property, liberties and customs from his ancestors, and

passing them on in a perpetual condition of refinement"
(p. 345).

Thus, Pocock provides a vivid glimpse of that other liberty
in a particular phase of its history—the early seventeenth century in England. Unerringly he has chosen for his formulation key words of its vocabulary at that historic point: "property," "law," "custom," "ancestors," "inheritance," "a perpetual condition." Thus he calls our attention to the other
conception of liberty only a few years before it was to con-
verge with the Aristotelian republican conception in England.

The two conceptions had converged during other time
spans on the long chronological line that parallels but does
not always coincide with *The Machiavellian Moment.* They
converged during one such span, for example, in antiquity,
around the beginning of our era. Pocock's own trajectory,
however, from Aristotle through Boethius and Fortescue to
the Florentine republicans, did not intersect with that convergence in antiquity, and consequently he took no note of
it. It was strikingly exemplified in the course of a brouhaha
in Jerusalem in the first half of the first century after the cru-
cifixion. There, as the Book of Acts tells us, the Apostle Paul
had occasion to make two divergent statements about his
citizenship within a single day. He had been mobbed in the
Temple, and then rescued and put under protective arrest
by the commander of the Roman troop of guards. Having
picked up from the babel of charges the peculiar notion that
Paul was the leader of an Egyptian outlaw band, the commander was surprised to hear Paul speak in Greek. "I,"
Paul complained, "am a man . . . of Tarsus, a city in Cilicia,
a citizen of no mean city." This unexpected evidence of civilization won Paul permission to speak to the crowd again.
Unfortunately, his harangue in Hebrew precipitated another

riot. The much tried commander ordered that Paul be scourged until he was ready to explain how he happened always to bring on uproars. Paul demanded to know, "Is it lawful . . . to scourge a man that is a Roman, and uncondemned?" Startled at the question, the commander asked Paul whether he was indeed a Roman. When Paul answered yes, the commander said, "With a great sum obtained I this freedom." And Paul replied, in what sounds like a put-down, "But I was freeborn." So in one day to the same officer Paul claimed twice to be a free citizen, once of Tarsus in Cilicia and once of Rome (Acts 21:27-39).

Here we have, it appears to me, materializations of both ideas of liberty that concern us. In Paul's proud avowal that he is a citizen of Tarsus—no mean city—we surely hear a late version of that sense of liberty as participation in the life of the *polis* that forms the core of Aristotle's politics. Paul's claim to being Roman, however, has nothing to do with a part in ruling and being ruled in the city of Rome. Paul had neither ruled nor been ruled in Rome; he had never been there at all. Yet at that moment in Jerusalem, being a freeborn Roman was of more importance to Paul than being a citizen of Tarsus. It meant that a Roman state official could not legally scourge the renegade Jew of Tarsus, because he was bound to treat him as a man under Roman law. To be a citizen of Rome was to be under Roman law, and to be under that law was civil liberty in the highest degree, the freedom for which the commander himself had paid a high price. And here we find the seed at least of "the other liberty" of citizen or subject. That liberty lies not in action and participation in politics but in such protection as the law gives to the free against all who would take away from them what the law allows them, even if the would-be taker is an officer of the state. Men are free when with respect to them their ruler as well as others is under law, bound by it.

Later to be born than the Aristotelian idea of liberty, the other, negative, law-oriented conception emerged from the convergence of Stoic ideals and Roman law practicalities; and it was more durable than the Aristotelian idea. Tied to the city and to citizenship, the Aristotelian idea vanished in the West after the fifth century when Germanic tribes inundated the Western Empire, and citizenship disappeared along with the cities themselves. This is no place to speak of the peculiar and complicated history of the other idea of liberty in the West in the following millennium. We may limit ourselves to pointing out that when the historical wits have finished demonstrating its deficiencies and class origin, Magna Carta—and especially its twenty-ninth chapter—is as good a place as any to look for a careful formulation of the medieval version of the other idea of liberty.

The next convergence of the two languages of liberty took place inevitably when the participatory idea of liberty re-emerged—that is, it took place in Renaissance Florence, and most conspicuously in Giannotti, Guicciardini, and even Machiavelli. Evidence of the convergence appears in *The Machiavellian Moment*, but Pocock does not focus his attention on it. Giannotti prefers the *popolo* over the ambitious few, he says, because "that *libertà* which the many desire to preserve [is] the condition in which each enjoys his own under law," and such liberty under law "is close to being the common good itself" (p. 310). But to say this is almost to identify the common good not with action and participation but with the enjoyment of common right under a common law. Far more specifically than Giannotti, Guicciardini confronts the idea of liberty as participation with the other idea of liberty in his *Dialogo del Reggimento di Firenze,* and comes down flatly on the side of the latter: "The purpose of *libertà* is not to ensure the participation of everyone at all levels of government *(che onguno intromettersi nel governo)* but to ensure the conservation of the rule of law and the common good *(si conservassino le leggi ed el bene commune)*" (p. 226 and n. 15).[14] And, Guicciardini continues, this end is better achieved under the rule of one man than under other forms of government. As Pocock points out, "A man might enjoy his own under the law with minimal or even no participation in decision-making . . . Guicciardini is here developing a negative as opposed to a positive concept of liberty, making it freedom from other men's ascendancy rather than freedom to develop positive human capacities and qualities" (p. 232).

Even Machiavelli occasionally veered toward the other language of liberty. For example, in chapter 5 of *Il Principe* he broaches problems a prince will have in holding a newly acquired state accustomed to live "con le loro legge et in libertà." If the "et" is conjunctive, the phrase suggests a negative conception of *libertà.* This fits with Machiavelli's earlier advice to a new prince to change neither the law of a newly conquered people nor the taxes taken from them.[15] Such an arrangement would leave them in possession of the indispensable elements of the other kind of liberty—property and the rule of law.

14. The speaker at this point in the *Dialogo* is Bernardo del Nero, who, according to Pocock, is Guicciardini's mouthpiece in the dialogue. The words Pocock uses here, "to ensure the participation of everyone at all levels of government," are—as one can see by looking at the original which he gives in parentheses—rather an extension of remarks than a translation. Literally, "everybody gets involved in governing."

15. Machiavelli, *Il Principe,* ch. 3.

It remains true that the Florentines did not develop a conception that would have placed legal limits on what the republic could rightfully demand of the citizenry. For all the Florentine Machiavellians, the other kind of liberty is the precarious yield of careful adjustments in the balance of participation, and therefore not separable from it. As participation alone yields the life of virtue in a civil society, in their opinion, it alone is worth their full attention. It seems likely that in Italy, as in all Western Christian lands, the other idea of liberty survived from the Middle Ages in the antithesis between freeman and bondman. However that may be, it remains true that the great Florentine theorists of civic virtue and republican politics did not make liberty as "freedom against" a main focus of their thought. On the evidence, thoughts about it crossed their minds. Equally on the evidence, those thoughts did not much occupy their minds, which were almost wholly taken up with the investigation of the necessary conditions of liberty as participation in governing a republic.

The next and historically the most consequential convergence of the two conceptions began in the mid-seventeenth century in England. The conceptions remained in constant conjunction for the next 150 years in England and in sporadic conjunction in her continental American colonies. As we have seen, Pocock is well aware of the presence of the other conception of liberty in the early seventeenth-century prologue to England's Machiavellian moment. But in his account of republican thought in the pre-Revolutionary Atlantic that other conception practically vanishes. He makes some thirty-odd direct references to liberty, yet in almost every reference the term is turned in the direction of participatory republicanism.[16] Occasionally we catch a glimpse that suggests the ghostly presence of the other idea of liberty, as when "legal militia" is linked with "English liberty" as against a "standing army" tied to "prerogative" (p. 410). The notion of liberty as freedom against recurs in Pocock's quotation from Burke to the effect that the Americans "snuff the approach of tyranny in every tainted breeze" (p. 489), and in the reference to Hume's views on the relations of "authority and liberty" (p. 509).

The separation of the ideas of liberty in *The Machiavellian Moment* hardly corresponds to the historical actualities. From the middle of the seventeenth century until the 1800s, the two conceptions of liberty inhabit the same political space —the Anglophone world. More than that, ideologically they just about fill that space. If they are not all that politics is about, they are pretty nearly all that writing and talking about politics is about. Yet the two conceptions were divergent in origin and in substance. The republican idea of liberty in England was generated in the crisis over the distribution of political power that resulted from the conflict between the king's government and the majority in the House of Commons in 1641. It received a clear articulation about a decade later when Harrington reflected on the significance of that conflict and its outcome. As set forth then and thereafter, it was primarily concerned with the conditions for achieving a durable republic of virtuous men, that is, with distributing power in a way that would keep the commonwealth secure from external enemies and internal corruption. Determining what those conditions were became increasingly difficult in the eighteenth century as the framework

16. In a few instances the context is too exiguous to permit even a guess as to the sense in which the term is being used.

of English society began to shift in ways discernible to men who thought seriously about politics. To many such men it was evident that England was undergoing transformation from the agrarian society that Harrington assumed it was into a commercial society. The free and independent yeomanry, the necessary foundation for a virtuous republic, was giving place to a rabble, dependent on their mercantile masters. Commerce was corrupting the English commonwealth; indeed commerce and corruption were identical. They corroded the very foundations of freedom. The political patrons of commerce, Walpole and his ilk, survived by corrupting the political process. Reflection on the effect of trade on a participatory free republic furnished food for thought for several generations of political thinkers not only in England but in the France of Montesquieu and Rousseau, the Scotland of Ferguson and Adam Smith, and the America of Jefferson, Hamilton, and Madison.

The other idea of liberty had no such sociological dimensions, since it supposed that liberty was a collection of rights belonging to free men regardless of the structure of society. Though it lacked a sociological dimension, the other idea of liberty had a long historical axis. Men's minds carried it back beyond Magna Carta into the immemorial Anglo-Saxon murk. Its major recent crisis had occurred in the early years of the reign of Charles I. In those years the prerogative actions of the king posed a direct threat to the property and liberty of Englishmen, and to the ability of the law to protect either of them. The question those actions raised was not "who is to govern?" but "what are and should be the limits in law on the governing authority?" The language of liberty that this view of politics generates does not allow much time in its ordinary discourse for talk about civic virtue, participation, patriotism, political animals, citizen militia, or corruption. It tends to go on and on about prerogative, authority, obedience, arbitrary power, and reason of state, about limited government, property, due process, rule of law, and fundamental law. The issues related to liberty as freedom against were almost as serious after the Restoration as before. It was after the Restoration, indeed after the Revolution of 1688, that freedom of worship, freedom of speech, and freedom of the press effectively established themselves in the Anglophone world, took roots so deep that they have up to now survived social and economic transformations of an intensity and magnitude that Harrington, the neo-Harringtons, and Thomas Jefferson scarcely dreamed of.

The two perceptions of liberty are not, however, wholly compatible. The classical-Machiavellian-republican theory of liberty takes a high view of politics as the only scene in which men can act out their human potentialities; implicitly, when not overtly, it takes a restricted and restricting view of the number of men to whom even in the best circumstances the road to the good life of liberty can be opened. Citizen liberty available only to the members of the Consiglio Maggiore or to the electorate of the unreformed House of Commons leaves an awful lot of people out.[17] The other idea of liberty is more ecumenical in its embrace. It does not profess, however, to give all that much to those it embraces. Mainly, it offers them some fairly clear constraints on the extent to which they can be rightfully booted about by current controllers of the machinery of political coercion.

That is the way things stood with respect to the word "liberty" for a century and a half in the Anglophone world: it was a shibboleth of political thinking; one could not get into the game without it. Yet it meant different things to differ-

17. In the case of England it leaves even more out if one feels, as Rousseau did, that representation cannot pass as legal tender in exchange for participation.

ent people or to the same person at different times. When two divergent conceptions, designated by the same term, simultaneously occupy the minds of men, they present a stiff challenge to a scholar's deftness. They test his skill in navigating long and difficult stretches of ambiguity. Such a test is worthy of the dexterity of a Pocock. Yet in the last section of *The Machiavellian Moment* Pocock slithers past this central problem and appears not to notice that the other conception of liberty is there at all. I think he noticed it all right. A mind like his, to which the making of connections and the exploring of relations is a vocation verging on an addiction, could scarcely help noticing, especially since the other conception of liberty is old territory for the author of *The Ancient Constitution and Feudal Law*. Unless I am greatly mistaken, Pocock's noticing but not exploring the other idea of liberty demanded of him an almost violent act of self-restraint. He had to keep his eye averted as he marched down a road marked all the way with signposts pointing toward the other idea of liberty. The debate on impositions, 1610; the Petition of Right, 1628; the Habeas Corpus Act, 1679; the Magdalen College Case, 1687; the Seven Bishops Case, 1688; the Bill of Rights, 1689; and so on up to the Declaration of Independence, the Constitution of the United States and its first ten amendments—all point vividly and insistently to that other idea. Pocock disregarded all that, although the temptation not to disregard it must have been enormous. We are indebted to him. Had he not resisted temptation, had he succumbed, we would not have *The Machiavellian Moment* now. Ten or fifteen years from now we might have had a book three times as long, called, perhaps, Two Languages of Liberty. Maybe he will give us that book someday. Meanwhile, I am happy for the bird in the hand.

1977

Index